The Collected Works of Sigurd F. Olson

The Early Writings: 1921-1934

The Collected Works of Sigurd F. Olson

The Early Writings: 1921-1934
Edited and with commentary by MIKE LINK

Illustrated by Dan Metz
Introduction by Robert Keith Olson

VOYAGEUR PRESS

ISBN 0-89658-091-1

Original material copyright © 1988 by Mike Link
Introduction copyright © 1988 by Robert Keith Olson
Illustrations copyright © 1988 by Daniel Metz

All rights reserved. No part of this work may be reproduced or used in any form by any means—graphic, electronic, or mechanical, including photocopying, recording, taping, or information storage and retrieval system—without written permission of the publisher.

Printed in the United States of America
90 91 92 93 94 5 4 3 2

Published by Voyageur Press, Inc.
P.O. Box 338
123 North Second Street
Stillwater, Minnesota 55082 U.S.A.
In Minn 612-430-2210
Toll Free 800-888-9653

Voyageur Press books are also available at discounts for quantities for educational, fundraising, premium, or sales-promotion use. For details contact the marketing manager. Please write or call for our free catalog of natural history publications.

Editor's note:
Sigurd Olson's writings are reproduced here as accurately as possible, preserving older spellings and occasional typographical errors.

Distributed in Canada by Whitecap Books, Ltd. Vancouver and Toronto.

To Kate
WITH ALL MY LOVE

Contents

ACKNOWLEDGMENTS *ix*
INTRODUCTION BY ROBERT KEITH OLSON *xi*
PERSPECTIVE — THE BEGINNING *xxv*
1899–1921 3
  Cruising God's Country 9
1922–1925 19
  Fishing Jewelry 22
  On the Fire Line with the Forest Service 30
  Rejection Letter 41
1925–1928 43
  Snow Wings 46
  Reflections of a Guide 63
1929–1931 74
  Confessions of a Duck Hunter 76

    Duck Heaven   90
    Stag Pants Galahads   104
    The Poison Trail   121
    Letters   134
    Spring Fever   145
    The Blue-Bills Are Coming!   158
1932   170
    Papette   171
    Learning to Write   187
    Search for the Wild   189
    Fortune at Lac La Croix   197
1933   210
    Trail's End   212
1934   227
    Roads or Planes in the Superior   230
    A New Policy Needed for the Superior   237
    Cruising in the Arrowhead   245
    En Roulant Parts I and II   258
PERSPECTIVE—THE CONTINUATION   *280*

Acknowledgments

THE EFFORT OF FINDING and gaining permission to print the articles and stories in this book was both a pleasure and a tangled web. It was a pleasure to go through the archives that contained many of Sig's personal notes and original copies. Tracking down other early pieces, however, involved me in a tangled web of endless correspondence, unexpected findings, and occasional dead ends.

I would like to thank Elizabeth, Sigurd Thorne, and Robert Keith Olson for their cooperation and assistance. I also appreciate the efforts of Kevin Proescholdt of the Friends of the Boundary Waters Canoe Area Wilderness.

The materials collected in this volume are reprinted with the permission of the following magazines: *Sports Afield, Boy's Life, Field and Stream, Outdoor Life, Minnesota Conservationist, Outdoors,* and *Minnesota Waltonian.* The newspaper stories are reprinted with the permission of the *Milwaukee Journal*. All rights are reserved by the original publication.

A portion of the proceeds from this book will go to the Friends of the Boundary Waters Canoe Area Wilderness to support them in their efforts to protect "Sig's country."

Introduction

HAD SIG OLSON been born at midcentury, he would have been all over the world, writing about the great ecological disaster overtaking the globe, condemning the polluters and exploiters, calling for a sustainable, ecologically sane society. In his private moments, he would be putting his experience into poetry and reflections. He would surely have been caught up in the fevers of the sixties, one way or another with Vietnam. Whatever, the spirit of the times would have set his course today as surely as it did during the half century in which he did grow up and during which he defined himself and his world. It is almost impossible now to imagine those early days of the century, before the wars and between them, the Depression, the mood of the times, and the simpler, more straightforward America. But they were important, for they were the days that must be understood to understand the man, his life, and his message.

This collection, therefore, will have performed a notable service in helping new generations to understand the real Sigurd Olson, who he was, what he stood for and why, and some of the constraints—and opportunities—he faced in striving to fulfill his own dreams. Republishing his mostly forgotten periodical writings, linked together by interpretive narrative, gives us a glimpse of the life and the man behind what has since become a legend. Indeed, reading the manuscript has reminded me of many things almost forgotten of those now far away times—memories long filed away with old papers and photo albums lying on the shelf at home.

The early stories, published in the outdoor magazines and here reprinted for the first time, are haunting. They bring back other places, other times, and another man lost in the achievements and recognition of his later life. He was young then, bronzed and handsome, tough as old boots, and rugged as the north country itself. He was a teacher, but what comes through in my recollections of my father is the woodsman, hunter, fisherman, and guide, strong masculine images that molded my own concepts of manhood and what a man should be. I have an old picture of him taken with his father sometime in the early thirties. He is in his summer work clothes, his clerical father meticulous and tidy in a vested suit. What, I have asked myself, did this straitlaced Swedish-American clergyman think of his big roughneck American son?

Those days come back as days of action, excitement, and the out-of-doors. Summers were spent guiding on the lakes or running the Border Lakes Outfitting Company at Winton. Fall started the school year, but more importantly, the hunting season. The basement would be full of gear, decoys, packsacks, and guns. An excitement pervaded the house, with early morning departures to Shagawa, Basswood, or the Stony River rice beds. There are pictures of golden autumn afternoons with the bag of ducks laid out in front of the canoe. There are unforgettable memories of annual duck dinners with friends—bluebills for the kids and mallards for the grown-ups, with wild rice, cranberries, and the little pile of bird shot by the plate when it was all over. With November and the snow came deer season and the atmosphere of the big game hunt, ending with a deer carcass hanging from the clothesline post in the backyard, tales of the hunt around the dinner table at night, and venison steaks. Winter was all about snowshoes, ice fishing, and skis. How we skied. We had brushed out miles of trails where we skied daily, sometimes before breakfast, always after school, often at night in the magic half-light of the full moon. Spring brought the delights of trout fishing. No matter what the time—six or eleven o'clock at night—when Dad came home, we cooked up a supper of "brookies," never so good as when they were fresh out of the creel, crisp tails and all.

These were the years when he was cutting his writer's teeth, putting his experiences and his thoughts into words. Each story then was a major or an unforgettable family event. The old titles "Papette" and "En Roulant" recall the whole business, family councils as the story took shape, everything discussed, shared, and, at daring moments, criticized. Why my father wrote these stories, I never asked nor thought to ask. All I knew was that it was important. We held our breath when the reply came back from the editors, then gloom and scattering to our respective retreats over a rejection, rejoicing and relief when a piece was accepted.

All that under difficult conditions, I might add. We lived

in a small house bursting with boys. In addition to my brother and me, our cousin Curtis came to live for two years to attend Ely Junior College. How Dad ever wrote I will never know. I can only remember some "desperate" moments. Finally, he acquired the "shack," the old garage converted to a study where he could be alone just a few paces from the house. It must have been a blessing, for all of us I think.

But there was another man, too, to those who knew him as a friend and father. I have never known anyone before or since who had such a rare and boyish appetite for action and experience. He loved living rough, bashing his way along through wind and weather, mosquitoes and alder swamp, the worse the better. He loved the elements, the icy bite of the winter wind, the hardness of the rocky land, and the truth of elemental things. To him it was a joy, and he sang and whistled his way through it all.

To live was to sing. As a family we sang in the living room at night, around the campfire, on long drives to the cities, laughing at mother who joined in but could never carry a tune. Our program was catch-as-catch-can, mainly the old folk songs, cowboy ballads, work songs, spirituals, "Frankie and Johnny," "The Streets of Laredo," World War I songs like "Tipperary" and "There's a Long Long Trail," old favorites like "Home on the Range," and "The Red River Valley."

My father loved horseplay and laughter. In a moment he could be like a kid, rolling around on the floor, laughing fit to split. He used to tell us "moose stories" at bedtime, raw material made up on the spur of the moment like "the moose with the rubber horns" or the adventures and misadventures of "Roscoe and Boscoe," the two little chipmunks, which sent us giggling and screeching with laughter under the covers at last. The only other people I have ever known

INTRODUCTION

with that capacity for such easy laughter were the old woodsmen and guides left over from the frontier days, who had about them a careless spirit that will probably never come again. Very American, and I am glad I knew it.

Indeed, it was the old woodsmen and guides who were to symbolize so much that mattered both to my father and myself and, I daresay, to my brother, Sig. Dad prided himself on being one of the best guides in the business (if not *the* best). The man with the pack and stag pants may have been a drifter or a drunk, like poor Canada Jack who wrote poetry in his spare time, but he also stood for the back-of-beyond, the frontier, and a man's world. We children scuttled and played among them with no doubt we would be woodsmen ourselves someday, the highest calling to which a boy could aspire. And guiding became a family trade for many years.

My father once told me how he had been tempted as a boy in college to sign up as a missionary to Africa. One night, he went to the roof of the YMCA in Madison, Wisconsin, to be alone and to think it out. "I realized then," he said, "that the main attraction of the missionary life was not to convert the heathen, but the prospect of travel and adventure." He had to be honest with himself and decided against it. But the thirst for adventure remained, which he played out in the North as a woodsman and guide and out of which he forged a philosophy, even a religion of his own.

It is not surprising, then, that the voyageurs, rough and ready, jolly and tough, became his folk heroes. Not surprising that he reveled in his role as "the Bourgeois" and relished the history of the fur trade days. It was an elemental part of his life, and out of it came the great trips with his Canadian friends to the far reaches of northern Canada and the material for his book *The Lonely Land*.

On a deeper level, Sig Olson was a sensitive and tender man, who felt things keenly and loved his world for its very self. He was a child of nature, if you like, to whom the sights and sounds and smells of the wild were a vivid language that we understood in our hearts, that spoke volumes to us if we would only listen. He loved the lakes and the names of the lakes—Kahnipi, Saganaga, Emerald, and Darky—the rocks, the pines, the campsites, and the smell of balsam boughs and rotting leaves. It was as if they existed in an eternity of their own, a northern Eden untrammeled by the prosaic purposes of everyday life. The lakes of the Quetico-Superior were to him a sort of Shangri-la, the fulfillment of man's oldest dream for a place of unspoiled perfection where he could live at peace with nature and himself. And he, Sig Olson, was its interpreter.

One day when he was old, we were walking back in the woods behind where I now live. The trail skirted the edge of the Namekagon River, where he had fished for many years. When we came to the river's edge, he stopped, gazed out over the water awhile. Then I heard him murmur softly to himself, "Dear old river."

Watching a sunset or a moonrise were moments of intense experience and meaning, for which he had an insatiable appetite. The call of the loon, the smell of autumn leaves flooded his consciousness with pleasure and meaning. The call of the wild was for him not the cry of the wolf pack, but the chatter of the squirrel, the mournful cheep of the nuthatch, the crackle of shore ice in the spring, the drumming of grouse in the fall. Or even silence.

It was a profound, probably the profoundest, need and experience all his life. One autumn afternoon we had been sitting in the sauna at the Point waiting for a rainshower to pass. When it was over, he walked out by himself toward the lake while I tidied up, swept the floor, and emptied the

INTRODUCTION

buckets. On my way back to the cabin I passed the little swimming dock where he was lying on his stomach, arms flung out, eyes closed, as if he had fallen. I stopped, and he must have heard me. Then he muttered, "I'm all right, Bob, I just want to lie here awhile and listen to the waves." The wind was singing through the trees and the waves chuckling under the dock. Day was fading into dusk, and I left him there to listen in peace and communion.

The days of his youth and young manhood were the most important days of his life, for they formed the man and laid the foundation for what came later. They were a bank where he stored his thoughts and feelings and the direct experience of the out-of-doors. He had tried to express them in gentle essays, but these were filed away along with the rejection slips. Those were the days when he gradually forged his wilderness ideas, which he was to carry to fruition in the years ahead. He had chosen a way of life, defined himself, established a home, and raised a family — all the conventional things. And then, so soon, it was all over.

We had spent an afternoon skating on a little bay of One Pine Lake outside of Ely. It was a grey day, as I remember, cold and rather bleak, with the dark pines frowning along the lakeshore, a landscape in black and white, like an old woodcut. But we had a fire and were having fun. Then we were standing around the car listening to the radio. The announcer was speaking excitedly about the Japanese attacking a United States base at Pearl Harbor. I had never heard of it and didn't know what it meant. But my parents were suddenly quite and grim. We packed up and went home, the fun gone from the day. A week later, we got the news that cousin Curtis, who had lived with us for those two years and then joined the navy, had gone down on the *Arizona*. I can still hear my mother's cry.

We didn't know it then, of course, but we had finally

been struck by a historical northwester that was to scatter everything to the winds forever. Soon my brother, Sig, joined the Tenth Mountain Division to become a ski trooper. Later, I left for the Army Air Corps. Dad went off to Europe to set up an educational program for GIs as the war in Europe ground to an end. So the life we'd known, our little idyl in the North, came to a close.

There must have been something of the pioneer and not a little of the independent Iron Ranger in all of us. After the war, we never looked back, never sentimentalized the past. Like everyone else we knew, my brother and I went off to make livings for ourselves. He headed for Alaska and the life of a wildlife biologist. I ended up in the United States Foreign Service, an entirely different life in many ways and yet somewhat the same: the world was my wilderness. My father shortly became involved in the national wilderness movement and especially the controversial fight for the preservation of what has become the Boundary Waters Canoe Area Wilderness. This battle took him all over the country. Despite the sharp break with the past, it seemed like the thing to do at the time, and none of us thought very much about any of it, except that each was engaged in a new adventure of his own. We just watched each other from afar, like people do if everything is going all right, each pretty much minding his own business.

Even the writing seemed to have become a thing of the past, except for an article or two here and there that was nothing to get excited about. I thought my father had put all that aside; it seemed pretty remote in those days of new ventures, something over and done with, a forgotten and not very important phase of the past. How wrong I was. In fact, it became and remained to his dying day the raison d'être of his life.

It took a new member of the family, my wife, Yvonne,

INTRODUCTION

to see things in a fresh light. It was she who one day discovered the old essays filed away and now all but forgotten. "Papa," she said, "these are beautiful and ought to be published. Why don't you put them together in a book?" By that time, even he had lost interest, I think. He was a busy man already—speaking and traveling all over the country. But she persisted. She typed them over in fresh copy and together they assembled them into a manuscript broken down by seasons. The result was *The Singing Wilderness*, a resounding success, reviewed on the front page of the *New York Times Book Review* section, runner-up for the American Library Association book-of-the-year award. We were dumbfounded, to tell the truth. But, more to the point, it opened the floodgates for a stream of books to follow.

How he did it is a lesson to all would-be writers. The reader may see him working quietly in solitude at the Point, where he could invite his soul and where deep thoughts would well up naturally, as a spring in the forest. It wasn't like that at all. Most of it was plain hard work under difficult and sometimes grim conditions. He wrote over the years wherever and whenever—nights, stray hours, weekends. He wrote on any kind of paper—envelopes, the margins of magazines, odd scraps of notepaper. I asked him once, "Dad, where do you find the time to write?" thinking of the enormous amount of business and correspondence he carried on without a secretary. "In hotel rooms and on airplanes," he said. It was difficult, but possible, because he wrote from the files of experience stored up in his heart and soul, thoughts and feelings harvested from those years of his youth when he'd steeped himself in the natural world. Like the singer from the *Kalevala*, quoted in the beginning of *Runes of the North*, he sang his tales from snatches of experience:

The frost squeaked out verses to me,
And the rain chanted runes,
The winds whistled other lays . . .
And the boughs of the trees whispered charms.

These he had collected and stored over the rafters of his heart. And then, when the time was ripe, he took them down and put them into words. From this process came a remarkable stream of writing that was vigorous, mature, fresh, and effective. It was always there.

During these busy, hectic years, his salvation, I think, was the Point. That became his retreat and his lodestone to remind him of who he really was and what he was all about. There he could relax among the pines and rocks, watch for the linnaea as it came up in the spring, listen to the call of the loon, dream by the fire, be alone with friends and family. It was an old dream, the Point. For years he had talked of having a writing shack somewhere away from it all. We used to tramp the country around Ely looking for just the right place. In the end, it became the Point on Burntside Lake, so important to him that he wrote a book about it.

We were back from the Middle East about that time, and he and Yvonne were discussing the Point and what to call it. We had served at the little American Embassy at Benghazi, Libya, which was a listening post during those days when the political winds were lashing the Middle East and Nasser was making big medicine out of Egyptian nationalism. "The Point," she said, "is like a listening post for you, isn't it, a place where you can tune into the world of the wilderness and its secret life?" He loved the idea and from that unlikely comparison came the name of the Point and the title for his second book, *Listening Point*.

But he never wrote there. His typewriter and tools remained at home in the writing shack in the corner of the

INTRODUCTION

yard. The Point was where he came back to earth, where he renewed his soul. We are back to the old man now, lying on the dock in the autumn twilight, listening to the waves chuckling among the rocks beneath.

I cling to this image because I like it and, perhaps, because I want to rescue the essential man from the myth that has grown up around him—the environmental guru and the public personality. After our career abroad came to an end and we came back home to live, it was to find a different man than we had known. During those years he had emerged from a decent obscurity to become a man of affairs and a nationally recognized author and environmentalist.

We rejoiced in his his well-deserved recognition and success. But it all came at a cost. The public increasingly took his time and demanded more. His life became a complicated schedule of telephone calls, commitments, and travel. Some of it he enjoyed. Some he did not. He would come back from trips to Washington and elsewhere grey and exhausted. At a banquet one night in the late sixties, where he was scheduled to speak, he had a near fatal heart attack. Yet the busy schedule continued for another ten years.

I cannot, therefore, write of these years without a sense of regret. I regretted the distortion of his life by his prominence, the expropriation of his time by the public. I regretted the personal cost to him. I regretted the books not being written. For he was, in essence, a simple person. He liked simple things and simple living. And he wanted to write about it. That's all. All the rest, I feel, was superfluous. He was a man of the early part of the century, caught up and blown about by the storms and powers of my generation, which staked out his soul and work as its own without, however, knowing much about who and what he really was.

I have also regretted the companionship we might have

shared had we not all gone off in different directions. My own years in the foreign service were totally absorbing. Those were the dramatic years of the high cold war and of the rise and decline of the Pax Americana. We moved to the Middle East, to Europe, to Canada, from Southeast Asia to Washington, D.C., and then back to Europe again. I became almost an expatriate at heart, more at home in Paris or London than in any American city. Absorbed in his own work, my father could have known little of mine, no more than I of his. In fact, we had much in common that could have made for a rich companionship.

Happily, in the end, but just barely, it all came together as we should have foreseen it would. His prominence in the environmental movement led him inexorably toward the great global issues of the day. My life in the foreign service brought me face-to-face with the forces degrading the planet—war, commercial exploitation, grinding poverty in the Third World, ignorance, greed, overpopulation, and massive environmental devastation. It was the beginning of the seventies when the world environmental movement really took off. After the Stockholm Conference of 1972, global environmental concerns became a priority on diplomatic agendas. We began to run into the same people. We exchanged books and ideas. I have on my desk a copy of Rolf Edberg's *On the Edge of a Cloud*, the little book that inspired the Stockholm Conference. I read it and gave it to Dad. He returned it heavily underlined in some parts, including the following short passage: "We must make peace with the natural forces on the surface of the earth if we are ever to make peace within our own species."

Paradoxically, it was my work overseas that finally brought home to me the real importance of my father's work. It was about that time, when I was working on the Sahelian Task Force and on organizing the World Food

INTRODUCTION

Conference at Rome, that I saw graphically for myself the global network of life into which we are all woven, how all parts are related to the whole. I came to realize that the balance and beauty of a wilderness lake and the life about it mesh naturally with the global picture of the interdependence of all things and all people. I can imagine the good talks we might have had. There is a lesson for us all in this.

I have said that Sigurd Olson was a man of his times, and he was. But in a deeper sense, he was a throwback to an agrarian age, to an ancient, more arcadian view of life. He cared nothing for machinery, for industry, for politics or trade. He loved nature, the land, and elemental things, literally fire, air, water, and earth. He liked to get his hands on it, smell it, play with it. He could have been some "pagan suckled on a creed outworn," for he did see "Proteus rising from the sea" and he did hear the voices of the old gods and the music of the spheres. Thoreau had been his inspiration and guide for cutting through the shallow pretensions of conventional life. He would have found a friend in old Hesiod or romanced his life away with Rousseau. He had the soul of a Wordsworth mixed with the rough-and-ready streak of the American frontier. Modern times have labeled him an environmentalist or conservationist. But he was that only by association or incidentally to his fight to preserve the Quetico-Superior wilderness. It was the whole system he defied, not, God bless him, by protest but by standing up for and expressing his own vision of the beautiful and the good. The man speaks best for himself.

> *Pipes of Pan, the little people, the spirit of trees, of animals and birds, of rocks and waters, of sun, wind, and storm, or night and morning, of a world all but forgotten in the hard cold light of the technological civilization we have built; these were part of my early childhood, a time before reason*

and knowledge colored perception, days that were not only mine but belonged to the childhood of the race.

It is a theme that runs through all his life and works.

He died literally with his boots on, on a cold January day, snowshoeing his favorite trail around the bog behind the house. The usual arrangements followed. But I wished we could have left him there, let the snow fall to cover him until he was only a mound beneath. We should have let nature have its way with his remains, to break him down into the soil of the forest. His body would have joined his spirit in the flow of life that had nourished him for over eighty years. In the fall, his shroud would be a blanket of autumn leaves, his anthem the far calling of strings of geese heading south, the low organ tones of the winter winds. It would have been fitting, I think, and a far, far better thing.

ROBERT KEITH OLSON

Perspective — The Beginning

Sigurd Olson represents more than an interesting historical character and literary personality. He was a philosopher and a friend, and I had the privilege of meeting him in "his" canoe country on one of my very first boundary waters experiences. At the time, I didn't fully realize how important that was.

Sig's life has the same number of twists and turns that all of our lives contain. He was successful and he was a good writer, but he also worked to achieve his fame and his influence. Few men have an institution named after them while they are still alive, but Sig did. He had an elementary school and the Sigurd Olson Environmental Institute named in honor of his status as one of the environment's foremost spokesmen.

His books gave voice to the average paddler's fascination

with the forest and the lake country. He spoke eloquently to what we all find important, and he gave prestige to the common place. He did not dwell on the long trip, the adventure beyond reach of most of us. He told of a cabin on a lake, a rock wall, a scrub oak, fishing, watching a sunset, sitting by a fire, and listening to rain on the tent.

In Sig's books, we learn that a portage is more than sweat and labor, it is an opportunity to place our footsteps in the flow of history. We learn to make the canoe an extension of the spirit of both the paddler and the lake. There are "white horses" in the windswept lake and open horizons to pursue. He challenges us, but he does it gently. He does not lecture, he leads. He puts us in the essays and teaches us to love the silence and the solitude. To comprehend timelessness, he takes away our watches and gives us the time clock of the wilderness.

I have had the privilege of being at Listening Point, and I have felt the strength of Sig's presence. It is a cabin on the lake, not set back in the wilderness but between other lake cottages. It is not wilderness. Motorboats cruise by, planes fly overhead, and I can drive to the path that leads to the cabin. Yet I find wilderness spirits there. I walk the ancient greenstone and touch Sig's love of geology and the earth. I walk beneath the red pines and know his love of trees and his fascination with the renewal of the natural landscape.

In the 1980 documentary "The Wildernerss World of Sigurd F. Olson" (Twin Cities Public Television Inc.), Sig touches a young tree and tells the audience that the youth of today are like the seedling, ready to replace the old trees when they come down if we give them the proper wisdom with which to grow. Sig's trees are still growing. The bearberry ledge, the lichens, the woodpile, the sauna, and the beach all have a special sense of significance to the students who visit the Point with me. But most important is Sig's suggestion that we can all find a listening point of our own. He challenges us with that thought, that there can be enough land saved, enough protection for nature that we can all find what he found.

We have to remember that the canoe country of Minnesota and Ontario was not a pristine landscape when he found it. Like Aldo Leopold's shack, Sig's Ely, Minnesota, landscape needed a visionary to see how it could recover from the ravages of man and become a monument to nature. The landscape was cutover, burned, logged, and developed in a haphazard way, but he could look past the slash and see the interior virgin forest.

He loved the land, but like John Muir and Aldo Leopold he had to take up the pen to help preserve it. He talked to us because he cared about the future. He had values far beyond his own life. Sig loved the opportunity to paddle and be immersed in the North. He liked to push himself physically, to paddle hard and long, to compare himself with the voyageurs and the Indians. He had a sense of history and a sense of the future.

He spoke as well as he wrote, at numerous hearings in St. Paul, Ely, Washington, D.C., and Canada. He faced opposition that was so hostile that others were looking for escape routes, and yet he never wavered in what he felt was right. He spoke with compassion, a scientist's background, a guide's sense of direction, and an artist's perspective.

In the environmental battles of the 1920s, Sig was there, and he was still leading the way into the 1980s. But despite battles that only seemed to end in time for the next ones to heat up, he never lost his dignity and self-control. Always a gentleman, he defended the opposition's right to express themselves. This is even more significant when you realize that he faced hostile groups in his chosen hometown, that they yelled and screamed at him, that they hung him in effigy. He never cowered in fear, nor did he succumb to the temptation to lower his behavior to their level.

Knowing Sig, I grew to admire and love him and had the opportunity to meet Elizabeth, Sig Jr., and Bob. I visited the farm, the cabin, the writing shack, and the house on the hill. I got a chance to know the depth of the person.

We all create images for famous and admirable people. We make internal decisions based on feelings rather than facts, and we conclude that the people we admire must live within the framework we create, with judgements being made on such an arbitrary and unknown basis that it is easy for these people to let their admirers down without realizing it. Sig was aware of this problem and anguished over the effects of a biography.

In *Open Horizons*, Sig told his own story in a limited autobiography, but he was afraid of the effects of going further. He was afraid that those people who had read his books or those who had heard him in testimony had created false images of him, and that those images might serve as self-created motivation. He worried that a real biography would leave him far short of those expectations. Sig never wanted to do anything that would diminish the efforts of those who worked for the wilderness. That is why he spent more time answering letters and greating visitors than he did writing for publication.

Visiting with the family, I found that this fear was unnecessary. In reading his archival materials, I found that there was nothing to be hidden, that the man did not fall short of any realistic standards. On the contrary, he became more of a model, a more realistic image for all of us to look up to. He had his moments of weakness and indecision like all of us, but once he made a decision, he followed through with it. He used all his talents, and he stood for the things that were important in his personal philosophy.

PERSPECTIVE — THE BEGINNING

I could see the influence of his father, the strict minister, his mother, compassionate and full of humor. I saw the family that he and Elizabeth created living like many families, with love and frustration, with a wife who made the home a place where Sig could bring home guests who were adventurers, writers, politicians, lobbyists, and admirers, and a husband who provided a good living to support them all. They were real people who accomplished significant things because a family that is strong supports its members.

When I finally defined what I wanted to do in these books, it came down to a desire to share the real Olson family, to present Sig as a person who accomplished what is possible for all of us to accomplish. Like Listening Point, the opportunity to be as effective as Sig is available to us all.

This book has been in the works for years — the time that was needed for research, reading, interviews, and personal reflection. It began in a conversation with Sig in 1978 and an effort to learn more about our environmental heritage and the people who have shaped our land values. I learned about many people, but of all of them, Sig and my grandfather had the greatest influence on my personal philosophy and life. This project was full of apprehension, and a feeling of inadequacy, difficult emotions for a writer to overcome, but the importance of this material was too great for me not to share. I want to share with you Sigurd F. Olson, his wife, Elizabeth (Uhrenholdt) Olson, Sigurd Thorne Olson, and Robert Keith Olson.

I also want to fill the need that all Sig readers have for more words of wisdom, more inspiration from his pen, and in putting together this collection of articles, letters, and stories, I also hope that I share with you some of the fun that this project has provided me.

This volume represents Sig's beginnings. The texts are not polished; the philosophy is not refined. They are closer to the popular literature of the time than to the *Reflections from the North Country* sage. Don't judge the work, enjoy it. Reflect on the advances in your own skills and judgement over time. For the love of open horizons, adventure, and the earth, share the life of one of America's foremost spokesmen.

The Collected Works of Sigurd F. Olson

The Early Writings: 1921-1934

1899–1921

SIG WAS BORN in Chicago in 1899, four years after the first logging took place in the future Boundary Waters Canoe Area Wilderness. At the age of six, his family moved to Sister Bay in Wisconsin's famous Door County. His father, Lawrence, a Baptist minister, had been given the first of a series of northern Wisconsin assignments. Even at this early age, Sig was observant and saw the contrast between the tall, crowded structures of Chicago and the quiet beauty of Sister Bay, on the shore of Green Bay. Chicago was sixty-two years old when Sig was born. It had suffered through the 1871 fire and rebuilt itself immediately in an undisciplined style that matched the hectic growth of its industry and commerce. The move took Sig from an urban environment of over 1.6 million people to a rural setting.

In Sig's essay "The Singing Wilderness," he remembered

"the first time I heard the music." In Sister Bay, foghorns and boat whistles added mystery and wonder to the night. They were so vivid that the boy of seven had to hike "through woods I had never traversed" to see the coastline, the vivid blue, the tall cliffs, the waves, and the horizon: "I was alone in a wild and lovely place, part at last of the wind and the water, part of the dark forest through which I had come, and of all the wild sounds and colors and feelings of the place I had found. That day I entered into a life of indescribable beauty and delight. There I believe I heard the singing wilderness for the first time."

Maybe it was the contrast with Chicago's bustle and constant din that caused such an alertness, or maybe Sig was just an exceptionally perceptive child. He walked the woods with his grandmother, shuffled through autumn leaves, and admired fresh trout for beauty as well as taste.

The family moved westward to Prentice, Wisconsin, and then to Ashland on the south shore of Lake Superior. In Ashland, Sig entered a school writing contest and won first prize. He was twelve years old when he first felt the satisfaction of creative writing. The thrill of that contest would be remembered all of his life, and in many ways it was a crucial turning point for him. His prize-winning essay was on "The Function of the Chamber of Commerce."

Sig's mother, Ida Mae, had a great sense of humor to offset Lawrence's strict Baptist demeanor. They had met in Bemidji, Minnesota, and Lawrence had been a minister in St. Cloud before moving to Chicago.

In Ashland, Sig's father was in charge of supplying the northern Wisconsin churches, and he would fill in when the congregation needed a Swedish sermon. He had come from Sweden at the age of seventeen, and Ida Mae had immigrated at the age of twelve.

The Ashland setting was valuable to Sig for many reasons. Besides his writing inspiration, Sig found an outlet for the explorer in his soul. In every direction, there were exciting discoveries to be made. He canoed Whittlesey and Fish creeks, as well as the White River with its large and untamed Bibon Swamp. He had Chequamegon Bay and the Apostle Islands spread out before him. The Kakagon and Fish creek sloughs were rich in waterfowl, and the cutover area was teeming with deer. His canoe, bike, and feet gave him access to great adventures.

Ashland was a large town, not like Chicago but one that bustled with the shipping of iron ore and lumber. The town was full of characters—fishermen, farmers, sailors, miners, trappers, Indians, Scandinavians, Germans, and Danes. It was a place for Sig to see the full diversity of the region's history and economy. He lived at a time and place of transition that he would weave into later essays as he bridged modern and historic times to make modern canoeists into historic voyageurs.

Sig graduated from Ashland High School and attended Northland College. He was an intelligent student; his later research projects, writing, and position as college dean would all attest to that fact. He was also an extremely active person, with a need to be on the move, seeing the land, exerting physical energy, breaking a sweat, extending himself mentally and bodily.

His most important accomplishment at Northland College may have been getting to know his roommate well. Andy Uhrenholdt was the son of a Danish farmer who lived near the village of Seeley, Wisconsin. Sig once recalled the conversation that first brought him to his roommate's farm:

"Andy, who's that good looking girl in the photograph on your bureau?"

"She happens to be my sister."

"Well, I'd like to meet her some time."

"Come down and spend Easter with me."

Although it was Elizabeth's picture that led Sig to the farm, Elizabeth would recall that as Sig and her father, Soren, built their friendship, she saw less and less of the young collegian. Her father put him to work, and when they weren't working, her father would tell Sig about the land, his visions, and his plans.

Soren Uhrenholdt could look at young trees and envision a forest. He could see value in planting trees as well as crops. He knew that the forest had value, and he pioneered a combination of agriculture and silviculture. Uhrenholdt was to become a leader in conservation who would receive awards and recognition in later years. Uhrenholdt Memorial Forest, north of Hayward, Wisconsin, is a living monument to his efforts.

During those early years visiting the farm, Sig helped the hard-working Danish immigrant clear the stumps out of his fields. This combination of sweat and philosophy would be the pattern for the rest of Sig's life. In later years when he placed a quotation on the pack or thwart in front of him, it was an extension of this work/think theme.

Seeley is just north of Hayward, and that put Sig in another culturally rich part of Wisconsin. Hayward had long been a major logging and Indian center. The Namekagon and Totagatic rivers flowing through the countryside served as the historical highway for the area. They also served as a backdrop to the Uhrenholdt farm. Sig not only farmed, he fished, hunted, and explored. Here he learned how to fly-fish as well as how to plow.

At the farm, Sig was exposed to a family of four boys and four girls as well as a new wealth of ideas. The Seeley church was visited by a variety of ministers who "held service" on Sunday, whether they were Presbyterian, Lutheran, or another denomination, and on Sunday evening the farm would host a dance for the youth.

Elizabeth taught Sig how to dance—"a sin in the Olson home." On a visit to Ashland, she said to Sig, "There's an Elk dance; let's go to it." Sig had to take her aside and let her know that his parents didn't know he danced and that they would not approve.

Rivers and lakes were always close to Sig's experience. The Yellow River, which enters the St. Croix near Danbury, Wisconsin, was the focal point for Sig's work on the Wisconsin Geologic Survey for two summers. While he mapped the topography, he was able to hike the landscape and to fuel his growing curiosity about all of nature. Ecology was not a recognized study as it is now. Ecology was too interdisciplined for that time. It ties pieces together from many sciences and crosses many traditional department lines. Sig may not have been aware of it, but he was becoming an ecologist because of his diverse passions.

It was this work that started Sig thinking about geology as well as biology. By then, he was at the University of Wisconsin at Madison, John Muir and Aldo Leopold's university, studying for a degree in agronomy. Uhrenholdt's influence was obvious in Sig's college direction. He was preparing to be a county agent and to share the Uhrenholdt philosophy with other farmers.

By his graduation in 1920, Sig began to have doubts about his direction. He had some interest in agriculture, but his farm experience was limited, and the prospect of dealing with a variety of farm concerns and working in an office did not appeal to him.

After graduation, he took a position as a county agent and agricultural instructor in Nashwauk, Minnesota. He lived in Nashwauk for one year. This was the Iron Range, a narrow strip of land that cuts across northern Minnesota.

In 1920, it was a booming country filled with immigrant miners and loggers. There was a blend of rich ethnic traditions and harsh labor conditions. The earth was exposed by deep open-pit gouges. The rich, reddish layers told the geologic story of the region in human "grand canyons," and the air and buildings were tinged with red dust.

This was Sig's first exposure to Minnesota. He was alone in a new country, and his discoverer's instincts took him on the Prairie and Mississippi rivers and into the lakes northwest of town. He walked and paddled whenever he could. He also met another major influence in his life—Al Kennedy.

Al was a mystery man, a recluse with his own trail through life. He had been convicted of killing a man in a logging fight and was later pardoned from prison by Theodore Roosevelt. His cabin was in the woods north of Nashwauk. Sig's wanderings crossed Kennedy's path and brought the two men together at Kennedy's cabin. It was Kennedy who told Sig that he needed to go farther north—to the boundary waters—if he wanted to find real canoe country. The suggestion found fertile ground in Sig's mind.

Sig went to canoe country and fell in love with it. He found that he could not stay in Nashwauk; it was time to prepare for a different future. In 1921, he returned to the University of Wisconsin and studied geology—his new intellectual challenge—and prepared for the biggest moves in his life.

Cruising God's Country
The Milwaukee Journal
JULY 31, 1921

THIS WAS SIG'S FIRST *published article. His brother Kenneth was on the staff of the* Milwaukee Journal, *which led to the publication of two pieces in that newspaper. Kenneth went on to head the journalism departments at Northwestern and Rutgers universities.*

This article is one of the few works that hints at Sig's background as a minister's son. The other is the chapter "Easter on the Prairie" in The Singing Wilderness. *"Cruising God's Country" is Sig's strongest description of wilderness in this decade and gives us a glimpse of what canoe country was like when it was all right to sleep on balsam boughs and visitor days were 200 instead of 200,000. Most of Sig's early writing deals with hunting and fishing, not the aesthetics of wilderness.*

THE EARLY WRITINGS

When the Great Creator had almost finished this wonderful country he stopped in his labors and pondered. There was one thing lacking, a spot more beautiful than all the rest where his children could come and soothe their weary spirits. A sanctuary, far from the smoke of cities and the discordant clamor of industry, a wilderness unsullied by the hand of man. God saw all that was to happen. He saw the ravaging of his forests, the despoiling of his streams and lakes by the greedy, unthinking hands of those who would know no beauty and see only in the wonders of nature, resources for filling their own already bursting coffers.

He also knew that some of his children would love nature and its beauties as they should. That the trees would be their temples and the glories of mountain and forest their religion. He knew that they would weep at the wanton destruction of the nature that would mean to them life itself. So for these who would deeply love and truly understand nature in all its moods, He set aside a little bit of Paradise, inaccessible for those who would despoil it.

East of the Rainy Lake country and north of the rugged shores of Lake Superior lies a virgin wilderness almost too beautiful to describe. It would be as easy to paint a perfect sunset or the northern lights as to do the country justice.

It is a primitive wilderness of lakes, streams and mountains where the only sounds are the laughing of the loons, the slap of the beaver's tail and the sloshing around of moose and deer in the bays. It is to-day as it was before Columbus discovered this country, untouched, untarnished. The winds still whisper through the virgin timber, the waves on Big Saganaga still lap hungrily at the rocky shore. The cry of the great northern loon echoes and reechoes from Lake Superior to Hudson Bay. The moose and deer come down to drink still unafraid, down trails deeply worn through centuries of use. The beaver build their dams and the crash of the falling popple and ash is unheard by human ears. The wilderness is teeming with life. Everything is yet as God left it; perfect. He had planned well.

Let us cruise for a while, just you and I, through this wonderland that was set aside for us.

We have passed through many lakes, made countless portages and now at last are in the heart of the wilderness. Our camp is on a rocky island covered with balsam and spruce. The canoe is pulled up high and dry. I am busy with the fire. You perhaps have just finished cutting balsam boughs for our beds, and being a little tired after the long day of paddling against the wind, you light your pipe and wander down to the shore. A fallen spruce offers a good resting place so you sit down and look out over the lake.

All is still, the water is smooth as glass except when disturbed by the jumping of lake trout. The heavily timbered shores are reflected as from a mirror in the waters and as you gaze you sometimes catch yourself wondering which is which, the reflection or the shore. A white throated sparrow calls so far away and sweetly, you can hardly believe a note could be so clear and faint and still be heard. You stand there in awe, the silence almost overcomes you, and a queer feeling comes to your throat. God! how beautiful it all is, and your soul unconsciously goes out in gratitude to the creator who has saved this little bit of heaven for you.

Suddenly you are startled. A weird screaming peal of maniacal laughter rends the silence like a knife. Not only once, but peal upon peal, each more exultant than the first. A cold shiver travels up and down your spine. You wish you could kill that thing that spoiled it all. But it is only the call of the loon and it is answered far off to the north. You can't help but wonder how far that call will travel, perhaps way up to the Hudson Bay, who knows. As the echoes come back again and again from nameless lakes far away and finally cease, the silence is deeper than ever for everything has a place in God's plan, even the laughing of the loon.

It is almost dark. The sun has set, leaving the west a lurid tumbled mass of burnished gold. The sunset seems almost fierce in its intensity, not peaceful and glowing but instead a sullen angry red. The tent gleams ghostly in the shadow of a huge spruce. I have been cooking supper and the odor of bacon and coffee assails your nostrils and you remember that you are still alive and ravenously hungry after the long day of paddling and portaging.

After supper, our pipes. The smoke curls up and its fragrance adds the final touch to a day that has been lived, not existed. We take out our map and by the light of the campfire find we are on an island on Ottertrack Lake. It is the most beautiful we have struck so far and if it were not for the restless call of that "Something lost behind the Ranges," we would camp here, but like Kipling's explorer we decide that upon the morrow we will look beyond to see what awaits us there.

We are sitting smoking in front of the tent. The smoke from our dying camp-fire curls lazily upward. It is dark now but over toward the east the tops of the spruces are faintly illumined. We watch expectantly up the water way. First, a thin rim of silver, then slowly, majestically, golden mellow, a glorious summer moon rises dripping out of the dark placid waters of Ottertrack. The spruces are sharply silhouetted for a moment and then the wilderness is bathed in mellow moonlight. Even the sharp old stub over on the shore has something soft and beautiful about it. We sit in silence drinking in the radiant glory about us. Words would be sacrilege. The mournful long drawn wail of a timber wolf comes down from the north and you can't help but shiver a little. A silvery waterway leads directly to our little island. Now it is smooth and polished and now strewn with a million diamonds as a riffle of wind roughens the surface. Peacefulness and contentment is our lot.

Though we are poor in worldly goods, can anyone else love the forests, lakes and streams any more than we do? Our bodies are still strong and full of the vigor of life. We look forward to years of happiness, for life is good to those who know how to live. We do not ever hope to accumulate vast worldly wealth but shall gather instead something far more valuable, a store of memories. When we reach the twilight of life we can look back and say, "We are glad we lived as we did." Life has been good to us. We will not be afraid of death, because we will have drunk to the full the cup of happiness and contentment that only close communion with nature can give.

Our pipes are out and the moon is rising high in the heavens. We turn in for the night and sleep as only men can in beds of balsam in the wilderness.

Awake at dawn, for dawn is the best part of the day in the wilderness. The trees and brush are dripping with dew. The birds are bursting their little throats with warbling melody. Everything is fresh and clean. A dip in the icy clear waters of the lake and our toilet is complete. The sun is just coming up over in the bay toward the east. The faint white, low, hanging mist quickly disappears before its warming rays. A bull moose that we hadn't seen before is revealed standing up to his knees in the water of a bay five hundred yards up shore. He hasn't seen us and is busy eating lily pad roots. We watch expectantly as ducking his head and neck under water he comes up in a shower of spray, a bunch of lily roots dripping in his mouth. The sunlight glints on his widely spreading horns as he stands transfixed and looks in our direction. He watches us a little while and then leisurely steps out of the water. We can hear the brush crack as he works his way up over the rise. We get one last glimpse of him as he stands on top of the ridge and looks down upon us.

The trout are jumping and a pair of loons are laughing and splashing water with their wings. The water is so clear that we can see the fish feeding along the shore.

After breakfast we break camp, dip our paddles and are off for new country and new adventures. We paddle close to shore as there is always more of interest there than anywhere else. A mallard hen flies out in front of the canoe, quacking and making believe she is crippled. We soon see the cause of her discomfiture. A flock of little brown chicks are skittering for the shore as fast as their little legs and wings will take them. They hide in all sorts of nooks and peep out timidly at us thinking they are hidden. We glide along through lake after lake, sometimes making portages from one lake to another. Some of the portages are steep and rocky so a man with a pack and a canoe has all he can do to keep his footing. In some places beaver dams have to be crossed and marshy places waded through, not wet enough to float a canoe but too wet to walk upon. The beaver are very active and evidences of their logging operations are to be seen everywhere. They are so tame that we see them swimming about in broad daylight. When we get too close, down they go with a mighty flap of their tails. We are paddling easily along when the sound of a waterfall reaches our ears.

Paddling in toward shore we leave the canoe and follow up the sound. It must be small because we hear only a faint trickling over the rock. After a hundred yards or so we come to a steep face of rock nearly perpendicular and perhaps one hundred feet in height. A spring fed brook breaks over the top and spreads over the face of the rock like a thin transparent veil. The sun breaking through the birches seems to touch the veil with silver light so we call it the

"Crystal Sheen." The little fall is in a grove of slender white birches. The ground and the rock itself is carpeted with the most delicately tinted green moss. Everything is so exquisitely beautiful that one can't help but wonder if this isn't really a part of fairyland. A troupe of tiny fairies with gauzelike wings bathing in the spray of the falls would have made the picture perfect.

Leaving reluctantly we resume our paddling. The steady swish, swish of our paddles soon carries us many miles northward. It's a pleasure to watch your paddle in the clear water, and the little ever present whirlpool that you make with every stroke. We go through a narrow neck and presently the water becomes swifter. We are in a river and before we know it are racing along very swiftly. White water breaking over jagged rocks warns us to keep our distance. A sharp rock almost seems to leap at us out of the foam but a quick swerve of the paddle and we slip past. Now we are bounding and shooting through spray and white water. It takes quick thinking, and quicker acting to keep away from the rocks now. The trees on shore seem to shoot past and the rocks are getting thicker. A patch of white water shows up ahead. You try your best to head the canoe to one side. Now we are in it. The sickening sound of a rock grating on the bottom of the canoe and we stop in mid stream. We paddle desperately, the canoe starts to swing. Two more feet and we are done for. A last desperate stroke and we slip off and into the current. The water soon becomes quieter and we find ourselves cruising smoothly along through another lake, ever northward. This lake is dotted with rocky islands covered with spruce and Norway pine. Gulls are flying around screaming and flying low over our heads. Evidently this must be their nesting ground.

We are both tired so head the canoe for a pretty little island near the center of the lake. It is a good camping place and the weird beauty of the lake with its many rocky islands and screaming gulls appeals to us so we decide to stop for the night. The rock is covered with heavy lichen which makes a fine bed. The tent is soon up and supper on the way. After supper, our pipes alight, we lay on our backs and gaze up at the lazily drifting clouds. One more day had been added to our stock of memories.

And so we travel through hundreds of lakes and rivers, drink in the beauties of countless water falls, rapids and virgin forests, see naked grandeur as God intended it to be, unscathed by the hand of man. When we end up our cruise and our canoes grate on a sandy beach for the last time, our hearts are heavy and yet how happy. We were ragged and unkempt but what mattered was that our hearts were filled to over-flowing. We came back empty handed but oh, how rich we were. We could say with Kipling's explorer on his return, "Have I named one single river? Have I claimed one single acre? Have I kept one single nugget? No not I. Because my price was paid me ten times over by my maker. But you wouldn't understand it. You go up and occupy."

1922–1925

SIG WAS A ROMANTIC in his writings, but Elizabeth doesn't recall that he ever formally proposed to her. They were married on August 8, 1922.

Sig offered Elizabeth the choice of a honeymoon canoe trip or a diamond, and after the sales job he did on canoeing she chose the trip. It was her first canoe trip, and it started at Fall Lake and went to Newton, Otter Track, Moose, Kawnipi, and many other lakes. It took three weeks, and Sig barely made it back in time for work.

When they first started out, everytime they would pass a new bend, Elizabeth would ask Sig, "Is this where we stop?" "Oh, no." And they would keep going. After crossing Basswood Lake, Elizabeth was so muscle sore she became ill and was laid up for three days. After that, everything went well.

When they returned home, Elizabeth felt great except for the fact that she had no letter waiting from her mother. She thought that if she had told her what she was going to do on her honeymoon, her mother would have been worried and written.

As it was, Elizabeth passed the test. A few years before his death, Sig asked her about the diamond and if she would like one. "Oh no, it's too late. I've gotten along fine without one."

In 1922, Sig and Elizabeth moved to Ely and the land he loved. His world came together with relative ease. Ely was a bustling mining community filled with immigrants and colorful men. This was comparable to the mix that he had found in Ashland and would help him further develop his view of history, ecology, and geography as components of the same continuum. This was combined with the love of literature and philosophy he learned from his father, his mother's love of life and sense of humor, the forest ethics of Soren Uhrenholdt, Elizabeth's dignity and sense of order, and the physical challenge of exploring an unmapped canoe country of over 1,000 lakes, where there was always an open northern horizon. The country around Ely held lots of promise, but at this time, much of the land was mined, logged, or burnt over.

Sig began teaching biology at Ely Junior College, where he infused an exciting mixture of field trips into the curriculum. His trips went to a variety of "special" places and were made in private vehicles, since the school considered the field trips foolish. If the administration felt that these field trips made for easy classes, they did not understand Sig. He believed in hard work. It wasn't enough for students to like nature, they had to understand it and have a knowledge of how it worked.

During this time, Sig taught evening classes for the immigrant miners who wanted to get their citizenship. Sig enjoyed these classes and felt that he really got to know the people who enrolled in them.

In 1923, Sigurd Thorne Olson was born on opening day of duck season. Sig Jr. would develop into one of the country's leading game managers. With the first study of loons in Minnesota as his thesis, he moved on to Alaska and helped organize the wildlife programs in this country's last great wilderness. Robert Keith Olson was born in 1925 at the dawn of Sig's writing career. He went on to distinguish himself in the diplomatic service with posts in Vietnam, Libya, Lebanon, France, Italy, Canada, and Central America.

Sig was dean of the junior college, head of its biology department, and ready to make his mark.

Fishing Jewelry
The Milwaukee Journal
1 9 2 5

IN 1925, *Sigurd Olson was a twenty-six-year-old biology instructor at Ely's community college. He had been married three years, and his second son, Robert, had just been born when a check for twenty-five dollars arrived in the mail from the* Milwaukee Journal. *The check was for an article called "Fishing Jewelry." Now Sig could pay off the hospital and take Elizabeth out to celebrate, for although "Fishing Jewelry" was his second published piece, it marked the real beginning of his writing career.*

Elizabeth has described "Fishing Jewelry" as "such a silly piece." Indeed, like all the pieces in this volume, it lacks the depth of both philosophy and technique of Sig's later writing. It does, however, have its points of interest. You can feel Sig's closeness to the mixed ethnic background of Ely, for instance, by the broken English he uses for all of his fictional characters. There is also a description of the bass on the moss that is reminiscent of his description in "Grand-

mother's Trout" (The Singing Wilderness). *As you read this and other pieces in this book, don't judge Sig by the standards of his books, but enjoy the insights into his life and personal growth.*

In that 1925 issue of the Milwaukee Journal, *Sig's article nestled among the following headlines: "Right-of ways of Busted Railroads to Be Auto Roads" (today we are making them into bike trails), "Bryan Camp Would Dodge Debate at Monkey Hearings," "Arctic Tragedy Feared in Amundsen's Silence," "Semi-camping New Idea for Timid City Motorist," "MacMillan off for North Pole," and "Rog Hornsby as Manager is this Year's Miracle Man."*

THE TWO OF US, "Wild Cat" Dan and I had just stowed away enough fish mulligan to last us a week and were enduring the ominous silence that always comes between such an achievement and the inevitable suggestion, "Well guess we'd better clean up the mess."

After some fifteen minutes of bliss, I looked at Dan and he at me, both with the same blank expression of helplessness. Finally Dan heaved a ponderous sigh and rose to his feet. "Well," he started in, "I suppose," and he looked at me rather pleadingly, "I guess partner, I've et too much. Let's leave the dishes tills mornin'."

"Good idea Dan," answered I, greatly relieved. "Guess we both feel the same way.

With one accord, we pushed the supper dishes to the end of the table, just far enough back in the dark, so that they couldn't reproach us visibly at least for not washing them. It was all we could do after that, to stagger over to our respective bunks. Our pipes were soon going and a feeling of lazy comfort and peace pervaded the cabin.

As I watched the blue smoke curl up around the rafters, I wouldn't have traded places then with anyone else in the world. I knew then as I have often known since, that there is nothing so soul-satisfying and conducive to perfect contentment, as a full stomach and a good place to rest, after a day in the brush. Then to top it off, the rain began to patter softly against the south windows. The hour was ripe for dreams.

Neither of us said a word for perhaps a half an hour. From my corner, I could see old Dan sitting on the edge of his bunk, eyes half closed, smoking contentedly. Presently, he started taking short spasmodic puffs and I waited expectantly. A few long puffs and he began, "You was askin' me t'other day 'bout bass, and since then I've been thinkin' 'bout a fellow that came up here some eight or nine years ago. He was plumb crazy 'bout fishin', and had the dangdest outfit along, you ever did see, little red flies, white ones, brown ones, and all sorts of funny wooden bugs. When I saw it the first time, I asked him what he planned on doin' with all that pile o' jewelry. He laffed and said, he was goin' to show us lumber-jacks how to ketch bass. Well, I'd caught plenty of 'em with frogs and minners and told him so, but never in all my life with such an ornery collection as what he had. Between you and me, I thought he was a little bit off, but told him to go ahead an' see what he could do.

"Then he started askin' me where they was any, and I told him we used to ketch 'em pretty plenty up at Grass Lake, some twenty years ago, when this camp was runnin' logs down the river, but that it hadn't been fished much since.

"Right away this feller gets interested and wants to know where it was. I told him as clost as I could figger, it was 'bout a mile northwest of Bray Lake, an' as far as I knew there wan'n't no trail. Just the same he was bound to go and stayed with me all that night.

"Well, next mornin' before daylight, he was hittin' the brush an' he didn't come back till just before dark, but dang

FISHING JEWELRY

it all if he didn't have the fines' string o' bass I ever did see. Right then and there, I took back all I'd said about his jewelry. Before he left he gave me a couple o' those bugs an' flies, but I never did get time to try 'em out. One o' those bass he brought in must a'weighed seven pounds if he weighed an ounce.

Then followed a long series of puffs.

"Son," he said after some time, "I'd like to see you go up an' try that lake. They must be some big ones in there yet. In the ole days we had a scow up there an' in the early mornin's, jus' when the mist was risin' off o' the rushes round the aidge, we'd ketch all we could eat with a couple o' frogs before breakfast.

By that time, I was sitting bolt upright on the edge of my bunk, wondering if I was really awake. Imagine having an old timer tell you of a lake that had hardly been fished for twenty years and full of bass up to seven pounds or more. Before I had time to ask him about the location of the lake Dan told me where I'd find a stub of a pencil and an old envelope.

"I'm pretty old and stiff to go up myself but I can tell you pretty close how to get there," he assured me. "Now if you'll gimme your pencil I'll try and draw you a map."

Slowly and laboriously he sketched a rough map on the back of the envelope, then with the stem of his pipe he traced the trail from Bray to Grass Lake.

"Foller up the shore of Bray Lake north from the cabin till you strike a swale, then strike straight northwest for three-quarters of a mile and there you'll find her right in front of you. You can' miss it."

I stowed the map away religiously in my shirt pocket. "That's news to me, Dan," I answered, "and if I don't bring back the brother to that seven pounder tomorrow night, I'll buy you grub for a month."

We smoked a while longer and talked bass, deer hunting, and game laws, till we were both sleepy and then turned in. I was far too excited to think of sleep, but finally dropped off only to dream of monster black bass striking insanely at every cast. Right in the midst of it, I was awakened by Dan's, "Roll out. Daylight in the swamp."

Breakfast was finished hurriedly, and I plunged into the rain-drenched brush just as daylight was breaking over the east shore of Bray Lake. I might just as well have taken an ice cold shower, for in a minute I was soaked to the skin. I followed Dan's map carefully and in half an hour found myself on a high brushy hill overlooking a tiny alder-fringed lake, not half a mile away. Then followed a mad scramble through some of the densest jumble I had ever seen. The entire slope was burned over and grown up thickly with popple brush and the ground itself, a maze of charred windfalls interlaced with the prickly vines of raspberry. Half the time, I was balanced precariously on downed timber or extricating myself from a network of tangled brush.

Arriving finally at the lake, I found the shore was partly sand and partly mud. All along the edge lay windfalls with inviting bunches of lily pads nestling around their submerged tips. I hit the shore at just such a spot and nervously rigged up my tackle.

While trying to fasten a brown fly to a swivel spinner, I succeeded in running the hook clean through the arm of my shirt. I tried most carefully to back it out, but try as I might, the barb refused to come. It seemed as though I had worked half the morning, before I finally ripped it out in sheer desperation.

Wading out to my waist, so that I could cast without encumbering myself with the whole shoreline, I unlimbered and let the fly sail out toward a bunch of lily pads. It settled gracefully on the edge of a leaf, rested just a second and slipped off. Bang! and a big green form splashed the whole end of the windfall. I let him have it and struck. Yes, I struck and my bedraggled fly came dancing merrily back over the disturbed ripples. I cast again and again, but not another rise did I get. Finally deciding that I must have hooked him pretty badly, I left the windfall and waded up the shore, casting at every likely spot. Some places literally screamed black bass, but no lure I had would bring even a half-hearted strike. By ten o'clock I had fished clear around the lake with only one strike to my record and that the first. I was pretty discouraged and was beginning to think that Old Dan's story was a fizzle or that I was a no good excuse for a fisherman.

I sat down on a log to think things over, wondering if there wasn't some place I had missed. I did remember one, where the mud had been so soft that I couldn't wade out to cast, and had gone back through the alders to the next likely spot. It was half way around the lake, but nevertheless I decided to try it, so back I went, creeping carefully through the brush until I was at the water's edge. The mud was much too soft to hold me, so I stepped on a log lying near, without touching the windfall at whose end I was to cast. It was rather a ticklish place at best, for the brush grew so close to the shore that casting was difficult.

Finding a little opening in the leaves, I tipped my rod back and sailed the fly out over the end of the windfall. It lit gently a few inches from a big lily pad at its very tip. Slap! A boiling swirl of water and the fly started for depths unknown. This time I hooked him firmly and the fight was on. First he dashed for a tangle of half-sunken brush, then just as wildly for the lily pads further out. At every run, I expected to see the line come floating limply to the top. Then down he went and by the fierce, tugging jerks I knew that he was sulking at the bottom. Keeping my balance on the slippery log made it doubly interesting. Once, as I lost my balance, I stepped in up to my knees in the soft ooze and let out ten feet of precious slack while getting back on.

I thought that was the finish but when I recovered my line, he was still on. Finally he seemed to be tiring, so I began to urge him a little, but no sooner did he feel the added pressure, than out he sped again for deep water. Out, out, he went, while the handle whizzed through my fingers. I tried to hold him back, but still the reel screeched. Only a few yards left, when all of a sudden he stopped dead and started to sulk. Here I got in a few yards of slack and thinking he was done for, began to bring him in. This time he changed his tactics. In he rushed straight toward me, while I reeled madly. When about twenty feet away, out of the water he came shaking his head in a last desperate effort. Not once, but three times did he come, making each jump wilder than the one before. All I could do was wind, wind, and keep the tip of my rod down.

The third jump took his last ounce of strength, for after that he came in sullenly. I slipped my hands into his gills and lifted from the water one of the finest bass it has ever been my joy to catch, and one of the best fighters. I laid him down tenderly on a bed of moss and for a long time watched the play of light on the bronze and green of his scales. It was one of those supreme moments that come in the life of every fisherman when he realizes for once, that the big one didn't get away.

After that Grass Lake seemed more cheerful. The sky was bluer and the birds sang more light heartedly than ever. I had solved the mystery and every windfall after that, was cast at not from the water, but from the shore. By late afternoon I had landed two more splendid fish, almost as large as the first and not a one under five pounds.

If I had used a boat, I would have had my limit, but I was more than satisfied. I had discovered a new sport, one as yet unrivaled for me, stalking black bass from the shore. It was almost dark before I reached the cabin at Bray Lake. As I came down the trail Old Dan saw me and yelled, "What luck?"

I answered as unconcernedly as I could, "Oh, I got a few Dan." It seemed as though I never would reach the cabin after that, even though it was only a scant hundred yards away. I did finally arrive however, and with great inward satisfaction spread out my catch for his appraisal.

For a moment he looked at them in silence. "Well I'll be danged," was all he said. "If that fool jewelry ain't turned the trick again."

On the Fire Line
with the Forest Service
Unpublished

WALTER WILWERDING *of* Sports Afield *was the first editor Sig dealt with. After reading one of his early pieces, Wilwerding wrote Sig:* "I've got this article of yours and there are places where your words sing. If you can write so that your writing sings, then you're on your way." *Sig commented,* "That changed my life, because ever since then I've tried to make my words sing."

"On the Fire Line with the Forest Service" *dates from some time in the twenties.*

The telephone in the Forest Service Headquarters jangled impatiently. The tired Ranger in charge answered wearily, knowing only too well what would be the message.
"Hello—"
"Cripple Creek Lookout? What in hell's the matter now?"

"Bad fire north of Bear Island Lake," answered another voice, also tired with weeks of fire fighting. "Send up a crew of forty men at once as the boundary of the Superior National Forest is in danger. Bad north wind driving fire due north."

"All right, we'll send out the last outfit we've got," snapped the Ranger, and at once the headquarters was galvanized into action.

"Dennison, go up town and round up the crew. Don't take 'No' from any man not working. It's six o'clock now. We will be leaving for the fire line by 7:30 tonight, and will be out on the line by midnight. You've got an hour and twenty-five minutes now, so pile 'em down here in a hurry. I'll attend to the equipment."

Ranger Denley's orders were always obeyed, no matter how impossible they seemed. This was a time for action, and although Dennison knew he could never get forty men, he answered, "Yes, sir," and stalked out into the street. Denley also knew that there were few men who would say "No" when Dennison's fighting blood was up.

Men were hard to get, as almost every available man was out on some fire line and had been ever since the dry spell started a month before. Since the snow had gone there hadn't been a drop of rain or so much as a cloud in the sky. The woods were as dry as tinder, even the heavy bog-mass in the swamps was dry and lifeless. For days the air had been so heavy with smoke that we could hardly see the sun. The sunsets were always dark red in the veil of smoke, dire and foreboding. Not a sign of rain and the thirsty earth fairly crying for it!

At 7:15 a group of about twenty men stood before the Forest Service Office, men who had spent their lives in the woods and knew what the fire call meant. Fire fighting was no new experience for them. Pack sacks full of blankets, tents, and grub, were stacked alongside the pile of firefighting equipment out in the street. There was no glamour to this battle. Every man knew that it meant long days and nights on the smoky fire line, wielding the axe and shovel, some days without water or food from dawn till dark. Still, they laughed and jested as men always will in the face of danger.

At 7:30 a big red truck hauled up to the small mountain of equipment. A short order from Denley and the men threw on the outfit and clambered on top.

"Dennison, you are in charge," ordered Denley. "You will have a hard fight as you're short of men, but don't leave until she is under control. Drive up as far as you can go toward Bear Island Lake. A team will meet you there to take in the equipment on the St. Croix Tote Road. Make your headquarters where the trail crosses Beaver Creek, if the fire doesn't cut you off. The Lookout says she is heading north fast, so you will have to hurry."

"I'll do my damnedest, Denley, so will every man here," answered Dennison.

The truck careened out of town with utter disregard of speeding violations, and the crew was on its way to the forest. Someone started playing "Home Sweet Home" on a mouth organ.

"Where d'you think you're going, Slim?" I asked, for it was he who was playing.

"Trying to kid myself into believing we're going home," Slim answered, and kept on playing.

We were all glad to have him with us, because no matter how tired and worn out we were, he would always keep us laughing. For two hours we jolted along, then the smoke was steadily growing thicker and more stifling. The headlights could hardly penetrate it, and several times we were on the verge of running off into the brush. Suddenly out of the smoke loomed two white horses, looking huge and grotesque in the yellow glare of the headlights. It was the team that was to take our outfit up the St. Croix Tote Road.

"Here we are!" yelled the truck driver.

We piled out of the equipment hurriedly, loaded the lumber wagon, and started on the rough twelve-mile tote into the fire. Our crew of men went ahead with lanterns and axes to clear away fallen windfalls. Another crew stayed in the rear to load on the outfit whenever the wagon spilt over.

The tote road was as rocky and precipitous as the bed of a mountain creek. It was a queer-looking procession that worked its way slowly in toward the fire line, scrambling over steep rocky ridges, where the horses' shoes struck fire as they sought desperately for a foothold, then down in the swamps bumping madly over the uneven corduroy.

While going up one of the sharpest of the ridges, one of the horses slipped on a smooth face of rock. The driver yelled, "Look out, we're coming back!" and came back they did. I was in the rear and could see the sparks fly as the straining beasts tried to keep their footing. They seemed to hang for a second on the summit, and we held our breath.

Then, the horses reared backward and wagon and all came crashing back down the trail. A big bowlder was rolled against one of the wheels in an effort to stop the mad rush, but the wheel went up and over it. We jumped to the side to avoid the smash and the team and wagon lurched past us, back into the darkness. A crash, and silence. We hurried down. The rear end of the wagon had smashed into a bunch of young birch which had broken its fall. The horses were scratched but otherwise unhurt, and the driver, an old lumber-jack who had driven a team of fours down the same St. Croix trail, when she was iced at that, wasn't even ruffled. The equipment was spilled all over the woods.

Loading was accomplished in a few minutes, and then a new start with every hand at the wheel. This time the summit was reached safely.

It proved to be a long twelve miles and it seemed to most of us more like forty.

Dennison, who was with me in the rear, summed up the situation about as aptly as any man could. We had just covered a particularly rough stretch of road and had stopped for a few minutes to rest the horses. Cigarettes were soon glowing.

"Say, old timer," he said, "this sure is romantic and all that sort of thing. Wouldn't some of those brave Northern Movie Stars just love to fight fire for a month. They would be just in their element. This romantic stuff is fine, but there is always too damned much packing, too many mosquitoes and sandflies, and smoke, before you get any action. This trip would make a rotten story, if it was told just as it is with no decorations and hero stuff."

"I'll take you up on that, Dennison," I answered. "I'll write up this story, just as it happened, and then you'll be falling in love with the whole outfit."

"You're crazier than a bat," he retorted laughingly, rising to his feet. "There goes the wagon!"

We were now getting within the fire area. The smoke was getting thicker and more acrid. The lanterns in the lead bobbed around like lightning bugs. The sound of the axes clearing the trail sounded sharply above the rumbling of the wagon and the creaking of horses' shoes on the bare rock.

Pieces of burning bark lit like fireflies in the darkness on either side of the trail and small flames would begin hungrily licking up the dry leaves and pine needles.

It was on the crest of a high ridge that we first saw the fire line. The sky was lit up luridly with a fierce reddish glow. Occasionally, a streak of flame would leap out in sharp relief against the darkness as the fire ran up a spruce. We could hear the faint crash of falling timber above the ever-increasing roar and crackle of the fire.

As we drew closer, we were forced to tie our handkerchiefs over our noses and mouths, so that we could breathe the smoke-laden air. On the low spots the smoke was intense. The horses were becoming more and more difficult to manage. When fire dropped nearby they would snort with terror and rear in their tracks. Finally, it became necessary to lead them as they refused to move any further toward the flames. We could see that the fire was almost at the boundary of the Superior National Forest. Our object was to skirt the edge of the fire line to the Beaver River, about a mile farther on, and there pitch our camp.

At times we despaired of making it as the old tote road seemed to lead directly into the path of the swiftly advancing waves of fire. If the wind kept on blowing due north we could perhaps make it, but if it shifted two degrees in our direction we would be cut off. That would mean the abandoning of our equipment and perhaps the horses.

The trail curved still farther in toward the fire as we drew closer and at the same time the wind shifted. The flames leapt towards us and it looked as if we would have to fight for our lives. I stepped up to Dennison, and between choking gasps for breath, asked what we should do.

"It looks bad—damned bad," he answered. "I'd hate like hell to lose the outfit. We can't camp in the path of the fire. I think we'd better push on for another quarter of a mile, and perhaps the trail will turn away from the blaze."

So push on we did. The horses were more frantic and the men almost blinded with smoke. Rabbits ran past us in scores. Coveys of frightened partridges settled among us or flew over. Several deer, wide-eyed with terror, walked past us within a stone's throw, all fear of man eclipsed by the fear of the *red death* behind them. Song birds sang in bewilderment, flew aimlessly about, some directly back into the flames.

We had gone perhaps two hundred yards when the trail began to turn away from the edge of the fire line. As we skirted its eastern edge, the heat was so intense that the green grass shriveled in the tote road and we were forced to shield our faces with our arms to keep the flesh from scorching.

For three hundred yards from the fire it was light as day. I looked back at the beautiful green standing timber in the path of the fire, and it seemed a pity that such a wilderness should have to be sacrificed to the flames.

We arrived at the river and quickly unloaded our equipment. Stopping just long enought to snatch a bite to eat and gulp down some coffee, we then set out for the fire line, armed with shovels, axes, and grub-hoes.

We skirted the edge of the fire again and went half a mile beyond. The front of the fire line was almost two miles in length. Our object was to make a fire break in the path of the flames. Men were strung out at intervals with orders to fell a swath of trees directly in front of the line of fire. This would check the mad sweep of the flames until trenches could be dug still farther back to stop the creeping ground fires.

The sound of axes ringing and trees crashing to earth was in strange contrast to the roaring crackle of the burning spruce and pine. For three hours we worked steadily and at the end of that time, a line of felled trees faced the rush of the blaze. The flames were quite close now and it looked as if we wouldn't have time to dig our trench in the rear of the fire break. Rabbits were coming past us again. Smoldering bark lit among the leaves and we knew it was time for us

to go. All we could do now was to hope and pray that our fire break would hold.

We gathered on a hilltop to watch the game between fire and man. The flames increased in volume as they advanced. The fire line was now within a hundred yards of the felled swath of trees and traveling fast. We looked on, with gritted teeth and set jaws. We had grown to love the forest that we had fought for so many times and to hate the flames that tried to rob it from us. The fire was now at the swath. A burning spruce crashed down into the felled timbers, and in a second the whole swath sprang into flame. The fire died down somewhat as it burned in the tree tops along the ground. We looked on expectantly, thinking our battle half won. Now, we could go and finish our trench to stop the creeping groundfires. Then the worst happened. A gust of wind sprang up out of the south and lifted the weakening billows of fire clear over our obstruction into the standing timber of the forest.

A deafening roar as a clump of spruce went up, and we realized our efforts had been for nothing! With the expectancy of victory before us, none had thought of sleep or fatigue, but now we all felt hopelessly tired and beaten. The wind increased and the red destruction ate its way onward! The forest was doomed; we could do nothing but watch and hope that the wind would die down. The fire was now past our line along the whole front, and had crossed our trail in the rear as if to make sure that nothing would hinder its progress again.

The roar of the fire and the crash of falling timber drowned all other sounds. Suddenly, a louder and more rumbling roar than all the rest made us look at one another in wonderment. Could it really be!

"That sounds a lot like thunder, Dennison," I said.

"God knows," he answered huskily, "I hope so."

Another rumble and in the east a jagged streak that was not fire showed in sharp relief—then the curtain of smoke! We could hardly believe our eyes. Could it be the rain we all hoped and prayed for?

The wind shifted toward the east and there seemed to be a lull in the fire. Each one of the blackened, smoke-begrimed crew prayed in his heart for the only thing that could save the forest from destruction.

Then it came. First single big drops, each one spurting up the white ashes on the ground. They came faster. The sky seemed to open up and the wonderful rain came down in sheets.

It settled into a steady downpour that drenched the thirsty suffering earth through and through. The fire line was no longer roaring. Fitful bursts of flame shot out venomously.

Within a quarter of an hour, the once seething inferno was nothing but a subdued, blackened, smoking line. We didn't bother to go back to camp, but dropped down where we happened to be. Our forest was saved. Nothing else mattered.

Rejection Letter

EVERY WRITER *knows discouragement. Rejections are more common than acceptances. In the following letter from his first agent, F. M. Holly, Sig received discouraging news indeed.*

The letter is addressed to Mr. Sigurd Thorne, a name Sig tried out during the earliest years of his writing career. "I never liked the name Olson," *he said.* "Too ordinary. For a while I adopted the maiden name of Elizabeth's mother and signed my articles Sigurd Thorne. Isn't that a beautiful name? I finally dropped it, but we gave the name to young Sig."

TELEPHONE:	**F. M. HOLLY**	CONSULTATION
CHELSEA 9924	**156 FIFTH AVENUE**	BY APPOINTMENT
CABLE: HOLLYHOCK	**NEW YORK**	

June 7th, 1926.

Mr. Sigurd Thorne,
Ely,
Minn.

Dear Mr. Thorne:

I am returning herewith your three manuscripts, with a report of their travels:

"THE FUGITIVE"

has been declined by:

Collier's
Shrine
Blue Book

"SNOW WINGS"

has been rejected by:

Country Gentleman
Everybodys
Collier's
Harper's.

"THE VENGEANCE OF PAPETTE"

turned down by:

Saturday Evening Post
Red Book
Short Stories.

Hoping to see the stories in their revised form, I am,
Very sincerely yours,
F. M. Holly

1925–1928

Sig did not transform quickly from teacher to writer. His next article would not appear until 1928. It is difficult for us to picture the mid-twenties and what our culture was like. We have never had a time in our country's history to match it. This was a time of good feelings. It was a period between wars, a time of prohibition, and a time of prosperity. After the close of World War I, President Harding said that "America's need is not heroics, but healing; not nostrums, but normalcy; not revolution, but restoration; not surgery, but serenity." This was the prescription for the twenties.

What we got was not normal, and it was not serene. There were mobsters and demonstrations by the Ku Klux Klan. And it was a time for achievers, whether Harding wished for them or not; there were heroes like we had never seen before. Lindberg changed the world, Louis Armstrong changed the direction for all future music, Rudy Vallee dazzled the airwaves, and Johnny Weissmuller, Red Grange, Babe Ruth, Bill Tilden, Helen Wills, Bobby Jones, Man O' War, and Jack Dempsey made sports into news. In literature, Fitzgerald, Benchley, Parker, Millay, O'Neill, and Sinclair Lewis captivated the public. Richard Byrd flew over the South Pole, Will Rogers was America's spokesman, Billy Mitchell founded an air force, Darrow and Bryan debated evolution in Tennessee, and on the screen, Greta Garbo and Rudolph Valentino led the Hollywood rise.

In the twenties, we had flagpole sitters, speakeasies, the growth of crossword puzzles, mah-jongg, dance marathons, and the first Miss America contest. Automobiles no longer looked like the Model T. There were Stutz and Pierce Arrow, luxury Lincoln Coaching Broughams, Cadillacs, Packards, and even imports like Mercedes and the Minerva Landaulet.

In Ely, the impact of these national fads and events might have been less than in the big towns, but they certainly affected the reception that Sig's writing would receive. Ultimately, all the battles for our resources revolve around the urban areas and the political power of these large population centers. The writer must not only express what is important for people to know but must also express it in a way that people will want to read it.

During the two and a half years between Sig's first and second articles, there were many important events in the conservation field. One of the nation's ecological problems was also a part of the era's fads and part of the economic trouble—land in Florida was being sold faster than the mangroves could produce it. Like so many of the ecological battles that have been fought, the ecological position was one that would have benefited the entire nation. But the battle, as always, was a frustrating one between immediate profits and long-term benefits.

In Minnesota and Wisconsin, there were many important trends in forestry that were established during these years. Northern Highland became Wisconsin's first state forest. Wisconsin Power and Light became the first public utility to do reforestation, in the Wisconsin Dells area near Aldo Leopold's shack. Nekoosa-Edwards Paper Company in Wisconsin followed this trend by hiring the first industrial forester. Wisconsin authorized the federal government to acquire national forest land, and the Nicolet and Chequamegon national forests were started. The final step in Wisconsin's forestry program initiated a private forestry program with the university.

In Minnesota, there were important forestry decisions as well. In International Falls, a logger by the name of Edward Wellington Backus initiated plans for dams that would raise the water level throughout the Superior National Forest. This began a conflict with Ernest Oberholtzer and the Quetico-Superior Council. It would evolve into a long-term struggle that would sweep in Sig and all the region's conservationists. Secretary of Agriculture Jardine set aside 1,000 square miles of national forest land as a primitive area in response to the Backus initiative. This act prohibited roads and limited logging in the designated area. In 1927, the last three caribou were seen in Minnesota, a response to the changes that were being wrought in the border country.

Snow Wings
Boy's Life
MARCH 1928

This story differs greatly from Sig's book essays. It is closer to the popular style of Seton and the other storytellers of the first quarter of the century. Boy's Life *magazine was and is the official magazine of the Boy Scouts of America.*

DEATH FLOATED SOFTLY over the tops of the spruce trees, death in the form of snow-white wings and talons black as jet. The arctic snow owl was abroad, the most feared of all the winged marauders of the north. Slipping in between shadowy masses of spruce, he skimmed like a phantom close to the snow, searching, always searching for that which might mean food. From the rocky pine-clad shores of Lake Superior to the bare frozen tundras of the arctic, he reigned supreme. Over it all the swish of his great feathered pinions had become an omen synonymous with tragedy.

For hours the old killer had winged his way over the frozen stillness, seeing nothing but the glittering moonlight and the long dark shadows of trees upon the crusted snow. Since the last big snow hunting had been poor, and where once had been game in abundance there was now only a trackless waste. Partridge were lying deep in their snowy tunnels and the white snowshoe rabbits which formed the major portion of his fare seemed also to have completely disappeared.

Even for Snow Wings, used as he was to going for long periods without food, the monotony of not eating was becoming tiresome. As he drifted along, watching the moonlit surface, he would have welcomed anything in the form of food. He had reached the stage where choice had become second to necessity and starvation made the master of caution. Without an instant's hesitation, he would have attacked even four-footed killers as large or larger than himself. Night after night it had been the same, the endless winging over hills and valleys, and the return to the resting place in the black spruce swamp, with nothing but an empty stomach. He was getting thinner and thinner and had it not been for nature's generous provision of thick fluffy body feathers, he would not have been pleasant to look upon. The powerful leg and wing muscles, once full and firm, were now shrunken until they resembled nothing so much as strips of seasoned leather covered loosely by an equally tough leathern skin. His body, worn down as it was to the consistency of steel and his natural ferocity, augmented by poor feeding, made of him an antagonist not to be dealt with lightly. Hunger he had known before, but never as acutely as now. His was an appetite that could only be quenched by hot blood and flesh still reeking with life.

Below him lay a grassy swale, a welcome break in the endless monotony of pointed tree tops. He swerved slightly, and as he did so a movement caught his eye. Swooping down on muffled wings, he circled the opening slowly, rising and dipping over the ragged border of balsam and spruce. Two brownish animals, locked fiercely together, rolled over and over upon the snow, tearing cat-like at each other's vitals. Engrossed with their battle, they did not see the shadow of wings that drifted over them. Snow Wings took in the situation at a glance and desperately hungry as he was, knew better than to attack. Circling the swale once more, he then soared to the top of a tall dead tamarack from which he could have full view of the opening. Content to bide his time, he knew that sooner or later, he would taste the blood of one of those below him.

The coming of the great snow had also wrought hardship upon the four-footed carnivores. Starvation had stalked boldly among them and the north had witnessed many an unnatural tragedy. The killers had at last been forced to resort to nature's most awful resource, cannibalism. Two pine martens, in their wanderings, had been attracted to the edge of the swale by the chattering of a red squirrel. At sight of each other, their prey had been forgotten in the greater blood lust that had engulfed them. The fact that both were of the same breed mattered nothing. Each represented hot flowing life and food, beyond that they did not want. They closed instantly, even though one was by far the larger, and fought with the savage intensity that only the great weasels know.

For a time neither had the advantage, the weight of the larger, being offset by the greater quickness of the smaller antagonist. At times they completely buried themselves in the deep snow, only to reappear again at some other point, fighting as fiercely as ever. The gruesomeness of the combat was augmented by the fact, that not a sound escaped them, for like all of their kind they fought and killed in silence.

Of a sudden they broke away from each other, the smaller pursued, running swiftly for a dense clump of spruce at the edge of the swale. A huge Norway pine stood about half-ways and a little to one side of his course. He ran desperately, but with every jump, the distance between them lessened. Realizing the futility of trying to reach his objective, the fleeing marten turned slightly from his course and ran directly for the big pine. He reached it a bare two jumps ahead of his pursuer and ran swiftly up the trunk. Hoping that his lighter weight would enable him to reach a branch, inaccessable to his enemy, he climbed until he reached the very tip of one of the highest, almost sixty feet above the snow. Here he crouched, every muscle tense, clinging desperately to the rough scaly bark. Weak from loss of blood and terribly torn about the head and throat, it was all he could do to keep himself from slipping.

The larger marten had followed closely, and now crouched at the base of the branch that held his prey, glaring his malevolence. For a time he did not stir, secure in the knowledge that escape was impossible. Then almost imperceptibly he began to move. Belly flat to the bark, the short powerful leg muscles barely rippling, he crept along a fraction of an inch at a time, until at last, he was within two feet of his victim. The smaller marten now turned his head ever so slightly, and their eyes met in a gaze of mutual hatred and ferocity. Keeping his gaze fastened on the object of his venom, the hunter advanced a few inches further. The branch swayed dangerously and bent until the foremost was hanging head downward, legs and claws wrapped tightly about the bunches of long pine needles. Only a small space separated them now, a distance relentlessly being cut down to nothing.

Snow Wings, from his perch on the dead tamarack, not forty yards away, had been watching their every move with keen excitement. He had been sorely tempted on several occasions during the struggle, to swoop down in an effort to carry off one of the fighters. Each time, however, he had withheld in the hope that a better opportunity would present itself. Now with the two hanging helplessly upon the end of the branch far above the ground, he realized that at last his chance had come. Leaving the tamarack, he sailed swiftly through the intervening space. The flash of his wings had been seen, however, and just as the great owl was about to strike, the hunted marten loosed his hold and plunged downward, legs and feet widely spread, to the snow beneath. The other followed instantly, striking the crust not two feet away from the first. Dumfounded by their move, Snow Wings flapped wildly for an instant to regain his balance, then soared back to his perch.

Here he watched the pursuit across the snow, as the smaller tried again to reach his first objective, the spruce thicket. The distance between them was cut down rapidly, and once more they closed, fighting now a battle to the death. Snow Wings could stand it no longer. His taste for blood had been roused and regardless of consequences, he could not wait. Down he came and hovered like an angel of death over the two fighters, watching for a chance to strike. At the smell and taste of each other's blood the fury of the two killers had increased. Both of a race, noted for its fierceness and tenacity, it was a battle as bloodthirsty as any that had ever been fought in the northern snows. Suddenly the greater marten gained the advantage. Throwing his adversary to the side, he dashed in, secured a throat hold, and tore savagely at the life blood underneath.

Just then came a swoop of wings, battering them both down to the snow. For an instant they were enveloped in

SNOW WINGS

a cloud of white from whose cloudy softness extended claws sharp as steel. The topmost killer felt the vice-like grip in his neck and back and squirmed in agony. Then he was lifted clear of the snow. Twisting and doubling, he did his utmost to free himself. When he saw that his struggles availed him nothing, he gave vent to a snarling screech so venomous and filled with hatred that all the evil in the race of killers might have for that one instant been concentrated in the body of one. His weight was too great, however, even for the big snow owl. After laboring along mightily for a few rods, with the tail and feet of his victim dragging the snow, he was forced to earth. Wings widely spread, he nevertheless retained his hold upon the squirming beast and struck fierce slashing blows with his powerful beak at its head and eyes. The thrashing of the now sorely wounded animal increased until finally it was all the owl could do to hold on. With a last desperate effort, the marten doubled up and wrenched himself free from the murderous talons. Blinded with his own blood, and crazed by the terrible laceration, he hurled himself at the white phantom before him. Snow Wings, however, had anticipated the attack, and knowing that should his enemy ever secure a hold upon his slender body, he would be doomed, had taken to the air at once. He circled slowly over the swale, then once more resumed his perch on the old tamarck to wait until his victim weakened.

The smaller marten who had been dazedly watching the strange combat from the shelter of the spruce thicket, now came stealthily forward, belly to the snow, and revenge in his blood-reddened eyes. His once powerful enemy, now crawled slowly around in a circle, stone blind, his eyes nothing but gaping bloody pits. For an instant the avenger gloated, then sprang in, fastened his teeth in the already torn throat and drank the hot blood that soon would have been enriched by his own, had not fate intervened. After eating his fill of the warm red flesh, he left the carcass and melted away among the shadows of the spruces.

    Snow Wings now dropped to the kill and ate ravenously. When he had gorged himself to repletion, he flew again to the tamarack and sent forth a call for his mate. He had not long to wait for although Yellow Eyes was miles to the northward she heard the resonant booming notes distinctly and knowing that they meant food, came winging her way swiftly over the high popple covered ridges and valleys choked with the dark green tops of spruce trees. She found her way instinctively to the exact spot from which the call had come, and dropped without a sound beside her mate. Although Snow Wings was large, Yellow Eyes was even more huge, for among the arctic owls, the female is always the larger of the species. Nature for once had been lavish in her gift of strength to the sex whose chief duty is the protection of its young. She rested only a few moments, then flew down and devoured the remainder of the torn carcass, fur and all, leaving only a few of the largest bones.

    Leaving the scene of the kill, they then flew slowly back to the swamp from which they had begun their hunting, some hours before. By the time they reached their resting place the east had begun to redden and the semi darkness of the winter's dawn was fast disappearing before the light of day. Here in the very center of a thick clump of spruce they dozed sleepily during the glaring hours of sunlight. Only when the long shadows had begun to creep over the snow did they show any signs of life. Blinking sleepily they would then stretch, change their positions and flap their wings in expectation of the flight ahead of them. At the first hint of darkness away they would go, beginning again their tireless drifting flight over the snowy wilderness. So passed day after day, each one a repetition of the last.

The killing of the marten marked the end of winter's long starvation. From then on food became gradually more plentiful. The days grew steadily longer and under the burning heat of the bright March sun, the great drifts began to sink. The squirrels came out of hiding and chattered gaily from the cone-laden jack pines. Partridge forsook their burrows in the snow and fed boldly upon the buds of popple and birch. Even the great snowshoes ventured forth, to bask once more in the grateful warmth, so long denied them. Hunting was no longer the haphazard pastime it had been, during the long nights of midwinter.

It was then that the two great owls regained their strength, and not a night passed but what they did not feast in plenty. The snow melted most rapidly on the southern slopes and here it was, on the long jagged stretches of brown earth, that they found their best hunting. Still as white as they had been all winter the rabbits made easy marks against the background of last year's leaves. Upon sighting game one or other would skim close to earth and at the first soft swish of wings the defenseless creatures would freeze with terror. Then hovering for an instant the owl would drop like a plummet and sink his needle-pointed claws into the snow white fur. A startled scream would pierce the quiet, then again the silence of night.

Ofttimes they surprised a covey of partridge, roosting in a spruce tree, or if in the early evening picking buds in the top of a bare birch. Yellow Eyes was then in her glory. Down she would swoop and the poor bewildered birds would go fluttering and squawking off into the darkness. Seeking out the fattest she would fasten her talons while still in midair and without dropping to earth, continue her flight. Then finding a suitable resting place she would proceed at leisure to tear off the tender white meat of the breast.

Spring came at last to the north country, the enchanted

time of year when life resumes again its natural course and all nature unites in one cosmic effort to attain tranquility. The hillsides became bare of snow and only in the shaded valleys and swamps did it linger at all. The nights were filled with the sweet music of trickling rivulets and the hollow gurglings of hidden springs. Songs of returned migrants sounded everywhere. Long lines of Canadian geese flew by high in the heavens, their discordant clamor heralding widely their approach. Sap was beginning to flow and buds were swelling fast. The very air, filled with the smell of melting snow and wet brown earth was pregnant with the surge of growing life. The harsh struggle for existence was forgotten by the dwellers of the wild and now, actuated by one prime purpose, the recreation of their kind, peace reigned where death had stalked before.

Snow Wings and his mate grew more and more restless as the time went on, for they felt again the age-old call of the arctic. Other years they had summered far to the north, at the very edge of the barren lands. Here where the jagged growth of scrub spruce meets the dreary expanse of the moss and willow grown tundra, they had nested in peace and plenty. Game had been abundant and they had lived well during the short summer months of their stay. With the coming of cold and snow in the early fall, small game had disappeared and the pair had been forced to seek better hunting grounds to the southward. Further and further had they drifted, until finally they found themselves in the pine and spruce forests north of the shores of Lake Superior. Never before had they penetrated so far southward. They were content to stay, however, as here they found that life flowed on smoothly and hunting was always good. Only during the harsh days of midwinter had they suffered, but now that food was again plentiful, all thought of starvation had been forgotten and the land of the great Superior water shed, basking in the warmth of spring, seemed to them a natural paradise. Nevertheless the restlessness was upon them and they felt that the time to leave had come.

Then something happened which changed their plans completely. Winter, not content with lingering through the blustery days of March and early April, descended again in one final attempt to regain the kingdom it had lost. The soft breezes from the southwest suddenly changed to biting cold from the north and the patter of raindrops gave way to the stinging lash of hail and sleet. For three days the fury lasted and when it was over every vestige of spring had disappeared, and the earth was once more covered with a blanket of snow. Then came days and nights of bitter frost, killing the new born buds and blighting the hosts of tender green shoots that had already sprung up through the covering of last year's leaves. For two weeks winter stayed on, and then as though worn out by its last outburst of fury, departed almost as quickly as it had come, leaving the earth once more to its rightful heritage of sun and warmth.

The two snow owls had spent the unusual period in dumb stupefaction, unable to reconcile the cold with their natural instincts. All thought of going north had been immediately abandoned and during the cold they had stayed on in the shelter of the swamp that had been home to them all winter. With the return of warm weather Snow Wings grew restless once more but now to his great wonderment Yellow Eyes refused to move. One warm starlit night he started off alone on his way to the north but was forced to return because she would not follow. Days of uncertainty passed and Yellow Eyes acted more queerly than ever before. Occasionally she would disappear to be gone for hours at a time, always returning, however, to the old roosting place in the swamp. Her mate was sorely puzzled at her unusual behavior, particularly at a time when they both should have been winging their way northward, bending every effort toward reaching their old nesting ground in the arctic.

He was soon to see the reason for her reluctance, however. One day he followed her on one of her lone expeditions and found her on the bank of a creek, sitting contentedly underneath a huge cedar log. Here in a natural hollow, protected from the wind and rain, she had built a nest of leaves and grass, lined with down from her own breast. At sight of her mate she ruffled her feathers and stretched to her full height, snapping her beak viciously. There were four eggs in the nest, so light in color that in their bed of down, they were almost invisible. Snow Wings knew now the reason for her hesitance. They had tarried too long and for once their pilgrimage into the far north had been thwarted.

In the barren grounds Yellow Eyes had always built her nest upon the ground for the simple reason that nowhere were trees large enough to hold one. Although now in a country heavily timbered, it had not occurred to her to vary her habit. She did not realize that dangers entirely new and strange would threaten her eggs and thought that she had chosen wisely. Snow Wings philosophically accepted his astounding discovery and promptly forgot his restlessness. His mate now seldom left the nest, depending almost entirely upon him for food. He hunted tirelessly, bringing in field mice, young rabbits, and occasionally a fish that he had pounced upon in the creek below.

One night he killed a large snowshoe too heavy for him to carry. He called for his mate and though she hesitated at leaving her eggs, finally joined him a short ways up the creek. After eating their fill, they hurriedly winged their way back to the nest. To their horror they discovered that two of the eggs had been broken during their absence. Yellow Eyes was frantic. Round and round she flew, snapping her great beak in rage and searching every possible hiding place for the robber. Try as they might, no clue or trace of the marauder could they find. In the arctic she had often left her nest and never had her eggs been molested. She could not reconcile the loss with her absence. Instinctively, however, her vigilance increased and it was seldom from that time on that she left her nest even to feed. In spite of her watchfulness, however, the remaining two were found broken on the following day. The stricken pair was dumfounded and helplessly unable to cope with a menace new to them both. Three more eggs were laid and these more jealously guarded than the first. Then for days nothing happened and it looked as though they were to be allowed to raise the rest of their brood in peace. Both lived, however, in constant fear that a repetition of the crime that had robbed them of their young would occur.

From the nest, perched as it was on the bank of the creek, they could easily see the water flowing over a rapids below them. It was the time of year when pickerel and northern pike were ascending the streams in search of spawning beds. The rocks in the rapids formed an almost inaccessible barrier to their ascent. As a result, they gathered by the score in the deep pool below, awaiting their turn at the riffles. Occasionally one more adventurous than the rest would separate from the school, hurl himself out of the quiet water into the swirling shallows above. Here he would splash and flop until he had either forced himself over the obstruction or had by his own misdirected efforts worked himself back again into the pool below. Sometimes a luckless fish would in his frantic struggling throw himself clear of the water out upon the rocky bank. Snow Wings was always on the watch for just such an emergency. No sooner had the fish demonstrated his predicament than the big owl would be upon him. After eating what he wanted he would usually carry a portion of the carcass back to his mate. However, when her part was too heavy a load, she would come at his call to feed, eyes ever on the bank of the creek where was hidden her nest. Then hurriedly she would gulp down huge mouthfuls of the cold sweet flesh, never tarrying longer than to barely satisfy her appetite.

Then one day toward evening, just when the soft spring twilight was settling over the valley, they were startled by a tremendous splashing in the shallows below. Not having eaten since the night before, both were more than hungry and alert for anything that might savor of food. At the sound they both looked toward the creek. There in plain sight was a huge pike, flopping helplessly between two boulders. Snow Wings slipped down softly and perched himself on a rock close by. As soon as the struggling fish lay quietly, he dropped upon it and sank in his long black talons. At the feel of claws the imprisoned pike redoubled his thrashing and almost succeeded in dislodging his assailant. Only by flapping his wings mightily did the owl keep his balance at all. Then he tried to rise, but try as he might the weight was more than he could manage. Again and again he tried, but was finally forced to relinquish his hold entirely.

Yellow Eyes, who had been watching him interestedly, was very hungry and, though she knew it was hazardous, could resist the temptation no longer. Leaving the nest, she spread her wings and floated down quietly to her mate now perched upon a rock beside his prey. Larger and stronger than he, she had little trouble in dislodging the fish from the crevice in which it was wedged. Together they fell upon it, tore it to bits and ate ravenously of the still quivering flesh.

No sooner had the big female left her nest than a small reddish brown animal, with a long feathery tail, left the protection of a black spruce top close by and climbed swiftly down the trunk. Before leaving the tree it stopped, looked carefully around in all directions and then as though satisfied that danger had flown, approached the nest with long jerky jumps. The closer it drew the more cautious it became. Once out of sheer nervousness it ran swiftly up a small sapling close by, where it chattered foolishly. Then as if ashamed of its timidity, it leaped to earth and ran boldly forward.

For days the tiny red robber had awaited his chance. Since his last raid ordinary food had seemed tasteless. The remembrance of the stolen delicacy rankled strongly within him and he could not rest until he had again satisfied his craving. During the day time he had been given little chance for only at the approach of nightfall did the vigilance of the pair relax. Even then, if one left the nest, the other was sure to stand on guard. His long looked for chance had come, however, when Yellow Eyes had finally left the nest to help her mate in the killing of the pike. Barely waiting till she was out of sight he had left his hiding place for one more desperate attempt.

He stopped once again before reaching the nest and carefully surveyed the ground before him. The raucous chattering of a blue jay in a tree above half startled him out of his wits. Nervously he covered the remaining distance and with one last bound was in the nest. He proceeded at once to gnaw a hole in the first egg he touched. As he tasted its delicious contents he became oblivious to the world about him and drank greedily.

A scratching sound on the log above attracted his attention. The sight that met his eyes transfixed him with horror. There crouched ready to spring, was a long sinuous form golden brown in color. Small reddish eyes blazed forth from a head terribly scarred and disfigured. One ear was almost off and the other torn to ribbons. Scars naked of fur and still in the process of healing, extended from muzzle to throat and lent to the evil visage an unnatural ferocity. For an instant the squirrel was petrified, then with a wild leap he cleared the distance between him and the closest tree, a slender balsam. Like a flash he scurried up into the thick interlacing branches. Climbing rapidly, he did not stop until he had reached the very topmost sprig. Here clinging terror-stricken he waited for his pursuer.

The marten had reached the balsam not two feet behind his prey. As a climber he had no equal and of all the killers of the weasel family, except perhaps his cousin the fisher, he alone could catch the squirrel in his native element. He climbed leisurely and soon reached the top. In spite of the fact that it swayed dangerously with his weight he kept on climbing. The little red watched his progress until he could bear it no longer, then launched himself out into space. This was exactly what his enemy had been waiting for and both struck the ground at almost the same instant. One swift bound and the sharp pointed teeth of the killer closed. A brief struggle and it was all over. The marten then drank of the hot blood and ate what he wanted of the tender red meat. After carefully burying what was left of the tiny carcass, he continued his way down the creek. His great debt to Snow Wings had been paid in full.

Reflections of a Guide
Field and Stream
JUNE 1928

IN MANY WAYS *this article captures Sig's spirit and love of life. He was content in Ely, and it was his guiding business that gave him the most satisfaction. His outfitting company was located in Winton, a small town east of Ely. It was called Border Lakes Outfitting Company, and the trips often began with a portage from the train to Fall Lake. His partners were the businessmen of the operations, and on the surface, Sig was the field-man. In fact, Sig was involved in much of the business operations, but he really loved guiding, and many of the lessons that he received were from watching other, older guides. He met Buck Sletton, a big, burly ex-marine who specialized in short trips with easy portages. There was Arne, a thin, wiry, strong, and efficient guide who was both a good cook and an expert fisherman. Gunder Graves was a lumberjack who paddled when he couldn't find work for his ax. Sig's ideal guide was the first one he ever met—Mat Heikkila.*

In 1967, in a letter to the Wilderness Society, Sig wrote, "Those were the glorious years and I traveled many thousands of miles, not only by canoe, but in the winter on snowshoes and skis and with dogs. Those years convinced me that this area of wilderness lakes should be saved for primitive travel; that roads, airplanes, and resort developments should be kept out of the interior."

In 1979, he reflected, "The guide not only did all the cooking and all the routine around the camp, but he had to know how to take care of people . . . watch them like a hawk. Start early in the morning, work until ten at night. So much to do, so much to get ready, but I thought—it's a shame to take my guide's wages, I enjoy myself so much."

GUIDES HAVE BEEN classified, pawed over and discussed so thoroughly that readers of modern fiction have cause to feel reasonably well acquainted with them. As a breed, they are blessed of men, for they live a life more appealing to them than any other occupation on the face of the earth.

The hermit-like existence they are commonly supposed to enjoy is largely imaginative. True, they do live alone for long periods; but then again, they meet and mingle for months at a time with a variety of people of every class and calling that would be the envy of any social aspirant. In the woods, the bars of social position are let down, and your poor lonesome guide becomes a brother to lawyers, professors, millionaires and royalty. Fortunate is he who can count among his friends and acquaintances so diversified a list. No wonder, then, that by the time a guide has spent a lifetime living in the close association with people that camp life makes inevitable, he becomes a fair judge of human nature in the raw.

However, it has always been the viewpoint of the man being guided that has been aired. How the guide sees his

REFLECTIONS OF A GUIDE

party and their reactions to camp life is a subject sadly neglected.

In the cities, where discomforts and the ordinary physical struggle for existence have been reduced to the minimum, a man can cover up his normal feelings so well that even the most intimate of his friends know him not. Up in the brush, however, a hundred times a day a man has reason to open up and show what he is really like. Whatever he has been holding in leash will crop out then, be it good or bad.

The longer he lives away from civilization the more natural he becomes. Gone is the smooth veneer that makes him acceptable in society, and he is at last an individual with the God-given right to exercise his own free will. He realizes that civilization has cramped his spirit too long in its effort to mold and makes him live his life like millions of other human machines, with no outlet for his pent-up nature.

His new-found personality is often a revelation to him, and he revels in his freedom. Life opens up in a thousand different ways, and every hour spent in the wilderness is packed to the brim with the joyous fulfillment of long dormant desires.

We all have a pronounced streak of the primitive set deep within us, an instinctive longing that compels us to leave the confines of civilization and bury ourselves periodically in the most inaccessible spots we can penetrate. Here we gulp huge lungfuls of sun-washed air, lie on our bellies and drink from rivers and lakes, work, sweat, curse and sing with the sheer joy of being alive. And what makes guiding the sport of kings is just that. No two men react alike. There is always variety in human nature.

Tenderfoot or old-timer, it makes little difference, for both come into the wild for the same purpose. To the guide, both are adventures in friendship. From the man who has roughed it before he often learns secrets of the woods and waters that he has perhaps been blind to all of his life, and it is always a joy to initiate the tenderfoot into the countless mysteries of the out-of-doors. Both types are a pleasurable experience, and little does the average man know the value his guide places on his friendship.

The man who has lived long in the open is content to drink it in calmly and enjoy himself in the mellow light of life-long experience and understanding. His is the serene enjoyment of the man who has weighed his values and retained only those worth while. He is through with experimenting and knows that in his kinship with the wild he is deriving all those things that to him make living complete.

On the other hand, the man who is new cannot get his full of violent gratification. The long hours of bending to the paddle, oftentimes in the teeth of a gale, and the heart-wrenching work on swampy portages and steep rock trails are more than compensated for by the feeling that for once he is really alive and living as a man should live. To him there is no joy quite so complete or content quite so blissful as that which comes at the end of a killing portage, when he can flop down to rest, half dead of exhaustion.

He feels then, more than at any other time, that the void created by too much city life is gradually being filled up. Worry is a thing of the past, and all that matters is the glorious present. At night, after a long day of cruising through lakes, running rapids and making portages, his bodily wants satisfied, with nothing ahead but rest and peace under the stars, the full realization comes to him, and then he understands why men go into the wilderness.

Whether he is a woodsman or not, the average man likes at least to act like one and give to his guide and the members of his party that "been there feeling." When the last outposts of civilization have faded away, your city man begins to shed his air of reserve and adopts instead the sangfroid of the Canadian voyaguer. He sings songs he hasn't sung since boyhood and college days, tells stories and laughs uproariously at his own jokes, smokes and curses to his heart's content, and feels like the toughest sourdough in the north.

When the waves are rolling high, he grits his teeth and plows into them fearlessly. What does it matter if water is being shipped and the waves are piling high? Today he's an adventurer in the land of romance, ready to die with his boots on.

At the portages he singles out the heaviest packs, buckles down like a Hudson Bay packer and delights in showing up his guide. No matter if he is half dead at the end, he can glory in his strength and bay his prowess at the moon. A guide can't help but have a warm spot in his heart for men of that caliber, and he can't help but feel that most men are brothers under their skins when once they come down to earth.

The same spirit that makes a man want to act like a woodsman when he is up in the big sticks makes him also want to look like one. If he is imaginative at all, the more he looks like Daniel Boone or Davy Crockett the more he enjoys himself. I don't mean that men go to any extremes in the matter of dress, but most of them affect some article or other that for some reason appeals strongly to them.

When a man is trying to live another life entirely, he naturally wants to appear as romantic as his conscience will let him. It may be an old checkered shirt or battered hat. Whatever it is, it is usually something in which he thinks he looks or feels particularly well. If it has once become part and parcel of his outdoors life, he will wear it till it falls apart, rather than get a more serviceable garment.

I have an old army hat that I should have thrown away years ago. It is as full of holes and as disreputable as any old hat can be that has knocked around the woods for over a decade. Yet if I sally forth without it, there is a feeling of loss and incompleteness. I will probably have to wear it another ten years before I have the heart to discard it.

Of all the examples of masculine vanity, an old red shirt worn by my friend Donald Hough occupies the most prominent place in my memory. Years ago, when Don was still cruising for the Forest Service, the old red homespun was a familiar landmark in the border country. It was even then long past its prime.

Several years after, on a trip we took together, the old relic was still very much in evidence, though sadly faded and patched together. At the end of this cruise, I thought it was high time, if Don was to preserve his self-esteem, that someone take the matter in hand. Knowing it would be a delicate proceeding at best, I postponed it till the time came to say goodbye.

I felt that, as a result of my interference in a matter as vital to any man as doing away with an old shirt, our friendship might hang in the balance. Nevertheless I solemnly pleaded with him to put it gently out of the way and give it a decent interment. He promised faithfully to do what he could, and I left him, assured that I had gazed on the old red homespun for the very last time.

A year later, when in from a trip, what should I see but a familiar splotch of red come wandering down the street. Sure as life, it was Don Hough setting out on a snow-shoe trip through the Superior National Forest. He saw me at about the same time I saw him and approached warily. At about ten paces we both stopped. The moment was tense.

"Don," I said slowly, "can you explain why that thing is up here again?"

For a moment he said nothing, but our eyes met, and in that instant the great realization came to me—"It was the love that passeth all understanding." I promised Don then that as far as I was concerned, he could wear it until it rotted on his back. So the chances are that it is still doing valiant service and will for many a year to come.

Though the men who come into the Canadian border country react as a rule much the same to camp life, nevertheless they vary so widely that a rough classification would not be amiss. The guides group them usually as fishermen, long-distance record-breakers and true woodsmen. Of course, all three are fishermen, but when I classified one type as purely fishermen, I had in mind those who come up for the fishing alone.

This type is perhaps the hardest problem for the guide. When the fish are not striking, the cruise is a failure; and when they are, it soon becomes monotonous. After about three days of wonderful fishing, the excitement of pulling out more fish than the camp has any use for palls, and discontentment prevails. In vain are the beauties of the scenery extolled, but nothing can satisfy. The fishing for fishing's sake alone soon becomes mechanical; and no matter how ideal other conditions may be, the fisherman leaves dissatisfied.

The long-distance record-breaker is the busiest man of the season. To him the cruise means a wonderful chance for a work-out and nothing else. Going from dawn till dusk, he stops for nothing. He fishes for meat, not for sport, and travels through beautiful lakes at breakneck speed.

I well remember a doctor from Missouri, a record-breaker of the first degree. We had been out two weeks and had covered a stretch of country in that time that usually took a month of steady traveling. Our route one day led within a mile of Curtain Falls, one of the most wonderful spots in the border country. Parties traveled great distances to reach it and often camped near for days to take pictures and satisfy their craving for natural beauty. From where we were we could hear distinctly the roar of falling water. It was growing dark; and as we had cruised since dawn, I suggested that we go the half mile out of our way, view the falls and perhaps camp there.

Not stopping to take his paddle out of the water, the doctor answered hurriedly: "Don't think we'd better. Got to keep on paddling if we're going to make our thirty miles."

I knew there was no decent camp site within ten miles or so, but said nothing and dug in my paddle. It grew steadily darker, but instead of looking for a landing I kept right on as though we had all the time in the world. About 8:30 the doctor turned around and asked wonderingly, "Well, aren't we going to pitch camp and eat pretty soon?"

Without missing a stroke I answered: "I'm not hungry yet. Let's make her thirty-five before we quit."

He said nothing, but kept on paddling. We finally did land about 10:30 P.M., made a miserable camp in the dark, and ate a cold cheerless supper of cheese and hardtack. At the end of three weeks we had made a wonderful record of distance covered, but we had missed all of the beauty and restful peace that can only come when one takes time to let the wilderness soak in.

The man who gets the utmost in enjoyment out of his cruise is never in a hurry or too busy. He never has a goal he must reach at a certain time. Beauty he sees in everything and knows that to do anything merely for its own sake is a waste of time. He never keeps on fishing until he is tired of it and never keeps more than he can use. If the fish are not biting, he takes the fact for granted, does not blame the guide or the country, and proceeds to enjoy himself in other ways.

He swears by the seven gods that the scenery is the most wonderful he has ever seen. Though the guide is not responsible, as a good many seem to think, he nevertheless feels an inborn pride in the country and a sense of ownership that makes him extremely sensitive about it. A man who makes depreciatory remarks and comes with the attitude of "Is this all there is to see?" will never get next to the inner workings of his guide and never learn the countless secrets of wild life and wilderness legend that are woven in with the character of every country.

Contrary to popular opinion, scenery hunting is perhaps the most fickle of enjoyments. To the man steeped in wilderness life, it is always enjoyable; but to those whose sensibilities and values are still governed by their physical natures, it is a variable entity. Plainly speaking, in order to be appreciated, scenery must be viewed against a background of physical comfort and mental relaxation.

Under ideal conditions, I have seen tourists entranced at the beauty of a heavily timbered rock point jutting out into a wilderness lake. Again, I have seen them curse roundly at the same point and at the waves breaking over it. A man's point of view determines whether or not waves are "whitecapped billows rolling in the sun" or just so much damned water to be paddled through.

The most beautiful scenery is always seen after a meal. Then, more than at any other time, is a man at peace with the world and most receptive to all its wonders. This truth was brought strikingly home to me on a trip taken two years ago. It was late afternoon and we were up against it for a camp site. We had bucked the wind since morning on Big Saganaga, hoping to camp that night in Seagull Lake.

Try as we might, dusk found us working up the Seagull River, still a long way from our goal. Hungry and tired, we were in no mood to admire scenery, so paddled on in grim silence, searching the steep, inhospitable shores for a landing. Finally we heard the roar of a rapids around a bend in the river and realized, with sinking hearts, that another portage was ahead. Not a man in the party wanted to make that portage and each one knew it.

We landed at the foot of the rapids, unloaded without a word and started to pitch camp on one of the steepest, rockiest slopes we had seen. Somehow camp was made and supper gotten under way in spite of the unpromising character of the camp site.

After the meal, which was one of those rare affairs when everything happens to be just right, one by one, under the additional influence of good tobacco and dry moccasins, we began to notice what a truly marvelous spot we had stumbled into. The rapids tumbled down through a rocky gorge into a broad, placid pool below our camp. Tall spruces lined the shore, and where the rock was too steeply sloping for trees to secure a foothold it was covered by a carpet of varicolored mosses and lichen.

Gone was the weariness, gone the memories of portaging and miles of paddling; nothing was left but a feeling of lazy contentment. We all sat smoking and drinking it in for what seemed like a long while. Finally Bill, who had cussed at the camp site more than any one else, broke the silence. He had been sitting on a rock overlooking the river, watching the long streaks of foam float down from the rapids. When he spoke, it was from the bottom of his heart.

"Boys," he said slowly and with conviction, "this is one of the most beautiful places we have ever been in."

We all silently agreed with him, for it was as nearly perfect as anything could be. The wisdom of the old saying came back to me then more strongly than ever before, that "The source of all contentment comes from within."

To the true woodsman, the wilderness is always at its best. Of course, his appreciation of its beauties is tempered by his own physical well-being; but no matter what the weather or how adverse the conditions, he always enjoys it. The simple things give him the greatest pleasure—colors, sounds, smells and the countless other things that go to make life in the wild packed to the brim with the fulfillment of cherished longings.

He believes and adopts whole-heartedly the motto of the guides in the canoe country, that "No matter how wet and cold you are, you're always warm and dry." He applies this versatile philosophy to all situations and as a result is the most happy-go-lucky, care-free mortal in existence. Nothing phases him, and his resultant state of mind is one of rare receptiveness to the beauties and joys of life in the woods.

When in the wilderness, all else is forgotten. He does not count as wasted any time spent watching the clouds, the trees or the waters. To him, those hours are precious, for it is then that he is storing up a wealth of memories that will help him tide over the times when the stress of city life bears too heavily upon him, and make him forget the struggle in a vision of clear blue skies and sunlit woods and waters.

1929–1931

IN 1929, Sig wrote "A Wilderness Canoe Trip" for *Sports Afield*. This was the year that the Quetico-Superior Council was formed from the loose affiliation of canoe country activists. Ernest Oberholtzer, Fred Winston, Charlie Kelly, and Frank Hubachek were the driving forces in opposition to many plans that would have caused irreparable damage to the canoe country. All the conservation news, however, took second place to the economic news of the year. The stock market crashed on Black Thursday, October 4. It was the end of the roaring twenties and the good life for most of the country, but not for Sig.

In 1930, one of the canoe country's most significant laws was passed, the Shipstead-Nolan Act, which gave legislative strength to the measures that the secretary of agriculture had been mandating. It prohibited logging within 400 feet of recreational water, it forbade altering water levels, and it withdrew the Superior National Forest from the provisions of the Homestead Act. For the next decade, the Roosevelt administration would be purchasing tax-delinquent land and solidifying the forest. In this same year, more opposition arose. There was a strong local faction that advocated "a road to every lake!"

Sig returned to college for an advanced degree in 1930, a decision that was spawned by experiences he had had while guiding for Ralph King, Al Cahn, Henry Ward, and Harry Hanson. The opportunity to add research to his passion for paddling brought the canoe country together for Sig in both an intellectual and a physical sense.

Although Sig could not leave the security of teaching at this time, he did give his future a lot of consideration. His canoe trips and his snowshoe hikes were times of deep thought. Elizabeth recalled, "He spoke so little, I often wondered, 'What are you thinking?'"

On one of the hikes, she remembered how she trailed behind for him for miles, while he pondered his future. His only words were, "I must write."

Confessions of a Duck Hunter
Sports Afield
OCTOBER 1930

THIS STORY RECOUNTS *the day in 1923 that Sigurd Thorne Olson was born. Sig tells the story with a twinkle in his writer's eye.*

Sports Afield *was founded by Claude King in 1887. The writers that graced the magazine included Zane Grey, Ernest Hemingway, and many other famous writers of each period. Illustrations in the early editions included some by C. M. Russell. The magazine in 1894 made the editorial comment, "Sports Afield — has an ambition above that of simply entertaining and amusing the public; it wants to help propagate the true spirit of gentle sportsmanship, to encourage indulgence in outdoor recreations and to assist in the dissemination of knowledge regarding natural history, photography, fire-arms and kindred subjects." In its first decade, the magazine took a strong stand in opposition to the plume hunters. Sports Afield had just moved its offices from Chicago to Minneapolis in*

CONFESSIONS OF A DUCK HUNTER

1930, and the editors became friends of Sig's through his guiding and outfitting.

It was two o'clock in the morning on the opening day of duck season and for once in my life I was undecided whether to go or not. Never before had there been any ifs and ands, merely a case of being on my way, but this year it was different. Here was the situation and I think you will agree that it was one requiring tack and delicacy. Within the hour, I had become the proud father of a first born son and heir. Now don't misunderstand and accuse me of the slightest disloyalty.

To tell the truth, I was thrilled to the marrow and if I do say so myself, I had experienced to the nth degree all of the proverbial joys incidental to young fatherhood. Yes, it was wonderful, a son, a hunting partner had been born to me and all of our dreams had come true, but why, why in the name of all creation did it have to come on this particular morning. That was the point and I think my duck hunting friends will at least give me the benefit of a doubt before pronouncing final judgment.

You can imagine my predicament. In two short hours the guns would be booming and the first wild flight of the season would be on. Of course it was ridiculous to even think of going and martyr like I dismissed the thought summarily from my mind. This was one opening day at least I would have to miss and I might as well make the best of it. In a way, I was ashamed of being even tempted. My place was here today.

After all, what was duck hunting compared to this. First days were never very good even under the most ideal of conditions and there were many week ends coming. Yes, I might as well forget it entirely and play the man. I believe

I could have had I not gone to the window, involuntarily of course, and gotten a whiff of the damp air off the lake. That whiff almost unnerved me and was the beginning of my downfall. There was no good reason why I shouldn't go for just an hour or so. Of course, I couldn't go very far or with the rest of the gang. I didn't expect that, but I did know of a place close by where I might get some shooting and where I wouldn't be out of reach. There was really nothing I could do here, merely the idea of standing by.

Tip toeing into the darkened room, I stole a peek at the little bundle in the corner and wondered if he would ever be a duck hunter. In a way, he would be far better off if he went in for golf instead, a much saner and comfortable sport. Beautiful mop of hair he had. His mother opened her eyes and smiled at me appreciatively. It was half past two and I would have to leave soon in order to be there for the first racket. I made one final effort to dismiss the idea from my mind, but it would have been as easy to have stopped breathing.

In my set that sort of thing was simply not done and yet why not. I could go home to rest and not a word would be said but going duck hunting was a different matter entirely. I argued the matter from every possible angle until I was weary with the effort. There was no doubt about it. I was a brute for even considering it at all.

The nurse stopped outside the door and for lack of something better to say, I asked her if everything was all right.

"Yes, everything was as well as could be expected."

"Could, I be spared," did she suppose, "for just a few hours?"

"Oh, yes," if I didn't care any more than that sort of an answer.

Out in the hall, I met the doctor and tried to explain in a jovial sort of way just how things stood. All I got out of him was a raising of the eyebrows and a peculiar smile, as much as though he had said outright, "so that's the sort of a dub you are." I could have killed him but he probably played golf and there was naturally no sympathy there. I stole another peek into the bedroom. Junior was sleeping soundly and so was his mother. The nurse put a finger to her lips, and I backed out quickly.

Within an hour, I was at the shore of Shagwa Lake, loading my gun and shells into the canoe. From far out over the water came a sleepy quack and a faint splash. It was dark, peaceful and quiet, the sort of sedative I needed. It was good to be alive and I was filled with a sensation of well being and accomplishment. Wasn't I the father of a son and wasn't this the hour I had been waiting for for almost a year. Everything was as it should be and I might have been perfectly happy, had not the faintest tinge of remorse crept in upon me. I shook if off and stepped into the canoe. Just for the first flight and no more.

The first paddle stroke cleared the air and I set my course for the mouth of the Burntside River, four miles away. Thousands of stars were out and as I pushed along, I had the sensation of floating through the sky itself. Finally I could distinguish the dark mass of the opposite shore and I turned my course slightly to the left. The east was already turning grey and tinged along the rim of the horizon with just the faintest indication of pink and orange. It would not be long now. Suddenly right in front of the canoe loomed a clump of cattails. They seemed to pop right out of the blackness toward me. As I swerved, I was startled by a loud quack and a beating of wings. It was too dark to see a thing but I heard a whistle of wings heading toward the mouth of the river and then a splash. Perhaps a jump shot later on. It would be better to wait for daylight before pushing ahead.

I smoked a cigarette and relaxed or rather tried to. An owl hooted mournfully over in the timber and from Little Long over the ridge came the wild call of a loon. A white mist was rising over the river, hard shooting if it didn't lift. The air was good enough to eat, rich and sweet, with just enough of the smell of turning leaves to give it pungence. I opened a new box of shells and smelled of them too. They always are a treat, particularly on damp mornings. About fifteen minutes to go. I wondered how Junior was getting along, probably sound asleep by now.

Bang—Bang—Bang—came from far up stream, someone shooting ahead of time and I cursed inwardly all law breakers in general although I admitted the temptation. Another two minutes. Perhaps my watch was slow and time already up. The cattails rustled softly in a sudden breeze. That would clear the fog in a hurry. Placing my gun against the thwart before me, I pushed toward the mouth of the river and my adventure had begun.

A beaver swam across my path carrying a green poplar branch. When he saw me, he dove whacking his tail with a report like the cracking of a blacksnake. A little further on a pair of rats chased each other merrily through the rushes. Dead ahead was where the mallards had settled. I would have to watch myself. From up stream came a nervous quack and dropping my paddle, I got set. Nothing happened, still too far away. A few short swift strokes and as the canoe glided through the rice, I got ready once more. Suddenly with a wild beating of wings, the biggest and blackest mallard I'd ever seen climbed out of the water. Straight up for thirty feet he went and that was where I caught him before he straightened out for his getaway. First blood and I pushed forward joyously to where he had dropped. One long brown wing was raised upward still quivering. I took the top of it and lifted into the canoe my first mallard well colored and large.

Boom-boom-boom-boom came from Burntside Lake, five miles away. That should start something down the river. I pushed hurriedly into cover and no sooner had I done so than from up river came the whistle of wings. Then I saw them, two black dots tearing like mad down the center of the stream, dodging and twisting to allow for every curve. Off went my safety, eighty yards, sixty and now they were directly opposite. In that first split second of waiting, I was repaid as I am on the opening day of every year for all of the waiting and freezing, all the loss of sleep and discomfort that every season brings with it. My first shot was a clean miss but the second was different. The lead bird crumpled, continued for fifty feet on its own momentum and dropped breast downward with that all-gone limpness that betokens a dead hit. Full three feet in the air it bounced with a splash that could be heard for half a mile. In that splash was also compensation for a duck hunter knows no sweeter sound unless it be the whistle of wings after sundown when they're coming in to feed.

The drake I had missed flew up towards the the river's mouth, doubled back looking frantically for his mate. If my luck held there might be another chance. Once more I slipped into the rice, pulled out my caller and gave one of the most seductive quacks, I knew. High in the air he circled and circled and then satisfied that everything was as it should be, began to drop. This luck couldn't possibly hold and it didn't, for just at the limit of range, he swerved, set his wings and fluttered into the river a quarter of a mile away.

Now it was a case of stalking and to me there was no greater sport in the world, far more thrilling than shivering in a blind waiting for them to come over. This was real hunting, beating them at their own game. Waiting a few minutes for my bird to get accustomed to his new surroundings, I then pushed cautiously forward. Every paddle stroke sounded as though it could be easily heard a mile away and the noise of the rice against the sides of the canoe was abominable. The first two hundred feet was the worst, then came a stretch of smooth open water through which the canoe glided with scarcely a ripple. The sun was just beginning to peep over the tops of the spruces and the dew on the rice glittered with light. A big spider web strung with pearls draped itself over the bow of the canoe. Another hundred feet or so and I'd be within range. Dropping my paddle, I decided to eliminate part of the racket by pulling myself through the rice. Besides it would leave my hands freer when the big moment came. Too often had the fraction of a second necessary to change from paddle to gun spelled disaster.

For a moment, I stopped dead to get my bearings and to allow my heart to resume its normal functioning. Twenty feet more I pulled my way. This was far better than paddling. If discovered now my duck would be out like a bomb and it would be a case of sheer speed if I'd get in a shot at all. This was about as far as I dared to go and I carefully reached for my gun. For perhaps thirty seconds I waited all tense with excitement. What was the trouble? Had I misjudged the distance or had the mallard sneaked away, warned by my clumsy approach? Perhaps right now he was swimming away up stream far out of range. Finally in desperation, I did one of the many foolish things all duck hunters are guilty of on opening days. Not able to wait another second, I gave a long powerful shove with my paddle. I might have known what would happen for just as I was finishing my stroke and in the most awkward position imaginable, the rice exploded with mallards rising in all

CONFESSIONS OF A DUCK HUNTER

directions. Panicky quacks, wild beating of wings and confusion. It was glorious and for once I had duck fever and that badly. My first shot went off in no particular direction which was to be expected but the second held true on a lone bird going dead away. Reloading frantically, I dropped another spirally high above me. Two wasn't so bad as it might have been under the circumstance and I though of the many other times similar emergencies had left me empty handed. Now I knew why the lone drake came back and why he swerved.

The flock reformed its line and disappeared in the wavering line of black dots far over the eastern horizon. Now I had four, two greys and two blacks and I laid them side by side before me in the canoe where I could feast my eyes on their color. It was now about six o'clock and the flight was about over what there would be of it. All that was left was jump shooting to which I didn't object in the least. For the first mile, I saw nothing but blackbirds and there were literally hundreds and hundreds of them, flock after flock, warbling and chattering, drifting gaily from one clump of rice to the other, making merry before their long jaunt to the southland. They too have their place and any marsh in the fall would seem barren and desolate without their cheerful diverting music.

I was seriously considering starting home, when I saw something big and black move into the rice ahead of me, ducks again sure enough. Then I saw two more, the three of them bunched closely together, pushing farther and farther into shelter. A great covey of blackbirds now came to my rescue, flew directly overhead and lit in the very patch of rice I was going to enter. What could be better than stalking under cover of their racket. This time I would hold my fire until I had a bird in line. No more stage fright this season. Another twenty feet and still they didn't move. Finally my curiosity got the better of me and I stood up to look around. No sooner had I gotten off balance than the three flew into action. It never fails, and in spite of my good resolve the first shot went wild. It was just as well however for before I got in my second, I saw in a flash that my three mallards had degenerated into mudhens, half grown ones at that, skittering through the rice dragging their long yellow legs after them. All my excitement had been for nothing.

Then came an anticlimax totally unexpected for just out of range a couple of big mallards beat their way heavily into the air, quacked a couple of times in loud derision and were off. Another minute if I had used my eyes and I'd have had some real shooting. There was no use even cussing. It was bound to happen at least once in every well rounded season and perhaps more. I stood up to watch the sky. Not a thing in sight, clear blue with a few patches of fleecy white clouds and the air warming up. I would have to be going soon.

Then far over the western horizon drifted a long uneven line of ducks, by their slow measured flight mallards without a doubt. Down stream they came, directly toward me and I pushed into the best cover that I could find. On they came in perfect formation, growing bigger and blacker with every wing beat, flying high and far out of range but slowly enough to indicate that they were looking for a feeding ground. The first quack on my caller and they turned ever so slightly, new ducks and innocent. At the second, the leader hesitated, swung my way and began to flutter downward in that falling leaf tumble all duck hunters know so well. The rest of the flock followed suit. Then they straightened out and began to circle still hundreds of yards away. Once they swung almost within range and I clutched my gun nervously. If I'd only take twos and threes instead of sixes, I would be sitting pretty. Once more they came around just at the limit of range and the sun shone on green and bronze as they turned. Then for no good reason whatever they set their wings and headed for a patch of rice a short ways up stream and settled to the accompaniment of much quacking and splashing. I couldn't help but wonder at the time why it is that the other rice bed always looks the best to them even though the one you are in has better feed and you yourself are perfectly hidden. I would have to be more careful this time for those mallards evidently knew more than I gave them credit for at first sight. Perhaps an old seasoned drake in the lead.

At the edge of a clump of brush near shore, I stood up for one final survey before starting. I could see the birds plainly diving and feeding and just beyond something that all but took the wind out of my sails, something black moving through the rice toward them, a man's hat. If this wasn't awful luck but there was no use bemoaning the fact. We were both as far away and would stand an even chance of getting shooting.

I saw my rival was paddling as swiftly as he could. He had already seen me so throwing caution to the winds, I started too. Whoever got there first would get the best shooting. It was now a case of sheer speed and I paddled as I had never paddled before. Suddenly there was a roar of wings followed by the bang, bang, bang of my friend's automatic and out of the corner of my eye, I saw two birds drop, pretty shots just as they were climbing into the air for elevation. One lone single came over me so close that I could see its eyes and I almost fell out of the canoe getting in line for a shot. Another circled high above me, swung out and came back and at my shot dropped like a pinwheel, wings outspread. It wasn't a clean kill and I had to fire again to put it out of its misery. By the time that was over the rest of the flock was dropping over the ridge to more peaceful feeding grounds to the northward.

The black hat paddled away without so much as a greeting. It was a rotten break for him too and I did not much blame him, but what of it. I sat for a moment looking at my ducks and drinking in the warm freshness of the morning air. It was duck season and the world was young. Of a sudden, I came to earth with a crash. What was I doing out here in the marsh with a brand new son waiting for me back home? I had almost forgotten. He would in all probability be awake by now and they would be wondering where on earth I was. Over on the opposite shore was a bunch of maple leaves turned by the first frost. They would brighten up that room considerably. I paddled over, picked the prettiest bouquet I could find, then turned the bow of the canoe toward home. This first morning had been perfect.

I made the trip back in record time. The first person to greet me was the nurse. The speech I had prepared failed me utterly and the brace of beautiful greys I handed her were taken without so much as a word. I had done the unspeakable and no matter how hard I tried to make amends, I could see plainly that I was not to be forgiven. Junior was sleeping soundly and as I kissed his small red forehead, I knew that at least he bore me no grudge. His mother took the red leaves and greeted me with a smile. That helped.

"Did I have any shooting?"

"Yes, I had had a little." I couldn't really tell the truth without hurting her and that I wouldn't have done for the world and a year of opening days. I was sure of her forbearance at least and that was something. For understanding, I would have to wait until I could confess the whole affair to my duck hunting breathren. They would know and sympathize.

Junior is now quite a big lad. He has already sat beside me for hours at a time in a blind and though he hasn't as yet handled a gun, I know it is gradually working under his skin and some day when we are together watching a couple coming in over the rise, he will listen to my story and understand. If he doesn't, I will have to admit that I was wrong, but way down in my heart, I have a feeling that he will come across with a knowing grin. After all, he should be the one to decide, because it was his party and the first day of season for him as well as for me. It was just his hard luck that he couldn't go too.

Duck Heaven
Outdoor Life
OCTOBER 1930

ONE OF THE *characters that shows up in many of Sig's early articles is "the dean." This is his predecessor at Ely Junior College. At the time of these tales, Sig is a biology instructor. After the dean retires, Sig will fill two roles.*

Readers of Sig's books are not exposed to Sig the hunter. He mentions hunting, but he does not emphasize it. In this early period, it is the voice of the hunter that found publishers and an audience. Sig loved to hunt and fish; it was part of his wilderness experience.

The transition that Sig made in his later writing was difficult. The publishers wanted action, and they resisted philosophy. But his hunting articles should not be dismissed as inconsequential. His chapter "The Sound of Rain" in Listening Point *covers lots of ground, but it certainly has one of its roots in "Duck Heaven."*

"If I were to die, and had my choice of where I wanted to go afterward," said the dean, as he gave the fire a kick with his boot, "I'd say to old St. Peter, 'Put me in your biggest celestial rice bed with a million shells and the ducks coming in.'"

"Boy, what a dream," I retorted, "but, to make it really perfect, you should ask for one thing more."

"And what more could any mortal want than that?" he exclaimed.

"Well," I answered, after some hesitation, "if it wouldn't seem altogether too selfish, I'd ask our friend, St. Peter, to keep all the other faithfuls out for just one day for our benefit."

It was in November, just before the freeze-up. We were camped that night on La Pond, a little lake near the southern boundary of the Superior National Forest and State Game Refuge. For us the season just passed had been particularly duckless, and, though we had pushed our canoe through every pothole and rice bed within a day's travel, very little shooting had come our way.

There were plenty of ducks in the country, to be sure, but, for some unknown reason, they insisted on staying in the great forbidden rice beds within the game refuge. Sometimes they did come in by the thousands to the lakes near by, but always it seemed, after dark. Then, long before daylight, we would hear the whistle of their wings as they left again for their protected feeding grounds to the north. We had puzzled over it many a night, and wondered how in the name of creation ducks could tell the boundaries.

For a long time, we sat watching the fire. It was getting perceptibly colder, and the air was full of sparkling frost crystals. From down along the shore came the uneasy swishing and crackling of newly formed ice.

"Do you know what I've been thinking of doing?" queried the dean, as he laid another stick of wood on the fire.

"Might be most anything," I replied.

"Some day, I'm going back to Mexico," he continued. "When I think of the mallards we used to get down there, I feel positively morbid."

"Mexico's all right," I agreed, "as far as tropical duck hunting goes, which isn't very far with me, but if I could find just one little rice bed up here that's not taboo, and not on the map either, I'd be satisfied. What's more, I think we'll find it if we keep on looking with patience and reasonable diligence."

"Guess you're not so far off at that either," he answered. "Duck hunting up here is different, what with the leaves and rice coloring up the way it does, frosty mornings, and that feel in the air. There's no doubt about it, this country would be nothing short of wonderful, if only there were ducks."

Our canoe had been everywhere and, though we had naturally picked up a few in our wanderings, we hadn't had, all fall, what could be called a good day's shooting. It was a problem.

The dean finally broke the silence. "Do you remember that old squawman we met last winter on one of our trout fishing trips? I'd almost forgotten, but, if I'm not mistaken, he mentioned something that sounded an awful lot like ducks."

I was instantly alert.

"I've been thinking about it for some time," he went on, "and, unless my memory fails me entirely, he said there was rice so thick on the upper river that you could hardly get through with a canoe."

"Why," I said, "there wasn't much of anything in there the last time we went through. Outside of a few scattered patches and a lonesome mud hen or two, we didn't see a thing to get excited about."

"That's just the reason I didn't put much stock in it, and I'll confess it never would have occurred to me now, if that new ice cracking down along the shore hadn't made me think of ice fishing." The dean rose to his feet. "What's more," he said, "a lot can happen in three or four years. I wouldn't be surprised but that the low water has had something to do with it. If rice is given half a chance, it will shoot up in an awful hurry."

"Sounds good to me," I answered. "Where there's rice, there's ducks. What's to prevent our looking into it next fall?"

Almost a year later, as we had planned, on the day before the season opened, our canoe was headed north. There are no roads into the section, all travel being by canoe and portage. The lake we sought has no name that I know of, being merely a widening of a wilderness creek. It lies north of Winton, Minn., and due south of Crooked Lake on the Canadian border.

We pushed on steadily through several small lakes, made a number of portages, and toward the middle of the afternoon found ourselves on the river.

For miles we followed its winding, sedge-bordered channel, and then, upon rounding a bend, saw before us a sight that only a duck hunter can fully appreciate — a great field of tall, waving rice, golden yellow in the September sunlight. We dropped our paddles and sat spellbound. It was really true, the river was full of rice, and such rice — stalks as big around as a little finger, and in places tall as a man. For a moment, we could hardly believe our good fortune.

Finally, the dean stood up and looked carefully around. "Not a duck in sight," he said disgustedly, "but what a patch of rice, and to think that it's all grown up since we were here last."

The words were not more than out of his mouth, when a big flock of mallards rose half a mile away, circled the lake slowly, and lit with that heavy, well-fed air of ducks that have never been molested. We sat as though in a trance, watching other bunches rise and move leisurely to new feeding grounds.

We had found, a little prematurely perhaps, the dean's celestial rice bed, and I, too, had been granted my wish, for not another faithful was in sight. For ten minutes, we didn't say a word. Then the dean turned around. On his face was a look of almost holy joy. For moment, he said nothing, though his lips tried hard to form the words and then, as though giving a toast to the king, he whispered, "Der Tag."

We paddled joyfully down the lake and made camp in the lee of a heavily timbered point, from which we had a gorgeous view of the entire rice bed below us.

The tent went up in a hurry. I busied myself with the firewood, while my partner went up the slope for some spruce boughs. He hadn't been gone more than a minute, before I heard him call. "Come up here, and I'll show you something."

I could tell by the tone of his voice that something was up, so, dropping my ax, I bolted through the brush to where he stood.

"Look," he shouted, pointing excitedly toward the lake. "See what's down below us."

I looked, and for moment could hardly believe my eyes. There, clustered around a small, timbered island, in the very center of the rice bed, were hundreds of black dots moving about leisurely, always changing position and sometimes disappearing altogether.

For an hour we sat and watched them. Ducks were

everywhere, flock after flock, feeding and quacking contentedly, unaware that this was their last day of peace. Occasionally, a flock would rise with a great beating of wings, wheel and circle, only to settle, with many noisy splashings, farther down the shore.

That afternoon we spent making camp as comfortable as possible, oiled our guns, tied new strings to our decoys, and talked strategy. When we could contain ourselves no longer, we climbed the rise to watch the feeding flock. It was an unforgettable afternoon, one of those rare occasions when a man knows, for once, that he'd rather be where he is than any place else in the world.

As we sat before our camp fire that evening, however, a vague doubt assailed us.

"What do you suppose is going to happen," said the dean, "if this weather keeps up until tomorrow? I've been a little worried, and, unless I miss my guess, that whole flock will clear out for good with the first racket. This isn't duck weather, and you know it."

"At the same time," I replied, "it isn't likely that they'll leave without giving us some shooting. Besides, there's a bank of cloud in the north that might blow up something."

In spite of my optimism, I, too, was worried. I had seen too many flocks get up on a clear, sunny day, and not come back. Then, too, the sun had set red and promising, and the sky above was bright with stars.

The dean rose to his feet, stretched, and yawned. "I'm too old at this game," he said at length, "not to know that you've got to be miserable in order to shoot ducks. Well, I'm getting sleepy, think I'll roll in."

I sat up, as I usually do, to smoke a last pipe and watch the fire die down. I had been sitting so for perhaps an hour, thinking of other camp fires and other opening days, when something hit my hand. For a moment, it startled me. No, it wasn't a leaf. It shone and glittered in the firelight. I looked at it in wonderment. It was a drop of water. I waited expectantly, but not for long. Another struck near the first. It couldn't possibly be raining. A short time ago the sky was clear. Perhaps that cloud in the north—. A big drop hissed into the coals. I looked up then, half-fearfully, to an overcast sky, and to rain coming down with that slow, steady precision that means storm.

I roused the dean with a whoop of delight, and together we sat in the shelter of our open tent, watching the drops put out our fire. It was too completely perfect to be true, and we sat as thrilled as two kids getting their first glimpse of Santa Claus. A rice bed to ourselves, rain and storm, and tomorrow the opening day. Who wouldn't be happy?

The fire died down to blackness, and only then did we roll in, but not to sleep. We were far too excited for that. The rhythmical dripping of the rain on the tent sounded for all the world like, "Ducks tomorrow, ducks, ducks, ducks, ducks, ducks tomorrow." To the tune of that, we finally fell asleep.

At 3:30 the weather was all that a duck hunting morning should be, dark, cold, and wet. A bright, cheerful fire and the smell of boiling coffee dispelled all thoughts of discomfort. It was still raining, a cold, steady drizzle coming out of the northeast. There would be misery enough for all today.

A full hour before dawn, we slid the canoe into the water, and headed out in the blackness toward the little island. Going through the rice, we made such an unearthly racket that it seemed as though every duck in the country would leave. Flocks rose ahead of us, and the deafening sound of their wings was everywhere.

We set our decoys carefully, picked our blinds close together, and began the nerve-racking wait for daylight.

Cigarettes glowed dully in the darkness, and the acrid smell of tobacco mingled with the rich, dank odor of wet leaves that were down.

For half an hour we saw nothing, then decoys came gradually into view — dark, uncertain blotches on the gray mist of the water. A lone mallard rose with a lusty quacking close by, and whistled swiftly over the island. Just as the east began to brighten, silhouetting darkly the spruce tops of the far shore, a coyote tuned up beyond our camp in a wild, rollicking medley of barks and howls. A whistle of wings came from behind us. It was still too dark to see. The flock passed close overhead, and in an instant was gone. They settled noisily over in the rice. A pair of bluebills came in unexpectedly, and lit with a plop in the very center of our decoys. For a while they swam about sociably, and then began their feeding. The east was now barred with red underneath the rain cloud. The darkness was lifting rapidly. I looked at my watch, a minute and a half to go.

I slipped the shell from the chamber of my gun. It slipped back with a click. The dean heard me and turned. His face was tense with excitement. Suddenly, he ducked, and I heard his whisper. "Here they come, don't move."

A bunch of mallards had dropped over the horizon and were circling the lake. I called them. They began to swing our way. Then, as though by prearrangement, flock after flock hove into view, until the air was alive with the whistling of many wings. Our bunch was coming closer. They swung over once, just out of range, veered, and came straight for the blind, wings set, necks outstretched.

"Pick one and take your time," I whispered to myself. "Take your time." They were now in range, close enough to see their eyes. I picked a big drake in the lead, coming straight at me, an impossible shot. At the report, he spiraled high into the air, only to crumple at my second load. He fell in a spout of water among the decoys. The dean had made a pretty shot, and I could see his bird flopping a hundred yards to the right.

I hastily reloaded my gun. Another bunch was circling the island. For a moment they turned to leave, but, just as they topped the horizon, our call brought them round. They began to drift our way along the shore.

To know that they were heading for our decoys alone, would swing and bank until we gave the word, was sweet satisfaction, to say the least. For once, no long range gun from down the shore would send them skyward. Now we could take our own good time.

We were watching the flock intently, every dip and swerve they made, when a pair of teal, going 90 miles an hour, whizzed over our heads. Not a chance in the world. The mallards were now heading our way, had seen the decoys, and were coming down. One last, agonized quack on my caller, and I got set. Just at the limit of range, two set their wings and sailed for the decoys. The others saw us and climbed. Our guns cracked as one. The dean's bird crumpled neatly. Mine faltered, and fell in a wide, air-beating circle, hovered for a moment uncertainly over the rice, and dropped like a plummet.

The dean was talking earnestly to himself, and I knew what had happened without his telling. He had missed a perfect straight-away with his second barrel.

We had no sooner reloaded than a group of three, startled by our last shooting, came over unannounced. They were upon us before we knew it.

As we fired, they rose straight up, pounded the air a moment in consternation, and kept on going. After flying around aimlessly, they lit in the rice, not 200 yards from us.

"How about going after them?" I suggested.

"Suits me," answered the dean, as he threw the brush off

the canoe and slid it into the water. We pulled straws for the bow, and he won.

No sooner had we gotten into the open than a flock came over the island, headed directly for the decoys, saw us, and passed by way out of range. We watched them ruefully and cursed our luck.

"It never fails," growled the dean. "One sure way to bring them in is to leave your blind."

We pushed our way through the rice as swiftly as the matted vegetation would let us. Big clumps of weed hung to our paddles and made such a racket that it didn't seem possible to get anywhere in range. Nevertheless, we drew closer. Still they didn't flush. We were now almost there.

"Grab your gun," I cautioned. As he laid his paddle behind him, a bunch of bluebills whistled by. He made a reach for his gun.

"Don't shoot," I whispered fiercely. He lowered it and, glowering, turned halfway around. "Next time," and he all but hissed as he said it, "I'm going to let them have it. We'll never get those blooming mallards anyway."

I pushed the canoe forward another 20 yards. They couldn't have lit much farther. My gunner shifted his weight to a better shooting position, and slipped off the safety. Ten feet more. I stood up to take a look around. Nothing but rice and blackbirds. Another push with the paddle. Then, with a loud quack and a beating of wings, a beautiful greenhead and his mate bounced high out of the water, not 30 yards away. The gun cracked twice, but the birds climbed swiftly on. I dropped my paddle, and all but fell out of the canoe getting in a parting shot. Not a feather, out of range and gone, as pretty a brace of birds as we would ever see. It was unbelievable.

We paddled back silently toward the blinds. Those things will happen. I tried to console myself with the thought that seeing them was enough, but small consolation there was in that. As we were pushing through the decoys, a pair of redheads came over. Dean made a clean kill with a vengeance. Mine wobbled, but kept on going. Retrieving our dead bird, we hastily pushed back to shore and crawled once more into the protecting shelter of the blinds.

It was now broad daylight. A freezing wind was howling out of the northwest, with occasional gusts of sleet and rain. For half an hour, nothing happened, though we stood facing the gale and shivering in a manner that should have brought in a carload of ducks.

"How's this for weather?" I yelled through chattering teeth.

"Perfect," answered the dean, blowing on his fingers. "This should bring them in."

I started to light a cigarette by way of diversion, when I heard again the whistle of wings. My cold hands refused to function, and I dropped half the package into the water, trying to get them back where they belonged. The flock was far to the east when I first saw them. A lone call brought them 'round, four black mallards aching to feed.

On they came, drifting warily along the shore line. They disappeared for an instant beyond the trees at our back, and then with a rush shot over our heads and dropped toward the decoys. One of us must have moved or rolled his eyes, for, just at the limit of range, they turned with baffling suddenness and headed away.

A muffled "Damn" came from the other blind.

I watched the speeding birds as they grew smaller and smaller. As they topped the horizon, two of them, for some unaccountable reason, turned and headed back the way they had come. "Here they come," whispered the dean, as though I hadn't seen every wing stroke those blacks had made. This time we froze. On they came. I felt for my safety. It was on. Nervously, I slipped it off. Another split second—in range. As I fired, the near mallard folded its wings, hit breast downward, and bounced high above the water. The dean missed his first barrel, but, with the second, his climbing bird crumpled, turned a pinwheel or two, and fell within 10 feet of the blind.

"That's getting 'em," I yelled. "Watch yourself." A single whizzed by directly over us, and was gone before we had time to move.

All morning long, we had wonderful shooting, black mallarads mostly, with an occasional gray. Once, after a long, quiet spell, a bunch of bluebills almost scared us out of a week's growth. There was a roar like that of a high-powered car. The sound grew louder, and then, with set wings, twisting and hurtling, they literally poured out of the sky, with that indescribable air-ripping racket that only bluebills can make.

For a bewildering instant the air was alive with ducks, but, when the smoke cleared away, there were only two down, and one of these was streaking it for the rice, with nothing but the tip of its bill out of the water. We had pulled the amateur's stunt of firing at the flock instead of picking our birds. There was no earthly use in chasing the wounded one. It had too good a start, and a bluebill can swim.

Toward noon the weather cleared. The clouds were moving south, and in the north was already a broad, blue streak of sky. For a moment, the sun came through, transforming the cold, gray lake into a dancing field of blue and gold. The flight was about over. We ate our lunch in peace, counted our ducks, and prepared happily for a long, dreamy afternoon. It didn't matter now if the sun did come out. We had had our fill of shooting, and for once could afford to be comfortable.

Nothing happened to disturb our ruminations until the middle of the afternoon. Then, without warning, two big gray mallards dropped from nowhere into the decoys. To my startled eyes they looked as big as a couple of geese and, no wonder, coming out of a clear sky the way they did.

I turned my head ever so slightly and looked toward the other blind. The dean smiled reassuringly and fingered his trigger. Out of the corner of his mouth came the old precaution, "Don't move." I smiled back and raised my hand, the signal we had agreed upon for just such an exigency. As we rose, they left the water in true mallard fashion, spent a frantic instant getting their directions, and then straightened out. At about 40 yards, we let them have it. Both birds hit the water.

"Pretty clever, aren't we?" I queried, as we reloaded.

"Don't be so sure," answered the dean, as he sprang for the canoe. "They're gone now."

I looked out over the water. Sure enough, our mallards, half-submerged, were heading for the nearest patch of rice and cat-tails, and even now were out of range. We paddled desperately, but to no avail. For half an hour, we beat the rice thoroughly, but not a feather did we raise. To say that we were dumfounded would be putting it mildly: knocking over two mallards almost within reaching distance, and losing them both.

"Do you suppose there's a grain of truth in the idea that they'll go down and hold on to the bottom?" I asked with huge disgust.

"Don't know," he replied, "but this I do know, that if I'm alive at this time, next year, I'm going to have the swimmingest Chesapeake that ever breathed. I'm through looking for down birds."

We paddled back to our island, crestfallen to say the least. It wasn't that we needed the two ducks, but it always hurt to lose a down and wounded bird, particularly when that bird was a mallard. The afternoon wore on, broken by an occasional single or a foray of jump shooting. At that we had had our share of excitement for one day, more than enough to make up for the preceding barren year.

We were content just to sit and watch the fast-coloring shore line, the waving rice, and the chattering flocks of blackbirds. The sun went down behind a lurid horizon. A bunch of five circled the lake a mile high, saw us as they started to drop, turned, and headed straight away into the west. They grew smaller and smaller, hung poised for a moment, five motionless black dots against the rose of the sunset, and disappeared. The first day's hunt was over.

We picked up our ducks and started for camp. As we paddled through the rice, the stars came out, one by one. It was now almost calm. High overhead came once more the whistle of wings—sss—sss—sss—sss. We dropped our paddles and listened, mallards coming in to feed. Fainter and fainter grew the sound, until it blended with the soft rustling of the night breeze through the rice. They settled with a splash somewhere over in the rice bed. A drake quacked loudly once, then all was still. There would be shooting again in the morning—perhaps.

Stag Pants Galahads
Sports Afield
NOVEMBER 1930

ALL OF US *have images of what makes up the woodsman. We may think in terms of plaid shirts, camouflage clothing, park ranger green and grey, or some favorite well-worn outfit that we save for the woods. We can picture Thoreau wandering the woods in white shirt and coat with the top hat that he used for storing botanical treasures. Aldo Leopold was extremely clothes and style conscious and wore only the latest attire to match whatever his activity was.*

As the title of this deer hunting article indicates, Sig's clothing was important too. In later years, his hat would become one of his trademarks.

The setting of this story is the Stony River, which extends from near Isabella, Minnesota, to Birch Lake in the Kawishiwi River. Highway 1 crosses the Stony. In addition to the dean, Sig introduces us to two more of his contemporaries. Glenn Powers was the principal of the local schools and was a target of much of Sig's kidding, since he was the more successful hunter when they were together. Hilliard was a local teacher in industrial arts, who went along on some occasions, but he was not an outdoorsman by the others' standards.

All writers develop favorite phrases and images that tend to reappear throughout their work. Editors are alert to this and try to keep them from reappearing in the same book. As you read this essay, pay particular attention to the last paragraph and then look for a very similar phrase in the story, "Papette."

"HEY YOU OLD WOODS RAT, wait a minute."

I turned around. It was the dean, hurrying up the street toward me. By the light in his eye, I knew something out of the ordinary was up.

"It won't be long now," was his greeting.

"What won't?" I asked stupidly.

"Come to," he said, "and take a look at this." Then with an air as momentous as though he was unveiling the only original draft of the Locarno treaty itself, he showed me a bit of yellow cardboard. Across the top, printed in bold black letters were three words and a figure. BIG GAME LICENSE 1928. I stared but said nothing.

"Better get some shells and limber up that trigger finger of yours," was his parting remark. "Another two weeks and we'll be on our way."

From that moment, my blood pressure was anything but normal. Until then, the coming of deer season had seemed rather indefinite and still too far away to worry about, but here it was, almost upon us and a million things to get done. Everyday affairs became suddenly of a secondary importance and I wandered around, my brain a whirl of pack sacks, tents, rifles and grub lists. My one consolation during those trying days, was that I was not alone in my travail. As time went on, others developed the symptoms and I revelled in such intimate companionship and understanding as seldom befalls one in these sophisticated times.

One evening Glenn Powers called me over to see his new thirty-thirty. As I drew beads on all the light bulbs in the house, he told me confidentially that he had traded in his old one and only forty dollars to boot. Didn't I think it was a buy? Of course I did, though I couldn't help secretly agreeing with his otherwise understanding wife who couldn't see for the life of her why the old one wouldn't have done just as well.

Hilliard was in the midst of a new sleeping bag. I came on him one day, knee deep in duck feathers and wool batt. He was working feverishly and I knew that for him it was a race against time. To my questions he only grunted and sewed all the faster. The strain was beginning to tell.

That last week was tense with suppressed excitement. The main topic of conversation was snow. Old-timers talked of other seasons and made sage predictions about the weather and things in general. The gaily decorated windows of the hardware stores with their show of rifles, deer heads, and neatly stacked mounds of ammunition, became the meeting places for men on the streets. Here they gathered any hour of the day or night to discuss in muffled tones the latest scrap of gossip. The game wardens had found several carcasses already in the brush just south of town. Someone had seen a buck and a doe on the Winton road not over a mile away. As the time drew close, men who hitherto had worn the calm placid look of substantial citizens, now had the preoccupied expressions of those about to embark upon great and desperate adventure.

Those last few days were interminable, then all of a sudden the hour was upon us. Final hurried preparations and checking over of supplies, all but tearful goodbyes from our wives. "There had been so many accidents already. We would be careful, wouldn't we? Good luck and have a good time," fell upon heedless ears and we were off.

As we roared out of town, the tension snapped and we were our old selves again. If we had cared to confess it however, there had been a lot of satisfaction in the fuss we had caused at that and in the incidental adulation that followed us out. My own little Junior had followed me around admiringly for a whole week, weighing my every word. But today when I donned my wool stag pants, checkered shirt and suspenders, his joy was unconcealed. To him I was as completely Sir Galahad as though I had worn a suit of shining armour. I had promised him faithfully a very rash promise, made I'll admit in a mood of braggadocia, to bring home the biggest buck in the woods, with horns a yard wide and full fashioned. For that matter, we were heroes to every youngster in town if not to our wives. It was satisfying to know that once again we could bask in the role of the primitive provider, faring forth to deeds of "derring do."

We were bound for the Stony River country, the choicest bit of hunting ground in northern Minnesota. Since the days of the lumberjacks, the word "Stony" has been one of more than ordinary meaning wherever the subject of deer hunting has come up. Just mention that name to any nimrod in the northern half of the state and see his eyes light up. Ten chances to one, he will start the inevitable "I remember" and then you'll be in for an all night session.

Thirty miles of driving over the crookedest road in creation brought us through the heart of the "Superior National Forest" to the banks of the Stony River. Here we left our car in the clearing of what used to be old camp six in the logging days, and struck due east into the brush. After following the north bank for several miles, we pitched camp just as it was getting dark in a heavy growth of mixed timber near the water.

After an hour or two of the usual milling around that accompanies the setting up of camp, we settled down to enjoy ourselves and make ready with the necessary word barrage for the morning's attack.

The fire of pine knots was burning merrily, throwing a ghostly light on the tall white trunks of birch and aspen. The dean looked at his watch. "Ten hours and twenty minutes to go," he announced. "Within half a day, we'll hear the crack of rifles."

We gave our guns a final polishing, while we planned the morning's hunt. Glenn would go up the narrows, the dean west along the river, Hilliard and I would work north toward Dunnigan Lake. One thing worried us more than anything else and that was the absence of snow. Deer hunting with the leaves dry and noisy and no possible chance of tracking was a condition to be dreaded. Yet here we were confronted by the very thing we had hoped and prayed wouldn't happen.

"I remember the season of '21," spoke Glenn. "The woods were so confoundedly noisy then that you couldn't get within a mile of anything. Didn't have a ghost of a chance."

"You're certainly a cheerful cuss," I answered. "Seems to me we had good shooting that year, although I will admit we had to work for what we got."

"The only way tomorrow," concluded Hilliard after an hour of reminiscing, "is to pick a spot and sit down. There's no earthly use in moving around.

"Guess you're right," agreed the dean. "Let 'em come to you. There's no use chasing 'em tomorrow."

I got up and walked out of the circle of firelight to take a look at the sky. It was cloudy and the wind was in the south. A slight chance but doubtful. Nine o'clock found us in our sleeping bags. The last long night was under way.

Long before daylight, I heard a whisper, "Pile out you swamp angels, it's almost time." It was the dean, as I might have guessed. He never could sleep worth a damn the night before. I looked at my watch. It was only four-thirty and wouldn't be light for another two hours.

"Start the fire," I mumbled, "and when it's nice and warm, call me." A disgusted snort was my only answer.

In a moment a candle sputtered into a sickly yellow flame. By this time, Glenn too was awake. "What's the idea," he roared. "This ain't duck season. Poor devil, he's gone completely off—." A flying boot hushed him up.

It wasn't long before a fire was blazing in front of the tent, throwing a warm and pleasant glow against the side of my sleeping bag. Never in all my life had I been so thoroughly comfortable. The fringe of trees outside the circle of firelight looked dark and mysterious. Somewhere back in the gloom, a branch snapped. It was a dark and forbidding world and I snuggled farther down in my bag. The smell of boiling coffee was tempting and so was the bacon.

"Come on you birds," growled the dean in desperation, "what sort of a tea party do you think this is?"

His sarcasm had the desired effect. "Here goes nothing," came from Hilliard, as he burst from his bag. I followed suit and so did Glenn. For the next few minutes, the tent was a nightmare of woolen underwear, stag pants and suspenders. Coffee over and cigarettes and still it wasn't daylight. We busied ourselves stowing away chocolate bars, sandwiches, shells and advice. The dean was pulling on his cap and without as much as a parting word, he lifted the flap and was gone. We were on our way.

There was not a breath of air and the woods so quiet it hurt to move. My first step in the dry crackly leaves all but unnerved me. After going a short distance, I stopped to listen. The others were gradually crunching off into the brush, Hilliard and Glenn to my right, the dean to my left. A partridge whirred up in front of me and lit in the top of a birch where he proceeded to make his breakfast on the frozen brown buds. From the timber in back came the rolling tattoo of a downy woodpecker drilling away at a dead pine stub.

I had gone perhaps a quarter of a mile, when I heard a different sound, the rapid pattering of running hoofs on a hard dry trail. I stopped again to listen, there was no mistake. The dean had jumped a couple and they were coming my way. Crouching, I ran swiftly forward toward a trail on the next ridge. The brush was so thick I couldn't see more than a few feet in front of me. When I reached the ridge, I climbed a stump and waited. The pattering sound had stopped. Had they gone or were they watching me? I stood it a moment longer and then stepped down. There was a snort and a crash and the deer burst from their cover in a thicket of alder and bounded away down the trail. As luck would have it, I didn't see a flash. Two seconds sooner and I'd have had shooting. I stood and listened until I could no longer hear them moving and then walked down the trail to where they had stood. It was as I had thought, a buck and a doe.

Picking out a likely looking spot, I sat down to wait. Perhaps the dean would scare up another. In a way I was glad I had missed my first chance. It would have been a shame to have made my kill so early. An hour passed without a sound but the nervous rustling of dry leaves.

Just as I rose to go, bang-bang-bang sounded far to my right toward the narrows. That must be Glenn. A little later came another shot, the "Coup de Grace." First blood of the season.

I wandered around the edge of a swamp grown thickly with black spruce and alder, and paused on top of a high ridge. Suddenly the brush cracked sharply down below me. All tense, I waited. Crash again, something was surely coming. Moving to a better vantage point, I slipped the safety off and got set. The whole valley was in plain view before me. Then out of the corner of my eye, I caught a telltale flash of red, brilliant eye-splitting red. I lowered my gun in disgust, not that I wouldn't have liked to shoot, but all that suspense for nothing.

I sat down carefully so as not to attract attention. On he came, someone else's Sir Galahad, running like a fool. Not once did he look my way and for that I was glad. In a short time he disappeared and I vaguely regretted the fact that he had proceeded in the direction my deer had taken.

Cutting across his trail, I started off at right angles to his course through the swamp. Five minutes later, I was startled by a series of rapid shots. My friend of the brilliant topknot had connected. After that, firing broke out in all directions. First came a volley from Deep Lake toward the east, then from old camp six, and last from the Dunnigan Lake country ahead of me. Everyone seemed to be getting shooting but me. It was disquieting to say the least, particularly when reflecting that I had hunted deer for almost twenty years, had guided scores of parties myself, and was generally considered an old hand at the game. Above all, I had my reputation with Junior to uphold. He could not be disappointed—the biggest buck in the woods—horns a yard wide and full fashioned.

I tightened up my belt and settled down to hunt in earnest. No more time for scenery or reflection. The leaves were so confoundedly noisy and though I took advantage of every moss covered rock and log, my progress must have been broadcasted for a mile. The racket I made was terrible. Today it was a case of pure luck.

Noon found me on a bare pine-covered ridge far to the northward. Here was a wonderful chance to watch. The sun came out and with it the shooting increased. The deer were moving around again. While I ate my lunch, I watched the country below me. Open rolling ridges extended in three directions and I could see for hundreds of yards. After all, the hunting wasn't everything and there were other days coming.

It was pleasant sitting there in the sun even though I knew that I ought to be moving around. A squirrel scrambled up the jackpine to my right and heaped upon my poor defenceless head all the vile squirrelish blasphemy he could think of. Then as if satisfied that anything as big and stupid as I was could certainly be of no importance, he scurried down the way he had come and continued his belated harvesting. A little later, a pair of soft grey whiskey jacks dropped in from nowhere and gave me the once over.

I don't know how long I sat there, but it was probably much longer than I should have. Leaving the hilltop almost regretfully, I turned south and headed toward camp. It was now the middle of the afternoon and by four-thirty it would be too dark to shoot. I would have to hurry.

Half a mile further on, I came to a beaver pond. This was good country, lots of swamp grass, willow and other feed around the edges. A beaver dam at the lower end of the pond served as a bridge. I made it across safely and strolled up a well marked trail on the other side. Everywhere were signs, places they had pawed the ground for roots and rubbing trees the bucks had used to polish the velvet off their horns. Here I would have to watch myself. As quietly as I could, I worked my way up the slope.

When I reached the top, I stopped to look the country

over. Suddenly there was a racket in the swamp below me. A ridge a hundred yards away would command the trail. There was only one thing to do, make a spurt for it. I made it in ten flat, of that I'm certain. Throwing myself down in true skirmish fashion, I waited. Something moved through the brush to my left. That was all, not a flash did I see, but I heard my deer crashing through the thin ice of the muskeg below. If I had only been two seconds sooner; another of the possibilities that pepper every hunting season.

A little later, while working through a brushy ravine, I stopped to take a look at my compass. While slipping off my glove, there was a crash ahead of me. For a frantic instant, I struggled to free my hand, while the white flag of a deer bounced gaily through the timber. One parting snap shot was all I got.

By now, I was fully convinced that I was the original "faux pas." Although I had just passed through a long season of duck shooting, where I had relearned for the ten thousandth time the old lesson not to be caught napping, here I was blundering around as though I had never had a gun in my hands.

It was dark before I reached the river. The fire showed up a long ways off, gleaming a steady red beacon through the trees. The others were in ahead of me and as I approached, I could see their red top knots shining in the firelight. There was no meat in camp as yet, at least none that I could see. Perhaps, I hadn't been so unfortunate after all.

Glenn was the first to look up. "Well," he remarked, "where's that heart and liver. We've got the frying pan all greased up and hot waiting for it."

That gave me my clue, or so I thought. Leaning my rifle against a tree, I took the place reserved for me in the circle, lit a cigarette and answered as casually as possible, "speaking of heart and liver, I guess mine is doing duty like the rest."

At that there was a raising of eyebrows and an exchange of glances that could only be interpreted in one way. Someone had killed a deer.

"Get any shooting at all?" asked the dean, after a weighty moment's silence.

"Nothing but a snap shot," I answered. "Couldn't get within a mile of anything today." Then remembering the shooting I had heard toward the narrows early in the morning, I turned around to Glenn and asked him to come across.

Without a word, he rose, walked over to a tree behind the tent and lifted something from a crotch. Then coming over to me, he held it under my nose for inspection. It was a heart and liver, sure enough.

Without any further urging, he told how a spike buck had all but walked over him on the trail alongside the narrows. Then as though that wasn't enough, Hilliard piped up and told how he too had dropped a nice little doe near Dunnigan Lake. The dean was still in my class and I could see that the situation rankled, for he too was supposed to be experienced.

That evening we spent praying for snow and cold, snow for tracking and cold to freeze the river solid enough so that we could snake our deer out on the ice. The prospect of a four mile carry through the woods was anything but pleasant. If it stayed warm, it might even necessitate cutting up our meat and packing it in quarters and that was a possibility that none of us relished. We all felt the same way about it. The wallop was half gone if we couldn't bring our deer in whole and then for me, there was my promise to Junior.

"We're never satisfied," spoke Hilliard at last. "During duck season, it's rain and cold, when we're fishing, it's got

to be cloudy, and now snow. You'd think that the only time it's possible for us to have any luck, is when it's miserable."

"It's all right for you to talk," grumbled the dean, "your reputation is safe."

Next morning, bright and early, we hit the trail. There were only two of us hunting, Glenn and Hilliard having planned to spend the day dragging theirs in to camp.

I hunted in the same general direction I had taken the day before. Mid-afternoon found me on a heavily timbered ridge overlooking a frozen grassy swale below. Here was as wild and likely a looking spot as I had ever seen, and strangely enough, I had the premonition that here I would make my kill. Not having kept track of my direction since leaving camp, it seemed as though I was miles away. I remember distinctly, wondering at the time, as though the kill were already a settled fact, how in the world I would ever get my meat out.

I settled down then to wait at a spot where I could overlook all but one small corner of the swale, hidden by a heavy clump of young jack pine half ways down the slope. I thought some of moving to the top of the ridge from where I knew I would have a clear view, but dismissed it as an unnecessary precaution. Besides, I was very comfortable where I was.

Ten minutes passed, then down across the swamp, a branch cracked sharply. I looked up. A brown form moved slowly through the alder brush bordering the opening and then disappeared. I waited expectantly. Presently, a big buck stalked boldly out and started crossing the swamp. Now I had occasion to curse, for the clump of jack pine was directly in line. Although I could see him plainly through the dense screen of branches, it was impossible to shoot. Why hadn't I followed my first hunch and moved? I sat there helplessly and watched him work his way to the center of the pothole. There he stopped and proceeded to paw through the thin ice for water. I could have tried a shot then, but decided to wait. Perhaps he would keep on coming toward me and cross the ridge I was on.

He drank daintily and started on once more. I could see now that he had a wonderful spread of horns. Never in all my life will I forget that moment. On he came, as though he had all the time in the world, as yet oblivious of the death that awaited him on the other side.

So far, I hadn't had a decent shot, though several times I saw him fairly well through the screen of branches before me. Once I thought of shooting, but he disappeared while I was getting my bead. He was now at the base of my ridge, well hidden in a dense growth of alder. I could hear him plainly, moving around, feeding on the brush. Now was my chance. Leaving my hiding place, I crawled swiftly to the top of the ridge where I should have been in the first place. There wasn't a sound from the thicket now and for a moment I was overwhelmed with the sickening thought that he was gone. Perhaps, he was standing still, listening and getting the wind.

It wasn't long before I heard him again, now coming directly toward me. Once I saw a movement in the brush, but it was gone in an instant. The buck was now within a hundred feet of me, but still I couldn't see him. If he should come out, it would be nothing but sheer murder and I instinctively recoiled at the thought of making a kill at that range.

Suddenly I saw a movement behind a bunch of balsams not seventy-five feet away; just a swaying of the branches, nothing more. Then he stopped dead and for the first time, I knew he was suspicious. Now things began to happen. With a wild snort, the deer wheeled, crashed down the slope and to my joy headed for the swamp the way he had come. He hit the grass going like the wind, flag up and horns back, twenty feet at a jump. I drew a hurried bead on his shoulder and fired. It was a clean miss. Another bead at the point of his nose and he dropped almost out of sight in the muskeg.

I waited a moment to see if he would get up and then ran down to where he lay. He was stone dead and queerly enough did not have a bullet mark on him. Not until I had him cleaned did a telltale drop of blood give the secret away. I had hit him at the base of the skull, the bullet having penetrated between the ears without even ruffling the hair.

I sat down upon a hummock of moss after I was all through and took a long deferred smoke. My buck was a nice one, about two hundred pounds in weight and with good horns, full fashioned too. I rested for half an hour and lived through once more every second of the time I'd spent on the jack pine ridge above me. By now the whiskey jacks had begun to gather and I was ready to move.

Throwing some brush over the carcass, I left, blazing a north-south line toward the river. To my surprise, it was only a little over a mile. My zigzagging had fooled me, but at that it was far enough.

No one was in camp, but a nice spike buck and a doe were hanging alongside the tent. Glenn and Hilliard had gotten theirs in. They must have gone out again to help bring in the dean's. Some time later, as I was enjoying a cup of coffee, I heard a yell from the direction of the river. I got up and ran down to the shore. It was the dean dragging his along the ice. Glenn and Hilliard came in shortly afterwards. They had struck the ice a mile above camp and the dean against their advice, had proceeded to take his deer down the river in spite of the fact that it had been thawing all day. Now we all went down to help and to the tune of cracking ice dragged the doe ashore and up to camp.

That night, we recounted our many adventures over and over again, elaborating and polishing, until each tale had become a finished product that could bear telling and re-telling without the danger of plagiarism. It was a night to be remembered. For once we were at peace with the world.

The next few days might better be gone over briefly. Much to our disgust, the weather turned warmer, making the swamps impassable and worst of all weakening the ice hopelessly on the river. Although we hated to admit it, we were up against it as far as getting our game out whole was concerned. We waited but in vain. The sun kept on shining and the wind stayed in the south. There was only one thing left to do, quarter our animals and pack them in as so much duffle. It was a disheartening joy to say the least, to bid goodbye to all hopes of a grand triumphant entry.

As we drove into town that last night my courage all but left me. Junior met me at the gate as I knew he would.

A wild yell of greeting and then, "Daddy, where's your deer?"

I pointed at the pack sack tied to the running board. He took one look and his jaw dropped. "Daddy, I thought—" and he buried his disappointment in the rough folds of my mackinaw. One Stag Pants Galahad had fallen from grace.

The Poison Trail
Sports Afield
DECEMBER 1930

THIS IS ONE OF *the more surprising articles among Sig's early works. It is surprising because in later years, Sig developed a true understanding of the wolf and its role in the ecology of the north country. Like Aldo Leopold, Sig began as an advocate of wolf elimination, then as his knowledge grew, he understood the mistake that he had made. In 1938, he published a study on wolves. It was the beginning of a long sequence of wolf studies in the Superior National Forest. He would no longer call them the "grey marauders" as he does in "The Poison Trail" and "Papette." If a person were to try to see significance in each article and story, one would have to conclude that this article points out the ability of all great intellects to change their minds as they learn new facts. It is not bad to be wrong, it is wrong not to learn.*

The trappers were Sig's source of wolf knowledge and the data base for his wolf research. And even after he developed an affection for the wolf, he never lost his admiration for these men who were an extension of the old voyageurs.

IT WAS NEW YEAR'S day and a howling northwester, the beginning of a long trek for the trappers, who had spent their holidays in town. The dry powdered snow whirled and eddied down the smooth beaten path of the dog team trail, leading straight away into the drifting whiteness of Fall Lake. Winton, headquarters for the Superior State Game Refuge and last outpost of civilization, was dropping rapidly behind us. The gale was at our backs and our skis all but flew over the hard brittle crust.

We were bound for the Frazer Lake country: Long Bill, of wolf trapping fame, Urho, his partner, and myself, to make the round of a line of poison bait set out some weeks before; a poison trail, one hundred miles in length. This was but a phase of the warfare between the predatory animal control and the hosts of grey marauders which each year descend from the wilds of Ontario to prey upon the herds of moose and deer across the border. Our trail lay along the eastern boundary through one of the finest big game areas on the continent and incidentally one of the most harassed by the killing packs.

At the end of Fall Lake we left the beaten trail and turned into the timber toward the southeast to make a thirty mile circle on our way toward Camp Twenty Five on Newfound Lake. After leaving the dog team route the going was more difficult for the snow was loose and deep. For a ways we followed a smooth winding creek, a wilderness boulevard, fringed with cat-tail and alder. Then, striking an old tote road, we plunged into a dark swamp of cedar and spruce and here we found our first evidence of game.

Tracks and signs were everywhere, and once we surprised a bunch of four deer feeding on the underbrush beside the trail. Startled, they watched us for a nerve-racking moment, and then like grey shadows, slipped away into the timber.

Other tracks we saw too, tracks that made us more than anxious to see the first of our poison sets. Following the deer runways, crossing and recrossing our path, were the huge dog-like imprints of the timber wolves. We stopped to examine one much larger than the rest, so broad that I could barely cover it with my closed hand.

"The deer are going to catch it now," spoke Bill. "As soon as the crust forms over all this loose stuff, there is goin' to be trouble."

"Yes," I answered, "and I wouldn't be surprised if they've started their murdering already."

I was breaking trail at the time and while crossing a small frozen pot-hole on the other side of the swamp, discovered the first evidence of their killing, the carcass of a doe dragged down the night before. I waited for Bill and Urho to come up, and together we examined it. What we most feared, had happened. Only the fat of the entrails had been eaten. They were already killing for fun.

"Fed up, are they?" spoke Urho. "What's goin' to happen towards spring if they're startin' that now?"

"There is only one thing that will save the deer now," answered Bill, with emphasis, "and that's to poison every lake this side of the boundary."

We set some scattering baits and pushed on. We soon struck another creek winding and doubling upon itself, until it seemed as though we never would reach its end. All along the stream were signs of beaver dams and houses down its entire length. Signs of starvation there were too, fresh cuttings of birch and poplar, and broad oval trails leading from the air holes up into the brush. Their stored supplies of food were running low.

The creek finally widened out and emptied into a rambling body of water known as Pine Lake, the location of our first poison stations. Naturally, we quickened our stride, for the first bait lay straight ahead, not half a mile from shore.

Urho was now in the lead. As he rounded the first point, he gave a yell and started to run. "There's something out there," he called back. "Looks like a couple of wolves."

We dug in our sticks and followed him closely. There, sure enough, within fifty feet of the first set, were two mounds drifted over by the snow. We uncovered them hastily and found that instead of wolves they were foxes, one a red and the other a beautiful silver black. Ordinarily, a catch like this would have given us cause to rejoice, but now we were thoughtful and somewhat saddened. We wondered just how costly a toll in fur bearers "The Poison Trail" would take.

But we were after wolves and we scouted around everywhere looking for larger mounds in the snow. An unnatural looking hummock a ways up the lake attracted my attention. I skied over, kicked off the drift, and uncovered an enormous timber wolf frozen solid to the ice. This was more like it, but now our work was cut out, still three miles from camp and a hundred pounds of frozen carcass to be toted in.

We pulled straws for the honor and Urho won. Without even waiting for our congratulations, he tossed the wolf onto his shoulders and was off. Bill and I each picked up a fox and followed, thanking our stars for luck. Our good fortune was short lived, however, for at our next station a mile up the lake, we picked up a couple of coyotes not a stone's throw from the bait. Now there was no choice, honor enough for all, and we each wore a solid fur collar the rest of the way in.

Leaving Pine Lake, we struck into the timber and just at dusk came to our first cabin on the shore of a tiny pond. Dropping our packs was plain luxury and for a while we just sat, enjoying the strange sensation to the utmost.

That night, we strung our animals to the ridge pole to thaw, and next morning skinned them out, throwing the carcasses to the chickadees and whiskey jacks. After breakfast, we headed north toward Newfound Lake. Crossing Moose we picked up another fox and a coyote and here adventure came to us from an unexpected source.

Bill left the trail half way down the lake to look at a trap he had set on a long, finger-like peninsula to our right. He hadn't been gone five minutes before we heard him yell. Leaving our packs, we hurried over to the point, cut into the timber and almost ran over him in our excitement. There he stood with a sprung trap in his hand, repeating over and over again, "Can you beat that, now ain't that the devil?"

"What's the trouble?" I asked, as soon as I could get my breath.

"Trouble," he blurted out, "look what's in this trap. That's trouble enough; twenty miles of trailin' to do, startin' right now."

I stepped over to where he stood, took the trap from his hands and examined it. Held neatly between the sharp steel teeth, was the heel of a timber wolf's foot, torn cleanly from its socket.

"Poor devil," I exclaimed, "he deserves to get away, after going through all that misery."

For twenty feet in every direction the snow and brush was beaten down and blood stained, giving every evidence of a terrific struggle. A bloody three-legged trail led off into the timber toward the point of the peninsula.

At a suggestion from Bill, I slipped again onto the ice and swiftly circled the point to see if the killer was still in the timber. At the very tip, I found what I was looking for. The trail emerged and zigzagged uncertainly toward the mainland. I followed it and noticed that the right front leg was dragging and probably broken.

For a hundred yards, the trail ran straight away and then to my surprise turned and circled back where it disappeared again in the timber of the point. I had just made this discovery, when I heard three shots and a yell, then three more in rapid succession.

When I got back, Bill and Urho were sitting on the ice skinning out a good sized wolf. Urho had stumbled on the crippled beast, shortly after my departure, and had fired the first three shots as it ran through the brush. Then Bill got into action, or rather was forced to, for the wolf bore down upon him, frothing at the mouth and snapping at its wounded leg. The last shot dropped him dead not twenty feet away. I lit a cigarette and watched the skinning with growing satisfaction. Luck was with us. No trailing through the brush and no carcass to be toted in.

It was late afternoon when we pulled into Twenty Five, and not having eaten or rested since daylight, we were tired and hungry. The dog team had been there with supplies and the three hundred pounds of chuck they had left looked more than welcome.

That night as we sat before the red-hot heater, I was regaled with story after story of trapping days before the law came to the border, of days when Twenty Five was a rendezvous for outlaws and its smoke-stained rafters had hung heavy with fortunes in smuggled furs. As I sat and listened and watched the play of candle light over our own shining hides, some of the romance of those old days crept into my blood. Even Bill, hardened old woodsman that he was, grew fondly reminiscent. It was ten o'clock before we knew it, and that is late for the woods; so we crawled into our bags, taking our dreams of the past in with us.

Daylight came all too quickly. Urho and I got the stove to roaring while Bill nursed his pan of bubbly sour dough, the pan that never failed or went dry. Pancakes and coffee and we were ready to talk plans. It was quickly decided that Bill should stay, skin out and stretch the fur we had, and comb the surrounding territory, while Urho and I should push on alone to Frazer Lake.

The range to the east was brightening up with streaks of orange and lavender as we shook the snow from our skis and started. It was considerably colder and two rainbow colored sun-dogs rode high on either side of the dawn. The trail for a mile was all downhill and icy and we shot along at breath-taking speed, rounding the turns with reckless abandon. Before we were even warmed up, we slipped through the last fringe of timber onto the smooth ice of Mountain Iron Lake.

Half a mile ahead lay the first narrows, a veritable death-trap for deer. As we drew closer, a game trail could be seen coming down one slope onto the ice and going up the other side. Skirting the edge of the weak ice, we counted four bloated carcasses floating in plain sight underneath the thin transparent crust. One, a young doe, we pulled out and cut off the rancid fat of her back and stomach for bait. The other three we marked for further use.

"Queer," I remarked to Urho as we were leaving, "that those fool deer insist on crossing where the ice is weak. You'd think that they would go down a hundred yards where there is no danger of breaking through."

"Yes, it is queer," he agreed. "They're worse than sheep.

Last year, Bill and I blocked up the trial, hopin' they'd detour, but after walkin' clear around the obstruction, they followed the shore and came back to their old tracks to drown themselves. We couldn't figure it out nohow."

The lake stretched eastward for a good five miles, miles of firm wind-rippled snow over which our skis glided with scarcely any effort. At the far end and towering skyward was a rugged range of hills, blocking our passage to Slate Lake. We stopped at several poison stations on the way, but none, as far as we could see, had been molested. At last we reached the portage and started the long climb over the divide. It was killing work in the deep snow with our loaded packs, but not as impossible as it had seemed from the lake and only once were we forced to shoulder our skis.

From the summit the view was well worth the effort. Far below us to the westward stretched the frozen whiteness of Mountain Iron, a broad glistening highway toward Camp Twenty Five.

We left the ridge reluctantly and headed eastward once more. Noon found us in the shelter of a huge rock on Slate Lake, boiling a kettle of tea. While I dug out the bannock and cheese, Urho took a run around the lake. Long before the water had even begun to bubble, I saw him coming back with something on his shoulders. As he came closer, I saw it was another timber wolf as big, if not bigger, than the one we had shot on Moose.

As he dropped it alongside our packs, he mentioned casually that five foxes were waiting for me around the point. Visions of an easy trip to Frazer vanished in smoke and I began to wonder if after all most of the romance of a trapper's life couldn't be translated into plain backbreaking work. As we sat watching the kettle come to a boil, I told Urho the story of the French voyageur who had carried a three hundred pound pack across the Grand Portage on the Pigeon River without stopping to rest.

"And how long was that portage?" he asked again.

"Nine miles," I answered.

Strangely enough, that gave us strength. After lunch, Urho wrapped his hard frostbitten choker around his neck and started. I followed until I reached the first point and there loaded on the foxes. As I mushed on, I discovered that five frozen foxes with twenty stiff legs jabbing me in the back and ribs wasn't nearly as amusing as I had thought.

On the lakes it wasn't so bad. But on the steep, drifted portages it was a different story; for in addition to the weight of a bulky pack was the added encumbrance of nine-foot skis and sticks. Sliding down was even worse, for no sooner did I gain momentum, then a frozen leg would catch on a branch or sapling. The pack would start to swing, gently at first, then a wild effort to regain my balance, ending usually in a swan dive to the foot of the hill, the heavy pack delivering the *coup de grace*, as I lit.

We crossed several small lakes and then struck Frazer with its beautifully timbered shores and islands, standing out dark green against the whiteness. For a time, I forgot my load in admiration of the scene before me. Suddenly, I stumbled over something. I was about to go on, when I noticed the tip of a coyote's tail sticking out of the snow.

From then on, scenery was only a blur. I was so heavily loaded, that my skis sank repeatedly through the crust. Urho strode on ahead as though carrying a hundred pound wolf was nothing out of the ordinary and I followed for ages, wondering vaguely how long it would be. At last in the very end of a long spruce-bordered bay, we saw the cabin. That last mile was sheer agony; slip—slide—crunch, slip—slide—crunch, I seemed to be in a treadmill getting nowhere. The moon was rising full and yellow in the rose tinted east before me, and behind me I knew was a sunset, but I was far too absorbed in my work to notice such everyday splendor.

Then before I was aware, we were unloading our packs and shaking the snow from our skis. That night the little cabin was full of thawing wolves and foxes. We had them hanging everywhere, and as their frozen hides began to warm, the perfume they gave off was one never to be forgotten.

The next few days were filled with activity — skins to be stretched and dried, baits to be looked after and reset, and the multitude of little jobs that are always waiting around any trapper's cabin.

It was here that we made the biggest catch of the season. One morning, Urho feeling ambitious, decided to take a run on the lake while I made breakfast. I puttered around for half an hour and had just stepped to the door to yell, "Come and get it," when he staggered up the trail, carrying on his shoulders the biggest, shaggiest looking monster I had ever seen. We carried him into the cabin and strung him to the ridge pole with a chain.

"Where in all creation did you find that?" I asked. "He looks more like an old lion than a wolf."

"And if you had carried him in, you'd have though he was bigger than that," answered Urho wiping the perspiration from his face.

From tip to tip, he measured well over seven feet and must have weighed as much as a man. Broad across the head and back and heavily furred, he was as savage a looking brute as one could imagine. Such jaws and teeth, it was little wonder that they could ham-string moose or deer and drag them down.

That afternoon, we picked up a cross fox on a little lake towards Saginaga, and Urho showed me where earlier in the season, shortly after the freeze-up, they had saved a moose from drowning. They had found him half dead, hind quarters broken through the ice and frozen in. After chopping him loose, they had finally hoisted him out with a long pole. But for a full day and night he had lain there, too exhausted by his struggles to move. Then with the return of his strength, he had ambled off slowly into the woods, a sadder but wiser moose.

The next morning, calamity descended upon us, the worst of all catastrophies that can befall a woodsman. Our sour dough batter went bad and our cakes instead of coming out their usually crispy brown were soggy and all but transparent. We tried everything but to no avail. The stuff was dead. I will never forget the look on Urho's face as he sank his teeth into that first anemic cake. Disgust and utter helplessness was written all over him.

"Let's go," we said in almost the same breath, and without further ado, packed our hides and duffle and left. The crust had frozen after the brilliant sunshine of the day before and a heavy frost had covered everything with a blanket of glistening crystals. The trees that morning were marvelous creations of fantastic lace-work and, as we skimmed over the trails, all of our troubles were forgotten.

We made good time and hove into camp by the middle of the afternoon, hungry enough to eat wolf stew. Bill, for some reason, had expected us and had a big pot of mulligan waiting to be dished out. The three of us laid to and cleaned up the entire mess before we had spoken a dozen words.

When I had finished, I pushed back my chair with a sigh of relief, lit my pipe and asked Bill if any excitement had happened during our absence.

"Nothin' much," he drawled. "Picked up a few more wolves and one morning on Mountain Iron, I saw a couple of eagles fightin' over a poisoned fox. I never heard such screechin' in all my life. They sure ripped up that hide before I got there, nothin' left but the head and ears and a few ribbons."

That evening while checking up our hides, Bill reminded me that I was due back on the twelfth and according to our new calendar this was the eleventh. I would have to leave in the morning.

As luck would have it, the clear cold weather came abruptly to an end and out of the southeast came a warm blizzard of soft sticky snow. Before rolling in, we stood in the doorway and watched it come down, white heavy gobs of it dropping out of the darkness. It was a beautiful sight, but when I thought of the twenty-six miles of mushing ahead of me, it was hard to wax sentimental.

We were awake long before daylight. It had stopped snowing, but in front of the door was a foot of loose fluffy stuff that spelled doom to easy travel. Bill's cakes were unusually good that morning and I'm afraid I lingered over them longer than I should have. I said goodbye reluctantly, slung my pack, and was on my way.

It was slow going at best and frequently I was forced to stop and rub the soft sticky snow from my skis. While crossing Moose Lake early that afternoon, I had what woodsmen term a run of pure fool luck. I was working along slowly watching the trail, when something squawked above me. Stopping, I looked up, and there not a hundred feet above my head, wheeling and circling about, were several black ravens.

Knowing their vulture-like habits was not at all reassuring knowledge and it was not hard to guess what they were waiting for. I was in danger, that I knew, but where to go to get out of it? Taking a chance, I went ahead testing the ice with my stick. I hadn't gone twenty feet before the steel-shod point went through. I stopped dead, hardly daring to breathe, and very carefully slipped one arm from its pack strap, "just in case." Then turning slowly around I pushed on my sticks ever so gently and glided away toward the mainland.

The ice cracked once, but I did not turn to look until I had gone a hundred yards. One glance was enough. Where I had stood a moment before was nothing but black water. The ravens followed me clear to shore and then left, deciding no doubt that it would be yet a little while before I would grace their menu.

It was dark before I hit the end of Fall Lake. As I pushed down the last seven mile stretch, one by one the lights of Winton hove into view. For an hour, they seemed to draw no closer. Then at last, I saw the welcome light of headquarters itself and heard the familiar chorus of husky dogs. Elijah had nothing on me. I too had come out of the sticks, thanks to the squawk of a raven.

Letters

EACH OF THE LETTERS *I have included in this section represents either an important friendship for Sig or a transition in his life, one that would involve a deeper commitment to canoe country.*

LETTER FROM SIGURD OLSON TO ALDO LEOPOLD
OCTOBER 14, 1930

THE FOLLOWING LETTER *was Sig's first contact with Aldo Leopold. In addressing it, he misspelled Leopold's first name, calling him Eldo. This contact would lead to a growing friendship between the two wilderness giants. At the time, Leopold was conducting the region's first systematic game surveys—for the Sporting Arms and Ammunition Manufacturers Institute.*

Dear Sir:

   A short time ago, I had the pleasure of making a trip with Mr. Ralph T. King who at the present time is carrying on a ruffed grouse investigation at the University Farm at St. Paul. He was up at the time securing live specimens of the native grouse and it was while doing this work that I met him. He broached the subject to me then of applying through you for one of the scholarships offered by the American Arms Association for research along game propagation lines. According to Mr. King, there is still one such scholarship available.

   Now a brief summary of my qualifications. I graduated from the Univ. of Wisconsin in 1920 majoring in Animal Husbandry. For two years immediately following my graduation, I taught Agriculture at Nashwauk, Minnesota, then I returned to the Univ. of Wisconsin to take a post graduate course in Geology of which I had taken almost enough for a major during my undergraduate work. The field in Geology did not look very promising at the time so after half a years work I together with a number of men who had come down for that work went into other lines of activity. This time I accepted a position teaching Biology at Ely, Minnesota, headquarters of the Superior National Forest, largely because it was in a section of country I liked and was very familiar with. The year following my coming a Junior College was established and I was placed in charge of the Zoology Dept.

   Since then I have been teaching high school and college zoology and related courses. My preparatory work for a Biology position, I will admit was rather scanty but during the years I have been here, I have kept up with my subject through reading and study, supplemented by a great deal of practical field work. I feel as a result of the work I have done since I came here that I have advanced considerably in my outlook and general knowledge. Every summer for the past ten years I have spent as a guide in the wilderness regions of the Superior National Forest and the Quetico Provincial park of Canada. As a result, I have become familiar with all forms of wild life and know the country thoroughly for several hundred miles north of the border, country that today is one of the last remaining untouched areas on the continent.

During the summer of 1928, I had the good fortune to collaborate with Dr. A. R. Cahn of the Univ. of Ill. on a parisitology investigation. We spent most of the summer in Ontario. We also made a survey of the birds of the Quetico. Since then, I have worked with Dr. Cahn on a number of similar problems. During the summer of 1927, I did some work in connection with Dr. Henry Ward of the Univ. of Ill. and also with Mr. Harry Hanson of the Biological Survey. During all of the time I was guiding and during the school year as well, I have had a splendid opportunity of getting first hand information on field problems. According to Mr. King, the scholarship committee needed men who had had some preliminary scientific training, who were enthusiastic above all else and who had had much field experience. After both Mr. King and Mr. Grange of the U.S. Biological Survey who was with him at the time had outlined for me the opportunities in the game conservation field, I determined to write you at their suggestion and see if at this late date there might not still be an opportunity for me. All of my life with the exception of the years I put in down at the University has been spent in the woods or near enough so that it has been always possible for me to indulge myself in the study and observation of wild life.

I shall be interested in hearing from you and if you would

like a personal conference, I should be glad to come down to Madison. I can furnish as references the following:

Dr. Alvin R. Cahn Zoology Dept. Univ. of Ill. Urbana.
Dr. Henry B. Ward
Dr. Chas. Bacon Presbyterian Hospital, Chicago.
Dean R. Shunway — Dean of Jr. Colleges, Univ. of Minn.
Dean J. H. Santo, Jr. College, Ely, Minn.

Sincerely yours,
Sigurd F. Olson

Excerpt from a Letter from Sigurd Olson to Ernest Oberholtzer
December 26, 1930

IN THE HISTORY *of the canoe country, Sigurd Olson is one of many prominent names who have recognized the significance of the region as a national asset. C. C. Andrews, who was a lawyer, Civil War general, and Minnesota forestry commissioner, had set aside the first land.*

In 1909, Ernest Oberholtzer (known later simply as Ober) left Harvard College to try and recover from the heart damage of rheumatic fever. He was told that he had only a year to live and sought the land of lakes as a source of energy.

Ober traveled with an Indian friend, Billie Magie, to the arctic and back. He wandered canoe country. His background as a landscape architect helped him to understand the ecology. His genuine interest in American Indians gained their confidence and earned him a place in a tribe. They also taught him the spiritual qualities of the borderlands.

Later, Ober was to settle on Mallard Island in Rainy Lake, conceive a plan for an international peace memorial forest, and establish himself as the godfather-guru of the Boundary Waters until his death in 1977.

I WAS GLAD to receive your resolution and am enclosing it herewith. For a long time, I have been following your work with more than passing interest and believe sincerely that what you are doing is a great thing. For the past ten years, I have been trying to do what little I could to stem the tide of exploitation that seems to be continually on the verge of wiping out our last wilderness, but as you know, it has been an uphill fight.

The business we are in gives us the opportunity of meeting thousands of people from all over the United States and if you could only see the interest they have in the fight to preserve their wilderness, you would be encouraged. No one has any idea how much that country is beginning to mean to the people of the middle west. During the days of my guiding particularly, I had occasion to talk to many men and with no exception whatever, they were all of the same opinion that the country should be set aside as a recreational preserve and not as a timber preserve. They know that the wilderness with its growing timber has value that can not be computed in dollars and cents, something that perhaps they cannot explain, an intangible spiritual value that they can find nowhere else but in the wilds. With them it is a religion.

Letter from Al Cahn to Sigurd Olson
February 22, 1929

SIG SERVED *as a guide to his friends Al Cahn and Jack Shelford, both ecologists from the University of Illinois who were engaged in field work. One was an ornithologist and the other an ichthyologist. The teacher-guide was intrigued by his clients: "We were gone from the fourth of July to the middle of September, clear through August!"*

LETTERS

In describing the influence of Professor Cahn in his life, Sig wrote, "He convinced me I should come down to the University and then do some ecological studies, which I did. We'd been in the bush all summer and he knew all about birds and I respected and learned a lot from him. When I got down there (Illinois) I had an instructor's assistanceship and part of my work was to take out ornithological field trips."

The following letter from Al Cahn is a good example of Sig's impact as a guide and of the long-term friendship between the two men.

Dear Sig:

I am heartily ashamed of myself for not having written you long ago. Your welcome (and unwelcome!) letter came just at the first of the two weeks exam period, and had to be laid aside while I played policeman (by University rules) over so-called students. Then the exams had to be graded—and I had more than my share, for I graded over 2800 answers! Then, without a break, came registration of 10,000, followed by the real task of the lot, getting classes started again for the second semester. That task is now finished, and things are running along smoothly once more, so I can turn my back on most of the machinery, and rest up a bit. And I need it. I take the responsibility of starting things off right a bit too seriously I am afraid, and I wear under it. Personally I am giving 4 courses this term: anatomy for 300 pre-medics, two different bird courses to some 100 or more maybe ornithologists, and a field course with Shelford. Outside of that my time is my own! That is, I have official permission to eat (occasionally) and sleep (some each night, if I have luck). And so it goes. We have had a gorgeous winter, the realest winter I have seen here, with skating ever since about Xmas. I have had no time for that, tho, for some weeks, but Jack gets in several a week.

For my part I am looking for signs of spring, for I have a tennis team to get into shape somehow, and I see no traces of a break yet. Last year this date I had the team out doors; to-day we have about 6 inches of snow, and it is 2 above zero! Not exactly tennis weather. I bet you have had some winter of it at Ely. My, I have so often wished I might have just a week of it: just a week to feel and see and smell and touch it. And during the last month I have had no taste or inclination to even dream about next summer. It has seemed so far away. But to-day a cardinal is singing, and a blue jay is calling, and it sounds more hopeful! Of course, your letter telling of the successful completion on your plans depressed Jack and me greatly. We neither of us can see just what a summer up north can become without Sig. But that is a selfish view point, and we have agreed to forget it (conversationally, at least) and hope for the best. Above all people I want you along; remember that—physically, morally and spiritually! But if I can not have you, I must make the best of what is left. So if I ever get to writing or talking cold bloodedly about others to take your place, remember it is all surface! As to the guide you mention: please, Sig, let me leave the picking of the man to you. You know what we are, for better and for worse; get me the man you think will come as near to filling the bill which you did so wonderfully. Tell him the truth, and if he is still interested, get him in touch with me. I don't know where to go at all; I want good fishing, good moose photographing (I am getting a new movie with a telephoto lens!) and at least 9 weeks of it, starting about the end of June. I don't want any gold rush stuff, and I do want solitude and good scenery; I don't want a trip that is all up-hill pushing. The party will be a four man affair this time (including the guide, I mean), and the fourth man is O.K. in every way, tho he has never had any trip like what is coming off. For that matter, neither have I! You know what I want; tell your friend all about it, and tell him I want *his* suggestions as to where we might go. You know without my repeating it every minute that I want yours too, Sig; have you any to offer? I have begun the indoor sport of getting things together. Already I have 300 cigarettes and 8 tubes (small size) of tooth paste! And my shoes are in the garage being rebuilt and hobnailed and Jack is ordering himself a pair of good shoes on the prize money he gets from his Trout Lake Lake Trout, which is places as per March Field and Stream, as you no doubt have seen by now. The weights are interesting all through, particularly in the lake trout and muskallunge groups; rather close, all of them. I wonder if either of us can place next year? See article on musky fishing in Outdoor America: do you know where any of this country is? Not the Lake of the Woods part, but the other lakes they mention. I would not mind hitting a real musky lake up in Ontario! A whole year and I never felt a musky! The first in about ten. But I would not go much out of my way to do it. Some year I hope to spend weeks on the Lake of the Woods after big muskies; I get an awful kick out of 'em. I can't imagine landing a 49 pounder, tho I have had several matches with fish that size; and have lost every fall. Not even broken tackle for an alibi; they just out-did me. Every dog has his day; mine will arrive sometime. That is why we always come back! Well, enough of this; I promise you to be more courteous and considerate in my writing in the future. But honestly, I was too indifferent even to think of the north lately. Someone ought to do a song: "The Northwoods Blues"—dedicated to the victims of that virulent bug. Write me Sig?

Yours ever,
Al

The Early Writings

Excerpt from a Letter from Al Cahn to Sigurd Olson
February 17, 1931

WHAT YOU WRITE about your thesis is interesting, but is not worrying me. I was in hopes that you would not find Ernest Thompson Seton so soon! But of course you had to. Don't let him worry you. What we want is a study of the wolf and coyote or other predators in the Superior National Forest and I believe E.T.S. never touched that region at all. Go right ahead; find out all you can about the animals in *your* region: never mind Manitoba or Newfoundland or the Labrador. Check him on every point you can; support him where you can with new evidence; contradict him at every point you can with new evidence. Remember that no one's work stands alone, unless it is supported by others. No one has supported E.T.S. or checked him on the mass of evidence he presents. Much of it may be good; some of it certainly needs checking, all of it needs support and verification or corrections. Pick the animals you would work with, and get every scrap of evidence you can in your territory. Digest what E.T.S. has reported; see what applies to your region; see wherein your region does not check with his observations elsewhere; try to re-check his discoveries and statements, never minding if your results support or contradict him; see where his observations are incomplete and try to fill the gaps if possible; use him as a stimulus, not a damper. Remember that no one knows all there is to know about any *one* animal; try to make your knowledge of that form as complete as possible. Try to go beyond surfaces; try to analyze *why* your wolf is doing what he is doing; what the factors are that determine his actions or reactions. What does he eat? What does he reject as food? Why does he not eat other things? Look at him as a reaction to the actions around him; then look at him as an action causing reactions around him. Only so can you possibly fit him into the picture as he really belongs in it. He is not a thing apart. Life is made up of actions, reactions, and interactions. Think, Sig, what that little sentence means! Turn it around and look at it carefully. It opens a new horizon, and paints a differently colored picture. Take your wolf from that point of view if you wish. No one has ever attempted it in any mammal before. Think it over.

Letter from Al Cahn to Sigurd Olson
March 12, 1931

Sig:
Old man, cut out the worrying! I wish I was as sure of heaven as I am of your assistantship here. Shelford had neither the right nor the authority to write that letter; he was simply over anxious about you. He wants you badly and he thought that there might be a slip, and did not wish to leave a rock unturned to help you get here. I took the matter up with Ward just now, and he dictated a letter to you in my presence; so I know what it says without your sending it to me. No further papers are needed; if so, Ward will demand them of you in no uncertain terms; you understand English, and will know when and if he wants anything! He is unmisunderstandable! Permit me to say that you stand No. 1 on the assistant list; out of some 40 applications, and there is not a thing to fret about at this end of the line. You see, you know me as a dreamer in the woods; down here I am Assistant Prof. of Zoology, and am, with all due modesty, inside of Ward's ear. Our system here is rather complicated for picking assistants. Every application is passed upon and graded by every member of the dept., after which Ward goes over the applications and the grading and picks the

men he wants. The papers are in his hands to-day, and I know whereof I speak when I say you were passed upon as highly desirable by *every* member of the staff. Hence I say cut the worrying! Drop Shelford a line thanking him for his interest, and assure him you will take care of the matter. Then forget it. Pay attention only to Ward officially.

Here all goes well. A terrific blizzard hit up last week end and burried us under 14 inches of snow. Now it is warm and bright again, and slush knee deep! Frost has been out of the ground for weeks, hence every drop of moisture will be conserved by the soil; there will be little run-off, which may mean millions to mid-western farmers. Robins are singing gaily, as are the cardinals; killdeer and mourning doves are back. Spring is around the corner. Glory be! Thanks for the poem; I like it much. Here's to you.

Ever,
Al

Spring Fever
Sports Afield
APRIL 1931

WHEN YOU TRY to correlate a life and published materials, it is important to understand the limitations of publishing. In the case of magazine publishing, the writer must first have the experience, then write about it, and then submit the finished piece to the magazine. In some instances, this can be a direct submission, while in other cases it follows a letter of inquiry. The magazine editors must then read the manuscript, decide if they like it, and if so, fit it into their publishing schedule. Normally, a magazine will have a number of articles scheduled in advance, with themes and seasonal considerations included in the schedule. People like to read articles that are timely, which means they are generally reading material written the year before so that they can be published in the proper season. Spring fishing is not something that people want to read about when their thoughts are on deer hunting.

    This article is much more descriptive than the earlier ones. Sig *paints word pictures that are closer to his book portraits. The trout is reminiscent of those in "Grandmother's Trout," and the opening sequence parallels "The Winds of March," both chapters in* The Singing Wilderness.

EVERY YEAR TOWARD the tail end of winter, something happens that plays havoc with our domestic natures. To some it's the advent of the first robin, to others the caress of a warm and balmy day, but to myself and a million others of my ilk, it comes in the form of an elusive feeling or hunch that jerks us bodily from our comfortable firesides and sends us forth in search of far horizons.

Strange though it may seem, my last rejuvenation came on a blustery day in March, a day of whirling snow and blizzard. What it was, I do not know, but the first breath I took that fateful morning told me that this was no ordinary kind of storm. Instinctively I knew that behind the false front of the gale rode a hint of something else, a promise of blue skies to come, thawing earth and gurgling rivulets.

Though doubting at first, as the day wore on I grew more and more confident and was filled at last with such inward joy and peace of soul that those who knew me best marveled.

All day I walked on air, and that very evening dug out from his burrow another who was as delicately attuned to the siren voice of spring as I was myself. Without even asking as to his state of mind, for I knew that in all probability he had breathed the same intoxication, I broached the subject, a twenty-mile hike to Snowbank Lake with the avowed intention of catching trout.

The dean of our local college, for he it was, looked at me quizzically for a moment, weighing the issues at hand. Then his tongue went into his cheek and I knew the spirit of high adventure that had hounded him through Mexico and a couple of continents was gnawing again at his vitals.

"When do we start?" was the only question he asked.

"Tomorrow at White Iron Rapids on the Kawishoway," I answered. "I'll bring the outfit, all you'll need will be your sleeping bag. This is Tuesday, we will be back by Sunday night. See you in the morning," and I turned to go.

Daylight found us at the rapids, loading on our packs. Before us stretched the Kawishoway, miles and miles of brittle frozen crust. We started down the river just as the eastern horizon began to color up. The crisp morning air was a tonic in itself. It seemed good just to be moving and the forty-pound packs rode lightly.

As the first rays of sunlight shot over the ridge, the river was transformed into a brilliant crystal-studded boulevard, fringed by a silhouette of rugged timbered shore. The crust was hard and roughened just enough for perfect footing. Point after point disappeared behind us and landmarks far ahead approached with startling suddenness. Our spirits were high and hiking along was sheer exhilaration.

Within an hour we hove in sight of a notch in the hills that marked the beginning of our first portage. We passed between islands, wooded thickly with jackpine and spruce, threaded a narrows choked with the gaunt spires of trees killed by high water of years before and then approached lower Deadman's Rapids. Below was a pool of open water eating its way into the blackening ice along its edges. As we drew closer a flock of wintering bluebills flew up, circled widely only to return with a plop into the very spot from which they had flown.

Skirting the weak ice gingerly, we reached the shore near the portage. Our first sight of open water was a treat and for a while we rested watching the rapids tumble down over the ice-encrusted boulders to the pool below. The ducks decided at last that we were harmless and continued their feeding along the opposite edge.

While I was meditating happily on the whys and wherefores of things in general, the dean, always a man of action, had rigged up a line and even now was worming his way cautiously out over the ice toward the water. I watched him not without a few misgivings.

Upon reaching the edge of the ice, he unlimbered, dropped a silver smelt into the swirling water before him and began to play out line. He hadn't long to wait. Presently he stiffened and turning his head, said in a stage whisper, "There's one down there, just took hold."

I waited expectantly. Then with a stifled, "I've got him," saw him strike, followed by a very unstifled, "Damn! Say that was a whopper."

I was enjoying myself hugely from my safe perch on shore and waiting until the air had cleared sufficiently. I ventured, "What do you think he was?"

"Nothing but a pike," he answered, "but a whale at that. I could tell by the way he ran with it. Give me another smelt."

I slid one out to him and he baited his hook carefully. Fifteen minutes elapsed before any more action. This time when he struck, the line went taut and I knew there was trouble down below. But now the dean was in a predicament for the ice was too weak to stand the strain of very much pulling.

"Hold everything," I yelled, dashing into a clump of dead alder. Breaking off a long, dry sapling, I hurried back and shoved it out to him over the ice. Grasping his line with one hand, he manipulated the pole under him with the other and then proceeded to play his fish. After a minute of suspense,

SPRING FEVER

a monster great northern pike rolled lazily to the surface, jaws wide open, fanning the water with his fins.

The dean lay there helplessly and with popping eyes gazed at the wicked array of teeth a few inches from his face. He tried to change his position but the ice cracked sharply under him.

"Look out," I yelled. "Don't let him grab you."

At the sound of my voice the pike did a double flop and drenched his captor with a bucket-full of icy water. That last wild rush took most of the slack and ended in a long sulk on the bottom. A few moments later he rolled again to the surface, but this time the valiant dean, at the risk of drowning, lifted the pike flopping onto the ice.

He was a beautiful fish of about twenty pounds in weight, well fleshed and colored. The way those bronze speckles gleamed against their background of silver-grey was indeed a picture. For a space we were content to watch the heaving sides and gills, speculating upon the havoc he might have wrought on a light bamboo in June. Then to show our guileless natures, we let him go the way he had come. It was trout we were after anyway and not extra ballast just then.

"Say, that was a thriller," spoke the dean as we made ready to go. "Who says ice fishing is tame sport?"

"The only thing wrong with that picture," I answered, "was that the ice didn't cave in under you."

We packed away the tackle and crossed the portage. The snow was three feet deep and frozen hard as yet, so we had little trouble. Before us lay Haystack Rock, a huge pyramidal bit of granite as big as a house, stranded in mid-channel by the glacier. Two more short detours around open rapids and several thrilling moments on honeycombed ice brought us at last to a wide stretch of river this side of Murphy's Portage.

The shores on either side were now bold receding walls of rock; barren, burned over and desolate, some of the ridges towering hundreds of feet above the river. The south shore was still frozen and covered deeply with snow but the north bank, exposed like a sloping hotbed to the sun, was brown and dry for over a mile.

We were hiking along, feasting our eyes on the unusual sight of bare earth and leaves in March, when without warning the brush cracked and a deer scampered up the rocky slope to our left. Before it reached the summit, three others had joined it. For a good half mile we watched their white flags bouncing gaily along over rocks and windfalls and snow-filled gullies, 'til at last they disappeared over the crest of a far ridge.

A little further on, a buck and doe unaware of our approach, stalked boldly onto the ice. For a moment they regarded us nervously and then with a whistling snort from the buck, wheeled and sped for shore, gathering speed at every jump. Twenty feet at a time they flew, scaling the slippery ledges with the reckless and sure-footed abandon of mountain goats.

From then on, we saw deer everywhere. Once we startled a bunch of eighteen and sent them bounding up the slope after the rest. Flashing tails everywhere, big ones and little ones, crashing of brush and snorting; exciting moments!

At the very top of the ridge on a glaciated rock, they all stopped as though by prearrangement, faced us and stood in bold relief against the sky. It was a picture I shall never forget.

During the next half mile until we hit the portage, we were never out of sight of deer. They must have come from all over the country to feed on that lone bare strip of the Kawishoway. We couldn't keep track of them all but

counted well over seventy. Without a doubt, there were several hundred feeding that day on the dry southern hillsides within a short distance of the river.

Here the Kawishoway tumbled for a full mile through a rocky canyon. The trail followed closely its northern rim, winding in and out, now giving us a view of the ice-bordered rapids swirling angrily far below and again hiding us completely in the scrub jackpine and spruce.

The roar of water, flush with the first of the melting snow, was music to ears that for months had heard nothing but the howling wind and the rustle of powdery snow. Late that afternoon we saw before us the Fernberg Lookout on the highest peak in the district, a spidery tower of steel shining in the sunlight. An hour later we passed the ranger station a mile below. The river now narrowed down to cut its channel through a maze of rocky gorges and dells. On every hand were spots of rare beauty now more entrancing than ever in the slowly suffusing glow of the afternoon sun.

We left the main channel and turned into a low-lying bay, a labyrinth of spruce-fringed arms and swampy indentations and at last saw before us the portage that would take us from the valley of the Kawishoway to Snowbank Lake, famous for its lake trout.

Upon reaching shore we dropped our packs gladly and took a long deferred rest. For twenty minutes we did not move. An owl hooted solemnly back in the swamp. It was getting dusk and time to go.

Now we struck our first hard going and for once we longed for snowshoes. The warm sun during the day had weakened the crust and to make things worse a pair of moose had ambled down the trail ahead of us pitting it with two foot holes just big enough to stumble into.

A chorus of wolf howls greeted us from far across the bay. A mile from the portage we found the cabin half buried in snow underneath the spruces. A porky had made himself comfortable inside and resented our intrusion by chattering his teeth nervously in the darkest corner under the bunk. He left with little persuasion, however, for less crowded quarters outside. A roaring fire was soon under way in the Yukon stove, then supper, fresh boughs, and dreams.

Next morning found us hiking down the smooth, wind-polished surface of Snowbank Lake toward a group of islands to the northward. In places the ice was covered with huge frost crystals as big as butterflies and much the same shape. Long cracks were bordered with them, for all the world like rows of cut glass flowers, and clear stretches blown free of snow were covered with intricate clusters scattered haphazardly about. The sky was blue and cloudless, a sunny day in a sparkling world of ice. It was good to be alive.

We stopped in the lee of a timbered island to cut our first holes and found to our dismay that three feet of clear blue ice awaited our chisel. It was over an hour before we had finished. After baiting our lines with smelt, we cut boughs to lay on alongside our sets, and then, thoroughly comfortable, began our fishing.

For another hour, or it may have been two, nothing happened and we had to content ourselves by basking in the warm March sunshine and watching the mysterious green shorelines for signs of game. A lone wolf crossed the ice between us and the cabin and once I was sure I saw a moose in the far end of a bay to the east. A flock of ravens wheeled and circled over an insland down the lake. There was always something to look at and we were never without diversion. Besides we had time to think, which in these hurried days is rare enough sport at that.

Just as I hauled in my line for the twentieth time to inspect my bait, something heavy hung on and began to move slowly away. For a moment my heart all but stopped its beating. The impossible had happened. Automatically I played out line, ten, fifteen, twenty feet, and then struck. The hook set firmly. Something was on, there was no question about it and something big. What it was, I might never find out. Now the fun began, wild dashes 'round and 'round the hole, swirling dives to the bottom and long uncertain sulks, when it was hard to tell if I had lost my fish or was snagged. If only those who decry ice fishing so loudly could have held that line for just ten seconds, conversions to the sport would have been in order.

I finally started urging him in. He came slowly to within ten feet of the hole. Lowering my face until it almost touched the water, I peered down into the amber colored depths but could see nothing. Then a broad silver flash drifted across my line of vision. It was a lake trout and a beauty. At sight of me he made a wild dash for liberty and took all the slack I had gained. That last run took all of his strength, however, and I edged him up to the hole once more, now thoroughly exhausted. Slipping my fingers into the wide open gills, I flipped him onto the ice, a ten-pounder if an ounce.

Summer trout are beautiful, but a trout in the winter time when at its best both in flesh and color, is a gratifying sight to the eyes of the most sophisticated fisherman. The dean came over hurriedly to share in the excitement and together we admired the first of our catch.

"Look at that color," he exclaimed wonderingly, "all gold and silver, and red fins to match. It's almost a shame to take 'em out."

I agreed and had it not been for the mulligan pot waiting back at camp, I'm afraid my trout would have followed the example of the pike at Deadman's portage. The dean had just spoken when out of the corner of his eye, he noticed that his stick was down. With a whoop, he left me and charged toward his set. For a while, he played his fish carefully, but as far as I could see, made no apparent effort to land it. Finally out of curiosity I yelled, "What's the trouble? Is he too big to come through?"

"That's just it," he called back, "he's too big. Bring the chisel and hurry."

That meant excitement and I hurried over to where he lay. I soon saw his predicament, for a great trout snagged in the cheek was laying crosswise of the hole. There was work cut out for us now and delicate work at that. One slip of the chisel and the fun would be over.

We let out a few feet of slack and while the fish swam slowly 'round and 'round the hole, I tried to time my strokes with the chisel to miss the shifting line. It was nerve-racking work and several times I missed by a hair's breadth. At last, unable to stand the strain longer, the dean suddenly grabbed the chisel and yelled, "Hold on, I've got an idea." Holding the line in one hand, he fumbled nervously in his pocket with the other and brought out a large spoon hook attached to an eighteen-inch wire leader.

Forcing the trout up again to the hole, he slipped the treble hook in between the wide open jaws and hooked it firmly. "Now," he said, "cut as recklessly as you like."

It was a wise precaution, for at the very next blow, I severed the linen line neatly. The dean didn't say, "I told you so," but the look of triumphant scorn on his face was sufficient.

At last, the hole was large enough. The trout was completely played out and came up easily, another silver-bronze beauty even larger than the first. The strain of this last experience was too much for us and besides we had more than we could possibly hope to eat. Taking up our sets, we hiked happily back to camp.

That afternoon we cooked a trout mulligan, a dish called in politer circles, chowder. And what a mulligan! All of my ten-pound trout went into it with potatoes, onions, butter and milk to match. After cleaning it up, all thoughts of the strenuous life left us and we were content to loll around the cabin the rest of the afternoon.

The next few days, we fished and loafed and dreamed to our hearts' content, made friends with the chickadees and whiskey-jacks, and in the evenings listened to the quavering serenade of the wolves over toward Lake Disappointment.

One day, we did not fish at all, but wandered through the dense timber on the west shore of the lake. Once, we found a fresh bear trail and another time the carcass of a deer killed by the wolves. We followed for miles a winding sedge-bordered creek and looked for signs of beaver and otter. They were days filled to repletion with the simple, happy adventures that make life in the woods at all seasons of the year a joyous adventure. Long sunny hours we spent on the bare southern slopes. For us spring had come and we all but steeped ourselves in its benevolence.

The Blue-Bills are Coming!
Sports Afield
OCTOBER 1931

THE DEAN'S REAL NAME *was Julius Santo, but in all of the articles, Sig refers to him by his title, which served as his nickname as well. The dean and his family spent many hours with Sig, Elizabeth, Sig Jr., and Bob. Julius had been in Mexico as a mining engineer during the time of Pancho Villa, and the articles often refer to Julius's love of Mexico. Sig loved to tease, and those he loved the most received the most teasing. Because Julius liked to drive around to all the outfitters to get a deal on fishing tackle, for instance, Sig would chide him about spending more money on gasoline than he saved on tackle. Theirs was a lifelong friendship. When Julius suffered a severe heart attack and lay in the hospital awaiting the inevitable, Sig was sitting beside him, sharing with him all the way. The dean's last words were, "Let's put the decoys out." And in their minds they did, one last time.*

THE BLUE-BILLS ARE COMING!

LATE OCTOBER found us, Dean and I, stationed once again at the old mallard hole in Rice Lake, the one place where we had had more and better shooting for a month than we had ever dreamed could be possible. Yes, there had been mallards, all season long, plenty of them and that in a country ordinarily barren of ducks. This was the seventh consecutive week-end we had waited for daybreak and the whistle of wings.

It was still much too dark to see, quiet and breathless, and everything covered with snow and sleet from a storm of the night before, the kind of morning when most anything might happen. What worried us more than anything was that the mallards had perhaps gone down south with the storm and we knew that when that happened there would be nothing doing until the last flight of the blue-bills came through before the freeze-up two or three weeks later.

A bunch rose with a loud quacking and beating of wings somewhere off in the blackness and whistled over our point as they made their getaway. Mudhens hearing the commotion, splashed around vigorously in manful imitation of the glorious flight of their betters. Things were beginning to move. Toward daylight several other flocks moved out and were swallowed by the blackness. The stars faded one by one and gradually the east began to color up. To our disgust the storm had blown completely over and in all probability the day would be clear and sunny. As it grew lighter, our fears were justified for not a cloud was in the sky and not a breath from anywhere. We didn't have a chance.

One by one the decoys took form out on the water, riding with the set, spinsterish look they always wore on quiet mornings, none of the wild hilarious cavorting there should have been ordinarily. It was disheartening to say the least.

"Fine day," growled Dean from the blind next to mine.

I didn't answer as I was busy watching a bunch of small

ducks coming in just out of range, teal or butterballs, I couldn't tell which. For a moment they wavered but sped by and lit in the far end of the lake. Daylight ushered in a gorgeous sight, for every blade of grass, every bush and twig was sheathed in glittering ice. We were in a frozen, duckless fairyland. I looked at my watch. It was almost time to shoot. Signalling Dean, we settled down for the last wait before action. The next few minutes would tell the story.

Two mallards rising heavily out of the rice, circled once to my call and then veered sharply toward the decoys, but just as they set their wings for the drop, something must have frightened them, for they shot upward far out of range, pounding the air frantically and in an instant were down the lake and gone. I looked over at Dean. He was gripping his gun fiercely and watching the disappearing birds with the tragic set expression of one who has gambled heavily and lost. Those two were probably the last of the mallards and we both felt it. That was the end. Now unless something unforeseen happened there would be nothing but blackbirds and hawks until the next Arctic blizzard and the freeze-up.

For several hours we did not see a thing even slightly resembling a duck and had we not had our memories of other days and mallards coming in, and scores of empty shells under foot, it might have been a dreary, hopeless prospect. Warmed by the sun and with the smell of yellow rice and bog in the air, we grew lazy and indifferent. Dean got up finally, stretched and yawned luxuriously and sat down again. I knew he felt the same way I did, for the moment at least, far too comfortable to care much whether we got shooting or not. However, about ten o'clock our interest was stirred again, for a small flock of blue-bills dropped in out of nowhere and settled in the rice a couple

THE BLUE-BILLS ARE COMING!

of hundred yards from the blind. We watched them hungrily for a while.

"Let's try a little jump shooting," suggested Dean finally, "and find out whether or not they're locals or northerns."

For answer, I threw the brush off the canoe, shoved it in the water and we were off. If by chance they did happen to be northerns, it was the signal that the rest of the flight would not be far behind. If they were locals they would be alone. There was much at stake. Now they were bunching. Gun-shy birds didn't do that and we pushed on swiftly. Now we were almost in range.

"Grab your gun," I whispered, "I'll paddle."

A big black raised himself half out of the water and beat his wings lustily. They were getting worried. One more dig of the paddle and they rose. Dean dropped one with each barrel. As we were retrieving the birds, three of the original flock circled back giving me a long straight-away shot. Only northerns would come back after being flushed once.

My bird faltered, set his wings, and sailed away into the open water, towards the mouth of the river half a mile away. The ducks we picked up were northerns sure enough, big, black and heavily feathered birds. Dean looked at me and grinned. "Must have come down on the tail end of that blizzard last night, and there's probably more of 'em on the way.

I stood up and looked for my bird but all I could see was a black speck half submerged streaking away toward the rice. We would have to travel if we were to stop him in time. Then began one of those long, nerve-wracking pursuits that every blue-bill hunter knows, shot after shot at a black, swimming head, long dives and interminable, breathless waits with the bird coming up where you least expect it. Finally with a plop the poor, bewildered duck came to the surface within ten feet of the canoe, mouth wide open and thoroughly winded. Dean administered the "Coup de Grace" with the paddle. That made three.

"Let's push up the river a ways," I suggested, "we might run into a stray mallard or two around the bend. Won't be much doing until evening anyway."

We had no sooner started than we heard high above our heads the whistle of wings, blue-bills again and how they were traveling. "Come a long way or they wouldn't be moving like that," remarked Dean.

"Do you know," I answered, "I've had an idea growing on me the last hour or so and that is that things are beginning to brighten up, and that perhaps you're right about the flight. These birds don't come down without reason and they don't come down alone."

"Watch yourself," from Dean. A flock of three was coming downstream at ninety miles an hour. On they came about forty feet above the water and right at us, the most difficult shot in the world. I tried to remember all the hints I had heard for just that type of shot and at the last second abandoned them all for the only rule worth a whoop, holding dead on the tips of their bills. At the crack of our guns, one dropped into the brush, flapping wildly in its effort to secure a perch on a dead tamarack before it dropped into the alders. The other two climbed. Dean dropped one with his second barrel that almost fell in the canoe.

"Well, big boy," I exclaimed, "they're coming in now, and coming fast. Let's get set," and we tore down that lake as though we were going to a fire. Every few minutes a small bunch would come in. If they would only keep on and give us a chance to change our decoys to the mouth of the river, everything would be lovely. Minutes were precious and we paddled like mad. The flight might last only an hour or so. Pulling up the decoys was only the work of a moment and back we sped toward the river's mouth.

Strings and anchors never acted more contrarily and we worked in a frenzy getting them untangled while the ducks kept on coming in. Time and again we dropped our decoys, grabbed our guns nervously crouching down in the canoe, hoping against hope that they wouldn't see us. They always did however and we realized that the sooner we got set and under the cover the better for us. Finally the last one was out and we tore for the shore, threw up a hasty blind and waited breathlessly for the next bunch. Now they could come as fast as they liked.

The sun was high and shining right in our faces and the sky was clear and blue as a day in June. It was getting warm and we took off our jumpers. No sooner had we done so than we were aware of a dull approaching roar, like the sound of a gale on the rampage. We crouched, tense and on edge and waited for whatever it might be.

The sound came closer and closer, increasing in volume and then from around the bend the storm broke loose, a hurricane of twisting, hurtling bodies, each one a bomb in itself, cutting through the air with a sound like the ripping of canvas. It was enough to unnerve anyone and I don't remember exactly what did happen. This much I know, that after the shooting was over, there was only one duck on the water and that one swimming away for dear life. Whose it was we shall never know.

I glanced over at Dean. He was pale as a sheet and breathing hard and the light in his eye meant battle. We had pulled the old amateur's stunt of aiming at the flock instead of picking our birds. The flock reformed after our fusillade and was now dropping swiftly over the far horizon, a wavering line of black, shifting dots.

"Well, I'll be damned," was all Dean said. "Wasn't that

terrible, and they were so close, we could see their eyes. If they wouldn't make that unholy racket when they come in, I could stand it, but that roar gives me the willies."

I agreed with everything he said and loaded my gun hurriedly. Another bunch had come in over the hill behind us and were slowly circling the lower end of the lake. Occasionally, smaller bunches would drop out to feed in the rice patches. One flock separated but instead of settling like the rest, they headed our way toward the mouth of the river. A call and they swung toward us. Now we would show them.

"Get set," whispered Dean fiercely as they drew close. "Don't move," I cautioned in return. They were planing swiftly toward us, wings outspread and dropping. In they came twisting and turning, the most breathtaking entree in duckdom. Just before we fired, they saw us, climbed high and gave us just the kind of shot we wanted. Two birds dropped within ten feet of each other, each in a spout of spray and a third pinwheeled into the jack pines behind us.

"That's talking to 'em," I yelled. "No more duck fever today."

"Let 'em come," answered Dean, a holy light in his eye. "What's that!"

A lone bunch of mallards came over the rise, circled the old feeding hole warily at least a dozen times, beating slow and heavily, began once to settle, only to rise and continue their circling.

"Pretty wild, aren't they?" remarked Dean. "Two weeks ago, there wouldn't have been much hesitation, but now they are taking no chances. Too bad we couldn't have been there to bid them good-bye."

The sky was clouding up and the wind beginning to moan through the trees. We watched the signs of the coming storm joyfully. If it would only begin to snow, our happiness would be complete. It didn't seem quite natural to have good shooting and good weather too. Storm and ducks had always been one and the same to us. Dean interrupted my reveries with, "Isn't it almost time to boil the kettle?"

I looked at my watch. True, it was almost two o'clock but we had been so engrossed with our shooting that we hadn't even thought of food, and now the prospect of taking time off for even so important a duty wasn't exactly inviting. My partner evidently had the same idea for he suggested that we pull straws to see who would be the lucky one. I drew as nonchalantly as I could and to my surprise was in luck. Dean took it bravely, picked up the blackened tea pail and retreated into the brush.

"Don't make too much smoke," I warned him, but my advice went unheeded.

At last I was alone with the whole lake to myself and no one to start the shooting until I let go. I know it was a selfish pleasure on my part but what duck hunter hasn't wished time and again that some day he would have the whole field to himself for just a few minutes. I settled down for half an hour of as unadulterated bliss as has ever been mine.

A trio came over and caught me entirely by surprise. To tell the truth, I had been too absorbed for a moment watching a hawk worrying a flock of black birds and here they were almost within touching distance and gone again before I could bring my gun to bear. I watched them ruefully as they sped down to the lower end of the lake and then to my joy saw them swing and head straight back to the river's mouth and my blind.

Crouching down as far as I could get, I rearranged the brush hastily in front of me and got ready. On they came. Now they were setting their wings for the last glide and were beginning to drop. A fraction of a second more and then as I was getting the final squeeze on the trigger, they settled with a heart-warming plop right in the center of the decoys. I sat there feeling rather foolish and half thrilled at what had happened.

Now I couldn't shoot for the life of me. Beautiful birds they were in their shiny black and white, looking much larger than they really were with their down all fluffed out. No, I couldn't do it. Something else would have to happen before they would draw my fire.

In a short time, something did happen and I made the shot that every duck hunter dreams of making at least once every season. A whistle of wings from up river suddenly drew my attention away from the decoys, a flock of seven coming along high in the air in a perfect V, an almost impossible shot. I drew a prayerful bead on the leader, held it an instant, led just enough and pulled. To my utter surprise, the bird folded its wings and began to drop. Down, down it came through all that space and I watched, mouth open and thrilled to the bone.

It was a marvelous shot if I do say so myself and like most shots of its kind probably due more to luck than anything else. But the thrill was mine and that was enough. The bird hit the water, bounced once and lay still. So engrossed had I been, that I failed to see three ducks streak it out of the decoys in a panic of flight, gone before I had a chance to fire. In a way I was just as glad.

For a minute or two, I just sat there thinking it over and draining to the last every bit of satisfaction I could get out of it. I might never make another shot like it if I lived to be a hundred years. While sitting there half in a trance, the brush crashed and Dean came out looking drawn and worried. The past half hour had been a strain and no doubt about it.

"How many," he asked rather testily.

"One," I answered.

"One," he exploded, "one, what happened to the three that lit in your decoys? Don't suppose you even saw 'em?"

What could I say? There was no use trying to explain so I simply told him that I must have been asleep. With a withering look, he handed me my tea and I drank in disgrace, happy nevertheless. Sandwiches were unearthed from the pack and we began to eat. I say began for that was as far as we got for several hours after. Just as Dean lifted his cup to his lips, the first bunch whizzed by. One wild grab for the gun and the tea splattered over the ground. At that he made as pretty a snap shot as you could hope to see. Smiling triumphantly, he reloaded, gulped down the remaining mouthful and the rest of his half chewed bite. I had also winged one and our two birds lay close together kicking their heels at the sky.

From that moment on, we sat with guns in one hand, cups in the other trying to mix shooting with eating. Every few seconds something would come over and all the warning we would get was the ripping whistle of wings as they tore around the bend above us. Every shot meant quick action as they were coming like the wind at the end of a forty-mile flight from one of the big lakes to the northward. Not for a moment could we relax and finally realized the futility of trying to eat at all. Shooting with a mouth full of food isn't exactly conducive to accuracy and besides we were getting food mixed with our shells.

The prettiest shot we made was on a bunch of five that decoyed after they had flown over us once. The first time 'round, they were just out of range but the second they couldn't have been in more perfect formation. As our guns cracked two tumbled. The remaining three climbed for elevation. Two more shots and there were four on the water and the fifth scooting away with the jerky, panicky flight the ones that get away always seem to have.

"That's shooting," snapped Dean, "too bad one of us couldn't have made a double on the last one."

By now our limit in blue-bills was lying on the water and we decided to push out and pick them up and call it a day. No sooner had we got out in the open than the biggest flock we had yet seen, tore out of the sky behind us, saw the canoe and shot up far out of range, made a half circle giving us a scornful once over, then headed into the south. No need for words. We had seen it happen a hundred times. This time it didn't matter and we looked at each other and grinned. We finished picking up the dead ones and pushed back to the blind.

No need for secrecy any more and we built a fire out in the open close to the blind where we could watch them coming over. As it proved, the incoming birds weren't frightened in the least even though we sat out in plain sight. Still they continued to come and several bunches lit right out among the decoys. For once we had a chance to study their flight and our mistakes, something that is impossible to do when firing. We learned more in half an hour of aiming with empty guns than in weeks of actual shooting.

"Do you know what I believe?" remarked Dean after sizing up our chances with a particularly nice bunch that came through. "I believe that the main difference between good and poor shooting is keeping your head. If a man could feel as though he were just aiming for the fun of it, instead of its being a matter of life and death, there wouldn't be half the foolish misses we make on perfectly easy shots."

Toward sunset the flight ended as suddenly as it had begun and we bethought ourselves of the long portage we must make before dark. We pushed out almost regretfully,

THE BLUE-BILLS ARE COMING!

stowed away the decoys and headed down the lake. The air overhead was alive with the whistle of wings.

At the portage we turned for one last look, a great field of yellow rice and a glowing horizon. The mallards were through but what a day we had had, speed and action and that nerve-gripping racket as they came in; yes blue-bill shooting had its points. Dean was throwing on the canoe. I shouldered a pack, tossed on the decoys and stumbled after him down the trail.

1932

IN THE SUPERIOR NATIONAL FOREST area, Edward Backus, the International Falls lumber baron, tried to reinstitute his plan for damming the region. He would have flooded thousands of acres of forests, eliminated the free-flowing streams, and changed the landscape forever. The Quetico-Superior Council was effective on both sides of the international border and prevented this threat from becoming reality.

Sig was developing his writing and completing his degree, but he maintained contact with the council and tried to correspond with the guides to find out what was going on in the north country.

Papette

Sports Afield
FEBRUARY 1932

IN THIS ARTICLE, *we can see Sig the storyteller. "Papette" represents the fictional experimentation that was part of Sig's early writing. It is part of his growth as an author. Although "Papette" is a very anthropomorphic story, it fits the pattern of the popular literature of Seton, London, and other writers of adventure and the outdoors. It also reflects a strong anti-wolf sentiment. Today's readers and Sig enthusiasts might be shocked by this early story.*

THE STORY SO FAR:
 Papette heard that single long-drawn note and, though of a blooded Collie dam, she was anxious to be gone. Old Joe, her master, opened the cabin door and Papette disappeared into the night. She joined the wolf pack and would have been torn into shreds by the greedy pack had not Lop Ear,

the leader, defended her. But Grey Neck, a beautiful, pearl-gray bitch, the last year's mate of the killer, hated her and nursed her jealousy. Unswervingly, Lop Ear led them to where the moose yarded for the winter. There, Lop Ear made a kill. Papette now came up and fed of the entrail and quivering flesh, an honor seldom accorded even his seasoned killers. When the two had feasted, they trotted away. But Grey Neck had seen and followed, vengeance in her eyes. Straight for Papette she came.

The husky turned just in time and caught the charge full on her shoulder, a trick her Collie mother might have used. The teeth of the wolf tore through the heavy mat of hair, but hardly scratched the skin. Startled, Papette sprang away. Why now another battle? She was puzzled and not a little angered, still there was no choice, fight she must. They circled each other warily waiting for an opening.

In size and strength, they were fairly matched, but Grey Neck was far too infuriated to fight wisely. Maddened by the indiscretions of her mate, only one thought possessed her, to kill and taste at once the hated intruder's blood. Papette on the other hand, cool now and on guard, forgot for the moment her kinship with the pack, and saw only through her mother's eyes an ancient foe of her race.

They circled each other once more and then closed. Both of famous out-fighting breeds, their method of attack was the same, a swift rush and side slash followed by a lightning recovery. For a time they fought fiercely, neither having much advantage, then Grey Neck adopted a new tactic. Running swiftly away, she stopped dead, and as her enemy flew past, struck from the flank. Papette however, knew the ruse from other battles and side stepped in time, the murderous jaws missing by the breadth of a hair. The wolf was thrown off her balance for just an instant, but before she

could recover, the husky was at her throat, long white teeth ripping cleanly through the jugular.

Mortally wounded now, choking with her own blood, Grey Neck turned and with a last desperate effort, hurled herself at her enemy. Over and over they rolled upon the snow, spattering it with red wherever they touched. At last the wolf felt her strength ebbing and tearing herself away, she ran weakly over the snow, dripping blood at every step. Papette hesitated in surprise, then bore down upon her, caught once more the pearl grey throat and this time did not relinquish 'til every vestige of life had fled. Slowly she released her hold and gazed in wonder at the still grey form beside her.

For a time the husky did not move, but sat as though carven of stone, a silent vigil of death. The pack was still busy at the kill and Lop Ear nowhere to be seen. She was alone, and in her aloneness there awoke another longing, a vague emptiness that she knew could only be satisfied before the hearth fire of the cabin she had left.

So, leaving the scene of the triple killing, she followed the leader's tracks toward the shore. Upon reaching the timber, however, she left his trail and for along ways followed a winding ridge covered with a growth of scrub jackpine and spruce. Higher and higher she climbed, until from the topmost pinnacle, she could see far below her the island dotted whiteness of frozen Lac La Croix. On all sides, as far as she could see, were the billowing timbered ridges, dark green with their covering of spruce and pine. To the north for a thousand miles was the unbroken wilderness; to the south, but a day's travel, the clearings and habitations of man. For a long time she sat there motionless, surveying the scene below her. It was the answer to the craving she had always known. Still she was a stranger, not yet one of the pack.

Just as the eastern horizon was beginning to tint with the

color of dawn, she left the ridge and worked slowly down its southern slope. For an hour she ran steadily, and as the sun burst over the pointed spruce tops, she reached the valley of the Loon. Down the frozen stream she ran and rounding a bend found the cabin suddenly before her. A figure stood outside, the half-breed making ready to follow his trap-line. She let out a bark of pure joy, raced to him and buried her nose in the rough folds of his mackinaw.

He fondled her for a moment, then carefully examined her for wounds. "Ma poor li'l' Papette," he groaned, shaking his head woefully, "all cut an' tear lak dat. Ol' Joe know always best. You should have nevaire go dose woods las' night. Sacre Bleu! Look dose long deep slash, deep een to de bone. Damn dose wolf," he muttered close to her ear, "once I catch dose beeg rascal, I keel heem wid mine own bare han's."

After the moose hunt came the heavy snows and in their blustery wake, the bitter cold. For weeks the wilderness was held in the icy grip of the frost king, and all life resigned itself to a long, indeterminate struggle against the elements. Starvation stalked abroad and as winter wore slowly on, it seemed at last as though the burden that had been placed upon nature, could no longer be borne with fortitude.

Then, as suddenly as though a signal had been given, the frozen land found itself reviving under the warm caresses of a balmy south wind. The spell was broken, and days flooded with warm sunshine, and nights as soft as those of spring, stirred anew the spark of life that had so long lain dormant. It was the time of year, when tracks ran double in the snow; the time when the dogs of the wild forgot their endless search for food in the enchanting search for a mate.

Lop Ear, the killer, was restless, and no longer content with appeasing his hunger, he ranged far and wide, over great valleys bedded deeply in snow, and over wind-blown ridges from whose rocky crests he could see for many miles. Within him was gnawing desire, an uncontrollable longing that would not be thwarted, and he stopped neither for rest nor food.

One day, while crossing a high summit, a scent was borne to him, carried by the warm south wind, a scent so faint, but at once so filled with promise, that it made him tremble with eagerness. He immediately set off in the direction from which it had come. On and on he ran, head held high, following all the winding ridges in his path. Not that day did he find it, nor the next, but this he knew, that somewhere in the south lay his answer.

Toward evening of another day, just as the golden March moon was climbing over the eastern skyline, he found himself on a hilltop overlooking the valley of the Loon River. Far below him, in a clearing walled in by heavy, dark green timber, stood a cabin of logs. There he knew, dwelt his greatest enemy, the two-legged beast called man, and though he realized his danger, still he did not move. The scene fascinated him and the strange odors wafted from the valley, filled him with a new excitement.

For a long time he sat there, winnowing the mixture of unfamiliar smells through his nostrils, in the vain hope that the one he sought might be among them. Darkness gathered quickly, as it always does in the north, and he wondered at the flickering yellow lights that came and went like giant fireflies in the valley below him. Then came a scent different from the rest. He stiffened and rose to all fours, sniffing the breeze hungrily. It came again, more strongly than before, a vague enchantment that carried with it memories of days long dead. Then the revelation burst upon him and he drank to the full the hidden pleasure that comes only once during the mating moon, he sat back upon his haunches, pointed his nose skyward, and poured forth his longing in a weird full-throated howl filled with all the passionate desire of his sex.

To his surprise, came an answer from the valley and the hair along his shoulders bristled as he recognized in it not the voice of one of his kind, but that of an enemy. Still he was thrilled and waited impatiently. The scent came still more strongly from the gloom below. Then the snow crunched sharply. He was instantly alert. Something was coming toward him. As he moved to a better vantage point, a sleek tawny form emerged from the shadows across a moonlit opening, and as quickly disappeared. For a moment he was startled, then throwing caution to the winds, he pursued swiftly.

At any other time of year, the husky would have been in danger, reeking as she was with the scent of man, but now secure in the knowledge of her desirability, she ran unafraid. She had not seen the grey loping form of the killer, nor had she gotten his scent, but by the old intuitive perception of her sex, she knew that she was being followed.

Straight into the north she ran, over the moonlit ridges smooth with snow, and down through valleys lying dark between them, holding her course for the shores of Lac La Croix. Not once during the first few miles did she even turn to look, though the blood within her pounded hotly with the chase. This at last was life, the final answer to her discontent, and she ran as she had never run before, burying herself more and more deeply in the timber.

For hours, Lop Ear pursued at a respectful distance, and not until the moonlight faded into the blackness of dawn, did he dare approach. She turned then to meet him, lips drawn back in a vicious snarl of warning, first greeting to her mate. Crestfallen and abashed, he left her, and henceforth kept away, careful that nothing again should happen, that might incur her slightest disfavor.

For days he was at her mercy, Lop Ear the killer, grovelling for the attention of a mere husky dog. Gradually, however, her attitude began to change, and no longer did she bare her teeth when he came near. He could have forced his suit then had he chosen. Instead, he left her as she wished, alone and free to go her way. Then one day after a hot exciting chase in a great spruce bog, he found her resting on a hummock of caribou moss. Surprised, he stopped to watch, and then all unconcern dropped down beside her. For a moment she regarded him quietly and then did something that the wolf had never seen, but somehow understood. She wagged her tail.

The next few weeks were spent crusing aimlessly over the country, hunting only when hungry, and resting when the desire overtook them. Farther and farther north they went, until at last, they were deep in the timbered valley of the Beaverhouse. Never before had Papette been so far from the fringe of civilization, never so completely buried in the wilderness of her longing.

Here, in happy companionship, they spent the rest of the winter, dozing together during the lengthening days on warm sunny slopes, and with the approach of night, hunting the alder choked gullies for the white snowshoe rabbits. The two were never apart, and the love Papette had borne her master in the cabin on the Loon, now went to her mate.

As the snowdrifts disappeared, game became more plentiful. Hunting took less and less of their time, and with the coming of the bright blue days of April, days of melting snows, blackening ice on the lakes, and creeks brim full of rushing water, Papette spent most of her time rambling over the bare brown slopes in search of a den.

At last, she found what she was looking for, a dry hollow

underneath a ledge of green rock, high above the shores of Beaverhouse Lake. Painstakingly, she cleaned it out, removing every single vestige of crumbled moss and last year's leaves. After that, she hunted very seldom, spending the days curled up on the floor of her shelter, dreaming of the momentous event to come.

In the mornings, she loved best of all to lie upon the flat rock before her den, basking in the warm sunshine, and gazing at the valley below, now a veritable fairyland of spruce tops, hung like dark green minarets in a misty haze of budding birch. She loved to watch the flash and sparkle of sunlit water through the trees, to breathe the pungence of thawing earth and new awakening life. Then was she most content. For this too had she come.

As the time drew close, Lop Ear did more and more of the hunting, bringing in freshly killed rabbits, tiny little field mice caught in grassy meadows, and sometimes a pike that he had pounced upon in the shallows of some stream; but no longer did his mate permit the little intimacies of their early wooing. Usually, after his return, Lop Ear would lie near, watching with satisfaction, her ravenous attack upon the food he had brought, sole compensation for the loss of her companionship. Then one day, he was even deprived of that privilege, for without any reason that he could see, Papette flew at him, and with a whine of impatience, drove him from the ledge. Stunned and mortified, he had hurried away, to roam disconsolate around the shores of the lake.

But next morning, fortified with a fat young marmot, he returned, hoping to make amends. To his surprise, Papette was nowhere to be seen. He worked his way warily toward the den, and dropping the luscious morsel from his jaws, sniffed the opening suspiciously. From its dark interior came a chorus of strange and hungry whimperings, and a scent entirely new. Something was wrong, of that he was sure, and for a moment he stood in hesitant wonder, uncertain of his course.

Just then, Papette, who had been nursing the soft grey bodies beneath her, turned. At sight of her mate, she bristled and half rose to her feet, lifting the suckling pups up with her. Lop Ear waited expectantly. For a time she did not move, but stared boldly at him, suspicion in her eyes. Then slowly the lips drew back, and a warning snarl trembled deep in her golden throat. His courting days were over.

By June, the pups had changed from shapeless balls of fur, to fat rollicking youngsters with bright black eyes and pointed upstanding ears. On warm afternoons, they played together in the sunlight before their den, rolling over and over on the slippery, needle-strewn rocks, then scrambling clumsily back up the slope, to nuzzle beside their adoring mother. The valley below was now even more entrancing than it had been in spring. The haze of bursting buds had changed to a dense wall of mottled green from whose depths sang warblers and vireos in a constant medley of joyous sound. Red squirrels and chipmunks chattered and scolded as they rustled in the underbrush for food. Kingfishers rattled noisily along the shoreline; and always from the water came the screaming of gulls, and the weird, unearthly calling of the loons. But on windy days, all wilderness sounds were merged in one, the long, uneasy roaring of the surf, and for hours Papette would lie watching her pups and listening.

Only one shadow was there to mar the brightness of those summer days, and that the ever growing fear she bore her mate. Why she distrusted him, she did not know, but in him she felt was her greatest enemy. So jealously had she guarded her young, that not once since the day of their birth, had Lop Ear seen them. He still brought them food, but only on rare occasions; so when Papette was certain that he was not near, she was forced to slip away on hunting trips of her own, always returning hurriedly for fear he had come during her absence.

Then one day as she lay sunning herself before the den, a snowshoe rabbit hopped past, not a rod away. Not having eaten since the day before, she was ravenous, and Lop Ear still gone. It was too great a temptation, and with a bound, she took the trail. Away she went, down along the lake shore, through a maze of alder and spruce, and a full mile along a ridge, before she made her kill. She feasted nervously on the warm red meat, and not 'til every edible bit had been eaten did she leave.

No sooner had she left her young, than Lop Ear hove into view below the ledge, a half-grown rabbit in his jaws. He approached warily, as was his wont, but just as he was about to drop his offering, he noticed that his mate was gone. For a moment it startled him, being alone with the pups, and pausing, he sniffed the opening of the den with growing curiosity. Then gathering courage, he crawled boldly inside.

There they were, four grey brown bundles of softness, sleeping together in the farthest corner. He watched them interestedly and listened to their drowsy whimperings, but as he stood there, the old resentment rose within him, the feeling of jealous intolerance that most males bear their young. Belly to earth, he moved slowly toward them, and as he drew in the warm, moist scent, the coarse hair of his back and shoulders stiffened. An instant longer, he regarded them, while the low rumble in his chest changed swiftly to a rising snarl of hatred. His crouching form quivered, hung poised, and like a flash, sprang at the huddle of helpless flesh.

It was over in a moment and the mangled little bodies lay scattered grotesquely about the den. As the killer turned to leave, a shadow crossed the opening. He whirled guiltily and found himself face to face with Papette, but a different Papette than he had ever known. For a breathless second they glared, Lop Ear in open defiance of his guilt, and she with the slow dawning horror of realization. With a terrible scream, she flew at him, and fought with the insane fury that only a mother knows, a mother robbed of her young. He did not try to protect himself, but fled howling from the cave. The stricken mother then returned, and for hours lay licking the warm, bleeding bodies of her pups, whimpering softly to little ears that never again would hear her.

Until far into the night, she lay there, too sick at heart to feel either hatred or pain. It was then that something died within her, and in its passing brought into being an old and dormant heritage, a smouldering spark of hatred and revulsion for the brutality of the wild. Long hidden by the wilderness life she had led, it now burst into a flame that consumed the last enduring vestige of her love for the pack. This she knew was the end, and in that knowledge, peace came at last, the peace of resignation. The lake below was misty with the dawn. Only one thing was left to do, go back to the cabin on the Loon River, and leave forever the valley of the Beaverhouse.

She rose slowly to her feet, and after one last look around, left the den and headed south and east toward the basin of Lac La Croix. Morning found her miles upon her way. All that day, she traveled steadily, and not until she had reached the north shore of the great lake, did she stop to rest. It was while working eastward in order to cross at the narrows, that she first caught sight of Lop Ear. That he would follow, she had been certain, but instead of flying at him, she ignored him utterly. Hatred had flown. For her there was no longer any mate.

Encouraged by her attitude, he now came near and followed dutifully wherever she chose to lead. For him, existence had now resolved itself into one purpose, one all engrossing desire, and the flash of golden brown through the timber, was the embodiment of it all. As they drew close to the valley of the Loon, man signs were increasingly in evidence, and once they crossed a trail, that fairly reeked with the dreaded smell. More than once would he have turned, had he not been drawn by a power far stronger than his natural inhibitions, the vision of his glorious mate ahead.

Toward sunset, they found themselves once more on the hill top overlooking the clearing with its cabin of logs. Lop Ear for the first time, now came close and together they watched the valley below. A thin curl of smoke rose straight above the cabin. There was no breeze, and the perfect stillness of late afternoon brooded over all. The sun was dropping slowly beneath a bank of clouds, and long dark shadows played over the open clearing. The horizon was now aflame with color, and reflecting its splendor, the winding, sedge bordered Loon was a river of blood.

A lone figure came out of the cabin, and for several minutes Papette watched, minutes that seemed hours long, and finally, unable to restrain herself longer, she broke away, and raced swiftly down the slope.

For a moment Lop Ear was dumbfounded by her action, then of a sudden he understood, and with a bound was on her trail. Gone now was his desire, and in its stead there arose a feeling of bitter hatred for his mate and all else that was not of the wild. His one passion now, was to kill. He gained rapidly and just as Papette left the timber, overtook her. Snarling fiercely, he rushed in and slashed at the golden brown throat. For a full hundred yards they ran, fighting desperately, drawing nearer and nearer to the cabin.

Suddenly from the darkness ahead came a spurt of flame and a crash, and Lop Ear felt a blow that stopped him dead. He wheeled and ran for the timber. Then something went wrong within him, and turning, he charged the kneeling figure of his new enemy. Again and again came the crashes, but still he ran on. Once something tore through the thick hide and fur of his shoulder, but it only served to increase his speed. Now he was almost there. One more bound and he hurled his hundred and fifty pounds of bone and sinew through the intervening space. A stinging blow met him, but the tremendous force of his charge bore down the man underneath. His great jaws slashed and tore, but at the same time, the long knife of the half breed plunged deep into his vitals. With a howl of surprise, the wolf threw himself backward, away from the biting steel, but the man fell upon him and buried his blade again and again.

For a long time they lay there, both as though dead. Then slowly the trapper raised himself, withdrew the knife and wiped its gore upon the long grey fur beneath him. Then staggering to his feet, he walked unsteadily toward the cabin. Close upon his heels followed the husky dog. At the doorway they stopped. "Ah Papette," he said, kneeling and stroking her still quivering form, "we bote have our revenge, don't we, you for de many slash and hurt and Ol' Joe for many odder t'ings you wouldn't understan'. Deedn't he say long tam ago, dat he would keel heem wid hees own bar han's dat Loup Garou?"

That night as she lay again before the leaping flames of her master's fireplace, a great contentment stole over her and the days she had spent in the Valley of the Beaverhouse seemed far away.

The half breed groaned and stirred uneasily. "Papette," he called, "Papette, come here ma leetle wan."

She stirred, rose to her feet and padded softly over to where he lay.

"No more you leave you ol' fren' Joe, weel you Papette," he murmured. For answer she buried her nose in the palm of his hand.

Learning to Write

"HAD THE POETS not been with me, I might have gone the other way, taken the well-worn trail I already knew." Sig had learned the value of books from his father, and it was important for him to both read and write. He bought a book that promised to teach him how to write—it still sits on the shelf at Listening Point—and in 1932 he put aside three days during which he intended to learn the craft. Each day was twenty hours long.

The book's title is *The Elinor Glyn System of Writing Book I* by Elinor Glyn, "author of Three Weeks, Beyond the Rocks, The Great Moment, etc., etc." It was published by The Authors Press, Auburn, New York, in 1922. A look through the book reveals some of its influence.

Chapter 8, "What Knowledge Must I Have to Succeed," includes the following quote under the heading "Nature a splendid teacher": "Of course, if one wished to be a doctor, a professor, a chemist, or a lawyer, he perforce must be well educated in one of those particular lines. The literary aspirant, on the other hand, has only to sit at the feet of nature, in its material and human aspects—listening carefully to what it has to say." Even though Sig did not mark it, it must have been a statement he could relate to.

Sig underlined only five parts of Glyn's book, and perhaps these three are the most pertinent: (1) "Success in anything rests on being greatly absorbed in some particular subject." (2) "It does not much matter what you stress in a story provided you give it a new twist and a new tone, provided the story arouses the emotions of your reader or the suspense of the reader regarding the outcome and with all this is sincerely told." (3) "The theme is that which the writer wishes to impress upon his reader, the central idea which he wishes to set forth as impressively and significantly as possible."

Search for the Wild

Sports Afield
FEBRUARY 1932

THIS ARTICLE BEGINS *a new trend for Sig. It is his most philosophical to date. When he and I talked, Sig would constantly refer to Thoreau, Muir, and other giants of both conservation and literature. They had been his companions since childhood, and in this piece he invites them to be part of his writing as well.*

The editor's note to this article reads, "In the May issue, Sig Olson, college professor, former guide, naturalist and biologist, pointed out that it is inherent in the sportsman to go out in search of the wilderness. Mr. Olson is manager of the Border Lakes Outfitting Co., Winton, Minn."

The photographs that accompanied this article were taken by Professor A. R. Cahn, Sig's friend and fellow ecologist from the University of Illinois.

THOSE WHO GO FORTH into the wild, unsettled regions, if asked the reason for their travels will give a variety of answers. For some it will be fishing, others hunting and the securing of trophies, still others to photograph, explore or conduct scientific investigations. Most men believe that they "go in" for some definite, concrete purpose. If they are made to admit the true motive behind their wilderness journeys they will, with few far-flung exceptions, agree that it is something entirely different, a purpose for which the very evident ulterior motive is only an excuse.

It is very true that when a man goes into the woods to fish, he in all probability heads for the lakes and streams; if it is ducks, the rice beds and marshes know him well. Whatever it is and wherever it takes him is really immaterial when compared to the underlying reason. What he is really looking for is that intangible something he calls "the Wild," and if he hunts or fishes hard enough, he will find it in the close contact with nature those pursuits entail. Thoreau expresses what most of us feel in Walden Pond.

"We need the tonic of wildness, to wade sometimes in marshes where the bittern and the meadow hen lurk, and hear the booming of the snipe, to smell the whispering sedge where only some wilder and more solitary wildfowl builds her nest, and the mink crawls with its belly close to the ground. At the same time that we are earnest to explore and learn all things, we require that all things be mysterious and unexplorable, that land and sea be infinitely wild, unsurveyed and unfathomed by us because unfathomable. We can never have enough of Nature. We must be refreshed by the sight of inexhaustible vigour, vast and titanic features, the seacoast with its wrecks, the wilderness with its living and decaying trees, the thunder cloud and the rain which lasts three weeks and produces freshets. We need to witness our own limits transgressed and some life pasturing freely where we never wander."

So spoke Thoreau, the naturalist and philosopher. To him the wilderness was a spring at which he continually refreshed himself and renewed his strength. John Burroughs speaking of him said, "He went to nature as to an oracle and though indeed very often questioned her as a naturalist and a poet, yet there was always another question in his mind. He ransacked the country about Concord, in all seasons and in all weathers, and all times of the day and night, he delved into the ground, he probed the swamps, he searched the waters, he dug into woodchuck holes, into muskrat dens, into the retreats of mice and squirrels, he saw every bird, heard every sound, found every wild flower, and brought home many a fresh bit of natural history; but he was always searching for something he did not find."

I do not agree with Burroughs' last sentence, for I am confident that the lifelong search of Thoreau was not entirely unfruitful. What he sought in his daily rambles through the woods and fields surrounding Concord and Walden Pond, is what we all seek when we go into the wilds. Sometimes we are successful and sometimes we are not, but we never come back without having found some slight vestige at least of that for which we sought. It is the underlying motive for trips and expeditions, this constant never-ending search for the wild, and it is compensation enough for all discomforts, trials and tribulations encountered enroute.

Those who have been much in the field have also learned long ago that although it is extremely pleasant to come back with the limit of birds or trout, still the day is not spoiled if there was only one or two or even none. The fact that during a day in the open a man may have absorbed some of the very essence of the Out-of-doors, itself, is then considered ample payment and no day in the wild is ever wasted.

To most men the wild and contact with it are a necessary part of existence. To some it means more than to others, all depending upon the potency of their primitive inheritance. Some are satisfied with a week or two out of the year; others must "go in" for months at a time. Many would go in more often than that if they only could. No matter what the classification to which you belong, the craving is there to a greater or lesser degree and must be satisfied, and more it is something which cannot be put off lightly or postponed. The penalty for disregard is too severe and self denial when the call is strong results inevitably in frayed nerves, loss of enthusiasm and appetite for present modes of existence. The urge to escape the rush and unnaturalness of urban life and make intimate and forceful contact with the earth once more is a more powerful incentive than most men care to admit even to themselves.

After all it is little wonder, when we consider that we are not far removed as yet from the day of the early pioneer and woodsman, not so far removed that the old ties may be severed with impunity. A half century ago, much of this country was still wild and unsettled. Many of us spent our boyhood days on wilderness farms or ranches, in the neighborhood of lumber camps or isolated frontier communities. If we did not, is is safe to assume that our parents or grandparents did. It is a long jump from the life of those days to the concentrated civilization of our cities and larger towns and it is rather hopeless to believe that in the short space of a generation or two, we can completely root out of our systems the love of the simple life and the primitive. It is still deeply rooted and it will be hundreds or thousands of years before we lose very much of it. It is an inheritance ingrained in our natures that it can never be stifled. We are still adventurers of the wilderness and must answer the call in order to keep our equilibrium. Once we lose our touch with the wild and we lose our perspective, too long a time on the pavements and we starve for the smell and touch of virile earth.

It was this that Thoreau meant when he said, "We need the tonic of the wild." Inasmuch as our natures are still rooted firmly in the soil, we need to renew frequently our contacat with the simplicity of life in the out-of-doors. Those who need artificial stimulation, crowds, and creature comforts without the necessity of working for them, have no place in the wilderness. Only those who can live frugally and simply can be really happy in the wild. They, on the other hand, who feel that they have been robbed of their inheritance by having had everything done for them, accept with joy the challenge of doing for themselves.

After all, what a man craves most is the old struggle for the bare necessities of existence, food, warmth and shelter, not to mention the stimulus and alertness due to constant battle with natural enemies. City life deprives a man of all that, and makes of the physical side of life so secure and easy a thing, that he revolts at the protection offered him.

Living happily in the out-of-doors means getting down to the bare essentials. The man who goes in with all of the clap-trap necessary to give him a semi-civilized existence in the wilderness is defeating at once the very purpose for which he went in. The mark of a real woodsman is one who can live comfortably in the wilderness with the least expenditure of energy, but that in the last analysis means living simply and with economy. If your wants are few and limited to only those things which are absolutely necessary for reasonable animal comfort, your life in the wild cannot help but be successful and happy. If, on the other hand, you are not attuned to the spirit of the out-of-doors and still feel the need of luxury and pampering, you have lost at the very beginning what you really came into the wild to find.

By renewing his contact with natural things a man recreates himself, by performing natural primitive tasks, by seeing and feeling things of the earth he is strengthened. That is why we get such keen and wholesome pleasure from simple tasks on the trail or in camp. We enjoy doing the primitive things we so long have been denied. Our muscles long for action and thrill at the performance of duties long forgotten. Then, too, there is a mental satisfaction which only comes from doing things with our hands and we delight in developing once again a skill with tool or weapon.

We all admit the marvelous convenience of municipal heat in town, nevertheless, we crave the sensation of direct contact with the flame. When we cut our own wood, we impart to it some of our own energy and when we warm our hands before the flame, it seems doubly good to us, because we were directly instrumental in bringing it about. We sit watching the coals at night, entranced by the mystery of their glow, watch the smoke curl up and disappear in the tree tops with an inward satisfaction we never knew in town.

How good and sweet water can taste that has been carried from a spring a quarter of a mile away over a dark and treacherous trail. How we husband every precious drop, measuring it out carefully, as though it was a high priced beverage, which in truth it is. How good to lie on the ground and drink from a gurgling riffle in some tiny stream. As we drink, we watch the shifting of the sand and gravel on the bottom and see the waving of the water plants and mosses in the current. The act of drinking itself becomes a pleasure and not merely a means of laving our thirst. A little more of a dip and the ripple flows over your face, a most delightful and legitimate sensation, but how ridiculous and criminal a performance at a public drinking fountain in town.

What a joy it is to pitch a tent, our home for a night or as long as we please. The very uncertainty and the possibility of choice amid new and strange surroundings makes it a pleasure in itself, a real adventure at the close of the day. First we examine this spot and then that, finally deciding on a point that not only is smooth and level but will give us air and view. The way the tent should face is a most important question and we weigh the factors concerned with solemnity. If it faces this way, we shall miss the morning sun and will sleep late; that way, we shall rise with the dawn and besides have a timbered island cruising before us. That decided, the tent smells soon again of balsam boughs. Everything is ready for the night and nothing to do but listen to sounds of the night birds, talk over the adventures of the day and rest.

And what a delightful sensation it is to relax and stretch weary muscles after a day of wilderness travel. In order to really appreciate rest we must first experience fatigue and without experiencing fatigue we cannot ever hope to know the complete mental relaxation that comes from muscular effort. That perhaps, more than anything, attunes a man to the wild and not until he can forget himself, his worries and the outside does he fit into the scheme of things in the wilderness.

These are only a few of the things we go into the wilderness for, the doing of which satisfies to some extent our craving for contact with the earth. There are countless other things that give us equal pleasure, dawns and sunsets, clouds, the color of leaves, the finding of a rare flower, watching a beaver build his house, listening to the whistle of wings over a marsh, not to forget the warble of birds in the sunlight of early morning and many others, all an intimate part of life in the wild and part and parcel of what we go in to find.

Fortune at Lac La Croix
Sports Afield
OCTOBER 1932

THIS IS SIG'S *second fictional work published in 1932. The years from 1921 to 1934 make up his experimental period. Later, he dropped some of the writing styles that are included in these selections, and he focused, as Elinor Glyn's book had told him to do.*

WHAT HAS GONE BEFORE:
It was high noon of a breathless day in August when Joe Mafreau, the old half-breed, "spotted" the magnificent silver black fox and her three pups on the ledge in the valley near Lac La Croix. His heart almost stopped beating when the fox came boldly out upon the ledge, followed by three romping balls of fur that rolled and tumbled over each other in excitement. Two were reds, but the third was a dark as his gorgeous mother.

In all his years of effort to bring back to the fur trading post a single specimen of the silver black, Joe had been frustrated. Other furs he had taken in abundance, but no silver black foxes.

Joe's enthusiasm leaped in unprecedented bounds as he thought of the fortune the foxes would bring him. He determined to mark the ledge indelibly in his mind and return to kill the foxes after the frost had set in, when furs would be at their prime.

Upon learning at Lac La Croix that fur breeders in the settlements were offering "wan tousan' dollars cash" for live "seelvaire black pups," Joe made hasty and secret preparations to return to the ledge immediately. He revealed his plans to no one. Jackfish Pete, a renegade Indian, just released from prison, guessed Joe's motives, however.

Early the next morning, while the settlers at the Lac La Croix trading post were still asleep, Joe paddled his canoe straight toward the rising sun. The flash of a paddle far out in the lake caught his eyes as he started out. For a moment he wondered, but he dismissed the thought with a shrug. No one could possibly know. By noon, he had paddled the length of Lac La Croix, up the Wild Goose river, and over Wild Goose lake. He beached his canoe and proceeded on foot. He hurried over a ridge and descended into a valley.

THE STORY CONTINUES:

He crossed the valley and climbed steadily, until he stood upon the topmost summit of the rise. Here from a bald rock, scoured smooth by glacial ice, he saw at last the creek, winding like a silver blue ribbon, through the level brown of the great bog, and there a full mile across, was the rocky ledge and the den.

The winding ridge from whose protection he had first seen the den, lay directly below him, pointing like a huge and crooked finger at his goal. By taking advantage of its

FORTUNE AT LAC LA CROIX

cover and the wind, he should if luck was with him, come within easy rifle shot of the crevice.

He rested a moment longer before continuing his journey; then adjusting his pack, he started down the slope toward the base of the ridge whose crest he was to follow across the marsh. Upon reaching it, he proceeded rapidly, the soft carpet of pine needles giving forth no sound.

As he neared its end, he stopped often to listen, and when at last he saw the opening through the fringe of pines, he dropped to his knees and crawled. A huge boulder, lodged between two trees, lay directly before him. He made that his objective and wriggled toward it flat upon his stomach. Not until he could touch it with his finger tips did he stop. For a long time he lay motionless, waiting for his heart to stop its pounding.

While he rested, he slipped out the shell from the chamber of his rifle, and polished it upon his sleeve, till it shone like a mirror in the sun. Holding the favored missile up to the light, he examined it critically, an old trick of his, when fortune hung in the balance. Satisfied that his work was good, he closed the breech noiselessly.

When he had regained his composure, he slipped off his pack, looked once more to his rifle and slowly raised his head. The sight that met his eyes made him fairly gasp, for there two hundred yards away was the ledge and sleeping peacefully in the afternoon sunlight was the old silver with two of her pups. But something was wrong. Where was the black? For a fraction of a second, he was panic stricken. Then to his joy, he discovered it curled up under a scrub Norway, not six feet from the rest.

For half a minute he did not move, then slowly, so slowly that one could hardly have perceived the movement, he raised the rifle, until the barrel came to rest on top of the rock. He drew a fine bead, held it for a breathless moment, and fired. At the report, the sleeping silver sprang high into the air, to fall into a quivering heap in the exact spot where she had lain. The pups jumped to their feet and bolted pellmell for the opening of their den.

With a bound the old trapper cleared the boulder, and ran with all the speed he could muster down the ridge and into the muskeg. Across the creek he splashed and up the slope of the other side, not stopping till he reached the ledge.

Tearing the net out of his pack, he strung it deftly over the mouth of the crevice, fastening the sides securely with poles and rocks. Then cutting a long sapling, he fastened to its end a roll of birchbark. This he touched off with a match and when it burst into flame, he thrust it under the net into the dark interior of the cave.

With excited yelps the two reds came plunging out, only to find themselves hopelessly entangled in the folds of the big fishing net. The half-breed laughed as he let them scramble out from underneath.

"Now you black rascal," he called into the darkness. "Now eet ees your turn. Come out an' meet your ole fren' Joe."

With that he thrust the flaming torch again and again, exploring every hidden recess he could reach, but without result. Sickening fear overwhelmed him. Perhaps he had been too late. Nervously, he cut a longer sapling and a bigger, more resinous piece of bark. It blazed up brilliantly as he thrust it clear to the very end of the cave.

This time the pup was cornered and with a terrified yelp he too charged out into the glaring sunlight, only to meet the fate of the others. He bit and tore in a frenzied effort to free himself, but succeeded in becoming only more and more enmeshed. Finally exhausted by his efforts, he lay panting and watched his captor malignantly.

"So my leetle black diamon'," laughed Mafreau, "I have

you at las', after all dese years." He wrapped the loose folds of the net still more securely around the pup, stood for a moment in satisfied contemplation of his strategy, then tucked the precious bundle snugly into the packsack.

Unsheathing his knife, he then knelt over the dead sliver and began to work. The hide was in poor condition, worth at that season, scarcely more than that of a red. Still that did not matter now. For half an hour he skinned steadily and when at last he had finished, rolled the unprime pelt into a ball and placed it with the net.

Leaving the scene of the killing, he started back across the swamp to the mainland, the way he had come. For once he did not notice the weight of his burden, though it was almost dusk before he reached his cache on the shore of Wild Goose lake. The sun had dropped below the western ridges in a lurid after glow of color and twilight was settling like a blanket of down over the waiting wilderness.

A cheery fire was soon under way, and by its light, he transferred the silver pup from the pack to the freedom of the willow cage. For a moment, he held the priceless captive in his hands, watching the play of firelight upon the shining fur.

"De fines' pup een de worl'," he gloated. "Eet ees a shame to put you een a cage wen de woods ees all around. Mebbe who knows, some day you come back to Lac La Croix." He placed him in the cage and closed the door tightly.

After his evening meal, a great weariness stole over him, a weariness not so much of fatigue as of the knowledge that his work was almost done. After three score years of waiting and dreaming, the big strike had come. He had often wondered as he sat before his fire at night, if the great day would ever come; wondered what would happen if it failed, and how long it would be, till they found his old bones beneath the winter's snow. Now he had his answer. The lakes and frozen trails would know him no more. He would die as he had dreamed he would, among friends, in his warm cabin at Lac La Croix.

Still as he watched the dying coals of his fire, he was aware of a feeling of sadness and regret. Like them, his cherished dreams were fading. The search was over. He was old and there was nothing left to do.

The coals gleamed brightly; a last flicker of flame, and then the blackness of night. A breeze sprang up from nowhere and riffles licked the shore uneasily.

With the coming of day, the surface of Wild Goose lake was dotted with whitecaps. The sky was clear except for a heavy bank of cloud that hung low over the western horizon. In the rising wind, was a low note of warning, a promise of combers and flying spray.

Mafreau crawled out of his sleeping bag and wandered down to the shore. The loons were right, she was going to blow. Old woodsman that he was, the roughened lake filled him with misgiving, for he knew he should make the post that day.

Breakfast over, he lashed the pack and cage to the bow thwart and pushed off into the breakers. Swirling streaks of foam tore across the surface and he paddled desperately to keep his head in the wind.

Foot by foot, he fought his way, taking what shelter he could behind points and islands. It was slow work and not till high noon did he make the outlet. When he glided at last into the quiet waters of Wild Goose river, he dropped his paddle out of sheer exhaustion and for half an hour did nothing but drift with the sluggish current. With the return of his strength, the miles of smooth water slipped swiftly behind him once more. He passed again through the spruce-fringed pot hole and at last heard the welcome roar of the rapids. The canoe dropped around a wooded point and landed on a sloping rock, just above the first foaming ripple of white water.

He untied the cage and carried it to a safe place away from the water's edge. Then picking up his pack, he threw the canoe onto his shoulders and started down the portage. For a full quarter mile he carried it, before the welcome gleam of water met his gaze. He reached the shore, dropped the canoe wearily, and sat down to rest. So far it had been rough traveling and he was tired. After all, there was no use in hurrying with the wind blowing a gale on Lac La Croix.

While sitting there quietly smoking, a branch cracked sharply not far behind him. Startled, he jumped to his feet, but saw nothing. It must have been a deer coming down to drink. He sat down again and leisurely finished his smoke.

Suddenly, remembering the most important part of his cargo, he rose slowly to his feet. He had rested long enough. Back up the portage he went. As he toiled up the crooked, rocky trail, a vague premonition seized him, a feeling of impending disaster and tragedy. He tried to shake if off. Surely, nothing could happen now.

Nevertheless, he increased his pace to a run. As he rounded the last turn before coming to the landing, he stopped in amazement, eyes wide with unbelief. It could not be. He must have forgotten. Then with a wild cry, he hurled himself forward to the place where he had left the cage not half an hour before. It was gone, gone as completely as though it had taken wings and flown.

For a time he did not move, but when the full realization crushed in upon him, he raised his clenched and knotted fists to the heavens and swore an oath horrible in its imprecation of the fate that again had tricked him.

On his hands and knees, he examined every inch of ground for fifty yards before he found a clue; only a leaf crushed by the heel of a moccasin. A little farther on, a broken blade of grass gave the direction the thief had taken, parallel to the portage and down the river toward the canoe. With a start, he remembered the snapping of the branch he had heard while resting.

Back to the portage he plunged and down the trail. Even so he might be too late. The rapids had now assumed a sinister note, one of foreboding and despair. He ran blindly, till he saw again the glint of blue through the trees. Down to the shore he reeled and as in a trance, saw that his canoe was also gone; and there just rounding the bend downstream, was an Indian, the outlaw, Jackfish Pete.

Fascinated, he watched the speeding craft till it dropped from sight behind a fringe of spruces. There was nothing he could do; too old to give chase, stranded, helpless. He sank down to the rocks and stared at the foam-flecked current stoney-eyed with grief, an old man, robbed of his last chance at fortune.

The heavy bank of cloud, that since dawn had lain over the horizon, now covered half the sky. Dark fragments tore themselves away from its edge and went skudding swiftly toward the east. As the half-breed watched and listened to the moan of the rising wind, hope welled up within him.

Jackfish would try to make the village by night and escape with the prize money before his return of that he was certain. Then to the god of the Chippewas, he breathed a prayer of vengeance and supplication, a prayer that the open reaches of the great La Croix be torn by storm that night as never before, and that its broad surface be covered with swirling whitecaps from the south.

He rose to his feet wearily. He would leave the river and cut through the timber to the shore of the lake. Forcing his way into the undergrowth bordering the stream, he worked slowly southwest toward its mouth. An insane desire for vengeance gripped him. Jackfish Pete must pay.

It was late in the afternoon before he emerged from the timber onto the bold, rugged shores of Lac La Croix. He scrambled out upon a bare rocky point, over which the spray dashed unceasingly. For a time he saw nothing but the marching rows of whitecaps, whole companies and battalions of them coming in slowly out of the southwest. Then he saw what he was looking for, a tiny black speck bobbing up and down over the huge rollers. It was the birchbark headed west for the village, eight miles away across the open. He laughed as he watched it, laughed with fierce elation when it dropped from sight in the trough of a wave. It could not make the channel, and it dared not come ashore, that much he knew.

Every second the wind increased, dashing spray high over the rocks. Unmindful of the wet, the old trapper watched the struggling speck, creeping inch by inch toward the narrows. It had hardly moved since he came, and was now in the broad open sweep of water, of the great south arm.

He leaped to his feet and yelled exultantly into the teeth of the gale, "Blow ye old devil, blow your damndest!" and he shook his old bony fists at the bobbing canoe.

Down the rock strewn shore he ran, stumbling and slipping over the wet, slimy boulders, watching the birchbark as a cat would watch a crippled mouse. Sometimes he lost it completely in the gathering dusk, only to discover it again a little further on, fighting its way gradually toward the west. It grew steadily darker and he was forced at last to give up, when he could no longer see ahead of him.

He left the shore and found a sheltered nook behind a rock. Here he built himself a fire and prepared to spend the night. For hours afterward, he sat and fed the flames and listened to the thundering crash of the surf. Sparks sucked up into the inky blackness above, hung for a brilliant glowing second and disappeared into the void. He watched them and wondered. Life was much like that. Despite the cold and wet, he fell finally into a troubled sleep.

He was awake long before dawn. The thunder had died and though the lake was far from placid, he knew the storm had spent itself. In spite of the dark, he picked his way down to the shore to wait for daylight. The combers had changed to long smooth swells, that washed the shoreline lazily, as though exhausted after their night's carousal.

As the darkness faded into the grey light of breaking day, he scanned the water anxiously for some sign of life. A rugged cliff rose up behind him. He climbed it, and from there could see a mile of shoreline on either side. A flock of seagulls were circling and screaming over something on a reef, far to the windward; there almost what looked like a log stranded high on a curving strip of sandy beach. The longer he looked the firmer grew his conviction.

Down the cliff he scrambled, and followed the water's edge as rapidly as the rough going would permit. It was now broad daylight, but even so, he often stumbled and fell. As he rounded a sharp jagged point, he saw the beach before him, and there turned high and dry upon the sand was a birchbark canoe, his own.

"Mon Dieu," he gasped and crossed himself. "Jackfeesh Pete ees drown."

He walked slowly down the sand, toward the wreck. One side was crushed completely in. He turned it over carefully. The cage was gone, but there still tied to the bow thwart was his own pack. Kneeling, he tore feverishly at the water soaked straps. Untouched and exactly as he had placed it, was the skin of the silver fox. He shook it out and laid it on the canoe to dry; then walked down the beach.

As he neared the far end, he saw something that made him catch his breath, something half buried in the sand. He hurried toward it. It was the willow cage, broken and empty. Then he made a discovery. Stuck to the splintered ends of the willows were several long black hairs. The "Fortune" had escaped.

"Sacre," he exclaimed, "perhaps hees live, perhaps hees sweem ashore."

A search confirmed his suspicions, for not far away was a nearly obliterated trail leading up and out of the water. The pup was gone, back into the wilds of his birth and somehow Joe Mafreau was glad.

He went back to the canoe, tucked the wet and unprime skin into his pack and started down the shore toward the village. His "Fortune" was gone, but that mattered not. It was still the day he had dreamed of, for he was bringing in a silver to the post at Lac La Croix."

1933

THE DEPRESSION caused Sig to take a cut in pay but not a cut in lifestyle. Across the nation, teachers made $1,227 a year and college techers made $3,111. Ely trailed the nation.

In the midst of monetary limits, however, the Olsons still enjoyed abundance. The outfitting business was going well and allowed them to buy a new home on the hill. At the time, everyone asked them why they moved so far out of town. It was the hill that was important to the family of skiers, and it would be their last move. The Olsons were settled, and the town gradually grew out to them.

Minnesota created twelve state forests, a new addition to the state's resource inventory. In Wisconsin, Sig's friend and contemporary Aldo Leopold was instrumental in the establishment of the first game management program in the

1933

nation, at Madison. The first true Civilian Conservation Corps (CCC) camps were established in Wisconsin's Nicolet National Forest. In nine years, the CCC would take two and a half million men from the unemployment ranks and pay them each $30 a month. The CCC was one of the nation's most massive efforts. It would be instrumental in many of the management decisions of the Superior National Forest in future years. Trails would be built, campsites developed, and the country mapped, with both positive and negative impact. All the nation's forests would be altered by this abundance of manpower.

On the national scale, the big news was the dust bowl, an environmental problem that got out of hand because of a desire for quick cash crops and an ignorance of ecology. The Soil Erosion Service began as a result. This was also the year of the extinction of the heath hen.

Also in the news that year was the appointment of Adolph Hitler as the chancellor of Germany and the end of prohibition in the United States.

Trail's End

Sports Afield
OCTOBER 1933

THIS IS THE THIRD *in the sequence of fictional pieces. It was illustrated in the original version by Walter J. Wilwerding. Many of the magazine pieces were photo illustrated, but the fictional stories "Papette," "Fortune at Lac La Croix," and "En Roulant" were accompanied by Wilwerding art.*

This Walter J. Wilwerding was not the same Walter Wilwerding who was the editor who gave Sig the important critique of his early submissions. Walter J. Wilwerding was a Minneapolis illustrator who worked at an art school for the Bureau of Engraving. He was prolific, and was especially well-known for his African work.

IT WAS EARLY MORNING in the northern wilderness, one of those rare breathless mornings, that come only in November, and though it was not yet light enough to see, the birds were stirring. A covey of partridge whirred up from their cozy burrows in the snow and lit in the top of a white birch, where they feasted noisily upon the frozen brown buds. The rolling tattoo of a downy woodpecker, also looking for his breakfast, reverberated again and again through the timber.

They were not the only ones astir however, for far down the trail leading from the Tamarack Swamp to Kennedy Lake browsed a big buck. He worked his way leisurely along, stopping now and then to scratch away the fresh snow and nibble daintily the still tender green things underneath. A large buck he was, even as deer run, and as smooth and sleek as good feeding could make him. His horns, almost too large, were queerly shaped, for instead of being rounded as in other deer, they were broad and palmate, the horns of a true swamp buck.

The eastern skyline was just beginning to tint with lavender as he reached the summit of the ridge overlooking the lake. He stopped for his usual morning survey of the landscape below him. For some reason, ever since his spike-buck days, he had always stopped there to look the country over before working down to water. He did not know that for countless generations before him, in the days when the pine timber stood tall and gloomy round the shores of the lake, other swamp bucks had also stopped, to scent the wind and listen, before going down to drink.

As he stood on the crest of the ridge, his gaze took in the long reaches of dark blue water far below him; the ice rimmed shores with long white windfalls reaching like frozen fingers out into the shallows, and the mottled green and grey of the brush covered slopes. His attention was finally centered on a little log cabin tucked away on the opposite shore in a clump of second growth spruce and balsam. Straight above it rose a thin wreath of pale blue smoke, almost as blue as the clear morning air. The metallic chuck, chuck of an axe ringing on a dry log came clearly across the water, and a breath of air brought to him strange odors that somehow filled him with a vague misgiving.

He was fascinated by the cabin and could not take his gaze from it. On other mornings, it had seemed as much a part of the shoreline as the trees themselves, but now it was different. A flood of almost forgotten memories surged back to him, of days long ago, when similar odors and sounds had brought with them a danger far greater than that of any natural enemy. He rubbed the top of a low hazel bush and stamped his forefeet nervously, undecided what to do. Then, in a flash, the full realization came to him. He understood the meaning of it all. This was the season of the year when man was no longer his friend and it was not safe to be seen in the logging roads or in the open clearings near the log houses. He sniffed the air keenly a moment longer to be sure, then snorted loudly as if to warn all the wilderness folk of their danger, and bounded back up the trail the way he had come.

Not until he had regained the heavy protecting timber of the Tamarack Swamp, north of Kennedy Lake, did he feel safe. What he had seen made him once again the wary old buck who had lived by his cunning and strength through many a hunting season. Although he was safe for the time being, he was too experienced not to know, that before may days had passed, the Tamarack Swamp would no longer be a haven of refuge.

As he worked deeper into the heavy moss hung timber, he stopped frequently to look into the shadows. The trail here was knee deep in moss and criss-crossed by a labyrinth of narrow rabbit runways. Soon his search was rewarded, for a sleek yearling doe met him at a place where two trails crossed. After nosing each other tenderly, by way of recognition, they began feeding together on the tender shoots of blueberries and still green tufts of swamp grass underneath the protecting blanket of snow.

All that morning they fed leisurely and when the sun was high in the heavens, they worked cautiously over to the edge of the swamp. Here was a warm sunny opening hedged in by huge windfalls grown over with a dense tangle of blackberry vines. They often came here for their afternoon sunning, as the ice-encrusted ovals in the snow attested. Leaping a big windfall that guarded the entrance to the opening, they carefully examined the ground, then picked their beds close together. There they rested contentedly with the warm sun shining upon them, little thinking that soon their peace would be broken.

The snow had fallen early that autumn and good feed had been scarce everywhere, except in the depths of the Tamarack Swamp, where the protecting timber had sheltered the grass and small green things. The plague had killed off most of the rabbits, and the few which survived were already forced to feed upon the bark of the poplar. The heavy crust, forming suddenly the night after the first heavy snow, had imprisoned countless partridge and grouse in their tunnels. As a result, small game was scarce and the wolves were lean and gaunt, although it was yet hardly winter. The stark famine months ahead gave promise of nothing but starvation and death, and the weird discordant music of the wolf pack had sounded almost every night since the last full moon.

The swamp buck and his doe had not as yet felt the pinch of hunger, but instinct told them to keep close to the shelter of the Tamarack Swamp, so except for the morning strolls of the buck to the shore of Kennedy Lake, they had seldom ventured far from the timber. They had often heard the wolf pack, but always so far away that there was little danger as long as they stayed under cover.

Several days had passed since the buck had been to the shore of Kennedy Lake. As yet the silence of the swamp had been unbroken except for the crunching of their own hoofs through the icy crust on the trails, and the buck was beginning to wonder if there was really anything to fear. Then one day, as they were again leisurely working their way over to the sunning place in the clearing, they were startled by strange noises far toward the east end of the swamp. They stopped, every nerve on edge. At times they could hear them quite plainly, then again they would be so faint as to be almost indistinguishable from the other sounds of the forest.

The two deer were not much concerned at first. After satisfying themselves that there was no real danger, they started again down the trail toward the clearing. They could still hear the noises occasionally, but could not tell whether they were coming closer or going further away.

Then just as they neared the edge of the swamp, the sound of heavy footsteps seemed suddenly to grow louder and more distinct. Once more they stopped and stood with heads high, ears pricked up, listening intently. This time they were thoroughly alarmed. Closer and closer came the racket. Now they could hear distinctly the crunching of snow and the crackling of twigs, and then whe whole east end of the timber seemed to be fairly alive with tumult, and the air reeked with danger.

The buck ran in a circle, sniffing keenly. The same scent that had come to him from the cabin, now rankled heavily in the air, and he knew the time had come to leave the shelter of the Tamarack Swamp. He hesitated, however, not knowing which way to turn. Back and forth he ran, stopping now and then to paw the ground, or to blow the air

through his nostrils with the sharp whistling noise that all deer use when in danger.

A branch cracked sharply close at hand, and the scent came doubly strong from the east. With a wild snort the buck wheeled and led the way toward the western end of the swamp followed closely by the doe. Their only hope lay in reaching a heavy belt of green hemlock timber which they knew was separated from the western end of the Tamarack Swamp by a broad stretch of barren, burned-over slashing. As they neared the edge of the swamp they stopped, dreading to leave its protection. From where they stood they could see the dark wall of timber half a mile away. A brushy gully ran diagonally toward it across the open slashing, offering some protection, but the hills on either side were as stark and bare as an open field.

Again came the crack and crunch, now so close that the very air burned with danger. It was time to go. They bounded out of the timber, their white flags waving defiance, and were soon in the brushy gully, going like the wind. Just as they sailed over a windfall, the buck caught a glimpse of something moving on a big black pine stump on top of the ridge to their right. Then the quiet was shattered by a succession of rending crashes and strange singing and whining sounds filled the air above them.

Again and again came the crashes. Suddenly the little doe stopped dead in her tracks. She gave a frightened baa-aa-a of pain and terror as the blood burst in a stream from a jagged wound in her throat. The buck stopped and ran back to where she stood, head down and swaying unsteadily. He watched her a moment, then, growing nervous, started down the trail again. The doe tried bravely to follow, but fell half way across a windfall too high for her to clear. Again the buck stopped and watched her anxiously. The snow by the windfall was soon stained bright red with blood, and the head of the little doe sank lower and lower in spite of her brave efforts to hold it up.

Hurriedly the buck looked about him. Several black figures were coming rapidly down the ridge. He nosed his doe gently, but this time she did not move. Raising his head he looked toward the approaching figures. Danger was close, but he could not leave his mate.

A spurt of smoke came from one of the figures, followed by another crash. This time the buck felt a blow so sharp that it made him stumble. Staggering to his feet, he plunged blindly down the gully. His flag was down, the sure sign of a wounded deer. Again and again came the crashes and the air above him whined and sang as the leaden pellets searched for their mark. The bark flew from a birch tree close by, spattering him with fragments. In spite of his wound, he ran swiftly and was soon out of range in the protecting green timber. He knew that he would not be tracked for at least an hour, as his pursuers would wait for him to lie down and stiffen.

He was bleeding badly from a long red scar cutting across his flank, and his back trail was sprinkled with tiny red dots. Where he stopped to rest and listen, little puddles of blood would form that quickly turned bluish black in the snow. For two hours he ran steadily, and then was so weakened by loss of blood that at last he was forced to lie down.

After a short rest he staggered to his feet, stiffened badly. The bed he had melted in the snow was stained dark red from his bleeding flank. The cold, however, had contracted the wound and had stopped the bleeding a little. He limped painfully down the trail, not caring much which direction it led. Every step was torture. Once when crossing a small gully, he stumbled and fell on his wounded leg. It rested him to lie there, and it was all he could do to force himself on.

While crossing a ridge, the wind bore the man scent strongly to him, and he knew that now he was being trailed. Once, he heard the brush crack behind him, and was so startled that the wound was jerked open and the bleeding started afresh. He watched his back trail nervously, expecting to see his pursuer at any moment and hear again the rending crash that would mean death.

He grew steadily weaker and knew that unless night came soon, he would be overtaken. He had to rest more often now, and when he did move it was to stagger aimlessly down the trail, stumbling on roots and stubs. It was much easier now to walk around the windfalls, than to try to jump over as he had always done before.

The shadows were growing longer and longer, and in the hollows it was already getting dusk. If he could last until nightfall he would be safe. But the man scent was getting still stronger, and he realized at last that speed alone could not save him. Strategy was the only course. If his pursuer could be thrown off the trail, only long enough to delay him half an hour, darkness would be upon the wilderness and he could rest.

So waiting until the trail ran down onto a steep ravine filled with brush and windfalls, the buck suddenly turned and walked back on his own trail as far as he dared. It was the old trick of back tracking that deer have used for ages to elude their pursuers. Then stopping suddenly, he jumped as far to the side as his strength would permit, landing with all four feet lightly bunched together in the very center of a scrubby hazel bush. From there, he worked his way slowly into a patch of scrub spruce and lay down exhausted under an old windfall. Weakened as he was from loss of blood and from the throbbing pain in his flank, it was all he could do to keep his eyes riveted on his back trail, and his ears strained for the rustling and crunching that he feared would come, unless darkness came first.

It seemed that he had barely lain down, when without warning, the brush cracked sharply, and not a hundred yards away appeared a black figure. The buck was petrified with terror. His ruse had failed. He shrank as far down as he could in the grass under the windfall and his eyes almost burst from their sockets. Frantically he thought of leaving his hiding place, but knew that would only invite death. The figure came closer and closer, bending low over the trail and peering keenly into the spruce thicket ahead. In the fading light the buck was well hidden by the windfall, but the blood spattered trail led straight to his hiding place. Discovery seemed certain.

The figure picked its way still nearer. It was now within thirty feet of the windfall. The buck watched, hardly daring to breathe. Then, in order to get a better view into the thicket, the hunter started to climb a snow covered stump close by. Suddenly, losing his balance, he slipped and plunged backwards into the snow. The buck saw his chance. Gathering all his remaining strength, he dashed out of his cover and was soon hidden in the thick growth of spruce.

In was almost dark now and he knew that as far as the hunter was concerned, he was safe. Circling slowly around, he soon found a sheltered hiding place in a dense clump of spruce where he could rest and allow his wound to heal.

Night came swiftly, bringing with it protection and peace. The stars came out one by one, and a full November moon climbed into the sky, flooding the snowy wilderness with its radiance.

Several hours had passed since the buck had lain down to rest in the spruce thicket. The moon was now riding high in the heavens and in the open places it was almost as light as day. Although well hidden, he dozed fitfully, waking at times with a start, thinking that again he was being trailed. He would then lie and listen, with nerves strained to the breaking point, for any sounds of the wild that might mean danger. An owl hooted over in a clump of timber, and the new forming ice on the shores of Kennedy Lake, half a mile away, rumbled ominously. Then he heard a long quavering call, so faint and far away that it almost blended with the whispering of the wind. The coarse hair on his shoulders bristled as he recognized the hunting call of the age-old enemy of his kind. It was answered again and again. The wolf pack was gathering, and for the first time in his life, the buck knew fear. In the shelter of the Tamarack Swamp there had been little danger, and even if he had been driven to the open, his strength and speed would have carried him far from harm. Now, sorely wounded and far from shelter, he would have hardly a fighting chance should the pack pick up his trail.

They were now running in full cry, having struck a trail in the direction of the big swamp far to the west. To the buck, the weird music was as a song of death. Circling and circling, for a time they seemed to draw no nearer. As yet he was not sure whether it was his own blood bespattered trail that they were unravelling, or that of some other one of his kind. Then, suddenly, the cries grew in fierceness and volume and sounded much closer than before. He listened spellbound as he finally realized the truth it was his own trail they were following. The fiendish chorus grew steadily louder and more venomous, and now had a new note of triumph in it that boded ill for whatever came in its way.

He could wait no longer and sprang to his feet. To his dismay, he was so stiffened and sore, that he could hardly take a step. Forcing himself on, he hobbled painfully through the poplar brush and clumps of timber in the direction of the lake. Small windfalls made him stumble, and having to walk around hummocks and hollows made progress slow and difficult. How he longed for his old strength and endurance. About two thirds of the distance to the lake had been covered and already occasional glimpses of water appeared between the openings.

Suddenly the cries of the pack burst out in redoubled fury behind him, and the buck knew they had found his warm blood-stained bed. Plunging blindly on, he used every ounce of strength and energy that he had left, for now the end was only a matter of minutes. The water was his only hope, for by reaching that he would at least escape being torn to shreds by the teeth of the pack. He could hear them coming swiftly down the ridge behind him and every strange shadow he mistook for one of the gliding forms of his pursuers. They were now so close that he could hear their snarls and yapping. Then a movement caught his eye in the checkered moonlight. A lone grey shape had slipped out of the darkness and was easily keeping pace with him. Another form crept in silently on the other side and both ran like phantoms with no apparent effort. He was terror stricken, but kept on desperately. Other ghost-like shapes filtered in from the timber, but still they did not close. The water was just ahead. They would wait till he broke from the brush that lined the shore. With a crash, he burst through the last fringe of alders and charged forward. As he did so, a huge grey form shot out of the shadows and launched itself at his throat. He saw the movement in time and caught the full force of the blow on his horns. A wild toss and the snarling shape splashed into the ice rimmed shallows. At the same instant the two that had been running along side closed, one for his throat and the other for his hamstrings. The first he hit a stunning blow with his sharp front hoof, but as he did so the teeth of the other fastened on the tendon of his hind leg. A frantic leap loosened his hold, and the buck half plunged and half slid over the ice into the waters of Kennedy Lake. Then the rest of the pack tore down to the beach with a deafening babble of snarls and howls, expecting to find their quarry down or at bay. When they realized that they had been outwitted, their anger was hideous and the air was rent with howls and yaps.

The cold water seemed to put new life into the buck and each stroke was stronger than the one before, Nevertheless, it was a long hard swim, and before he was half way across the benumbing cold had begun to tell. He fought on stubbornly, his breath coming in short, choking sobs and finally, after what seemed ages, touched the hard sandy bottom of the other shore. Dragging himself painfully out, he lay down, exhausted in the snow. All sense of feeling had left his tortured body, but the steady lap, lap of the waves against the tinkling shore ice soothed him into sleep.

When he awoke, the sun was high in the heavens. For a long time he lay as in a stupor, too weak and sorely stiffened to move. Then with a mighty effort he struggled to his feet, and stood motionless, bracing himself unsteadily. Slowly his strength returned and leaving his bed, he picked his way carefully along the beach, until he struck the trail, down which he had so often come to drink. He followed it to the summit of the ridge overlooking the lake.

The dark blue waters sparkled in the sun, and the rolling spruce covered ridges were green as they had always been. Nothing had really changed, yet never again would it be the same. He was a stranger in the land of his birth, a lonely fugitive where once he had roamed at will, his only choice to leave forever the ancient range of his breed. For a time he wavered torn between his emotions, then finally turned to go. Suddenly an overwhelming desire possessed him, to visit again the place where last he had seen his mate. He worked slowly down the trail to the old Tamarack Swamp and did not stop until he came to the old meeting place deep in the shadows where the two trails crossed. For a long time he did not move, then turned and headed into the north to a new wilderness far from the old, a land as yet untouched, the range of the Moose and Caribou.

1934

THIS WAS AN eventful year for the world and for the canoe country. Hitler and Mao Tse-Tung were emerging as leaders in their countries and were diverting the interest of the people of the United States to Europe and Asia. In the comics, Flash Gordon and Dale Arden tried to halt the collision between Mongo and Earth. On the screen, Shirley Temple debuted in "Stand Up and Cheer," and in Canada, the Dionne quintuplets were born. Politics centered on Roosevelt's "New Deal."

With attention drawn in so many directions, the environmental community still managed to focus its efforts. Edward Backus had his last dam project rejected by the International Joint Commission, while the state of Minnesota passed its own version of the Shipstead-Nolan Act and helped to preserve the integrity of the canoe country as a result. If the two governmental agencies had not been coordinated, piecemeal ownership of the land would not have allowed the natural evolution of its wilderness status.

President Roosevelt created the Quetico-Superior Committee in 1934, with Ernest Oberholtzer and Charles Kelly representing the Quetico-Superior Council. It was an unusual circumstance for one area's environmental views to have a special forum with the president, but it emphasized the uniqueness of the boundary waters.

There were problems in canoe country that were outside the realms of politics in 1934, however. White pine blister rust from Europe had infested one percent of the wilderness pines and threatened to eliminate them entirely. This introduced pathogen was running rampant across the Northeast, and only the action of the CCC in eliminating its intermediary host, the gooseberry, prevented the same kind of widespread catastrophe that has befallen the elms. The gooseberry had proliferated in recently logged areas.

Another impact of logging was the introduction of vast amounts of new browse in the cutover areas. This unnatural state of affairs made life easy for the white-tailed deer, which expanded both its range and its population. The north country had already lost the caribou, and now the large numbers of deer threatened the moose, whose population was already low for the region. The deer carried a brain worm that was not threatening to them but was lethal to the moose.

The public was entering a new era of public involvement with its wildlife. The publication of Roger Tory Peterson's *A Field Guide to the Birds* took wildlife out of dusty museum trays and put it into the hands of the public. With binoculars and feeders, people were now able to view wildlife, make their own studies, and identify what they observed. Prior to this time, wildlife belonged to the scientist, but after this, the legions of bird watchers would grow each year, and their interest would expand to all wildlife, land, and environmental issues. It would no longer be a handful of individuals who fought for wildness; it would now be part of the nation's conscience. The advent of field guides was more significant than we can imagine in today's age of field guide surplus.

Roads or Planes in the Superior
Minnesota Waltonian
APRIL 1934

THIS ARTICLE *is the beginning of Sig's involvement in issues. Here is the crusading writer-naturalist-guide. He would still write the hunting and fishing articles, but with less frequency as his attention was captured by the Quetico-Superior Council and the fight for wilderness. We can see a new, mature Sig rising from these pages. He made the transition from outdoorsman to environmentalist-activist just as John Muir and Aldo Leopold had.*

Among Sig's early canoe partners was Will Dilg, the original driving force of the Izaak Walton League. On a 1924 canoe trip, Dilg told Sig that the league would always be there to support canoe country when the issues were on the line. Even with the changes in leadership that are inevitable in any national organization, that promise has been kept.

Sig kept and cherished his association with the Izaak Walton League. Among the several national environmental organizations

Sig worked with, his first loyalty was "to the League." He always referred to himself professionally as "wilderness consultant to the IWL."

SINCE THE EARLY 1920's, the Superior National Forest together with the rest of the country, has been undergoing an era of road building. Conservationist organizations, such as the Izaak Walton League and others interested in preserving a remnant of the old Superior as a wilderness area, have fought constantly the steady encroachment of trails, but in every case it has been a losing battle. In spite of the ever growing appreciation by the populations of the middle west of the value of the Superior as a primitive type of recreational area, roads have been planned and built and at the present time even more extensive developmental projects are being considered.

Until 1924, there were no roads of any kind in the Superior proper and all travel was by the time honored method of pack and canoe. It was then practically all wilderness, accessible only by the water trails. Since then, however, the Gunflint Trail has been constructed from Grand Marais to Saganaga, opening the eastern half of the forest, the Echo Trail from Ely to Buyck, opening up the western half of the forest, the Fernberg trail to the Kawishowa River and innumerable, lateral branch roads, many of them private, to adjacent lake shore properties.

Past experience has proven that all roads designated by the Forest Service as truck and wagon roads, in spite of the fact that they were originally intended for fire protection purposes only, eventually in the course of time, become well graded public highways receiving annual maintenance not only from the Federal Government, but in some cases from the counties they traverse. When the I. W. L. A. protested the building of the Fernberg Road to the Kawishowa River and also the building of the 54 miles of the Echo Trail, they were told that these projects would merely be for the purpose of fire protection and that the trails in question would never become suitable as public highways. The League accepted this interpretation in good faith, trusting implicitly that the Forest Service would stand by its agreement and keep the fire protection trails always within that category. The last few years, however, have shown us that these so-called fire protection roads have slowly graduated from that lowly status to well graded, and smoothly surfaced highways over which automobiles can travel with safety and comfort. Some of these former fire fighting trails are swiftly becoming first class highways and at the present rate of improvement and development, will within a short time approach the classification of arterials. Such is the inevitable evolution of a fire protection trail in the Superior. What is more, as soon as these trails have assumed the character of fairly well travelled roads, private individuals invariably construct, often times with the aid of the counties, lateral branches into private holdings of lake shore property or timber. When this begins to happen, the country immediately adjacent to any main trail becomes a network and the former wilderness is a thing of the past.

Granted that there is a certain use for roads for purposes of fire protection, still when we consider the enormous annual toll of fires which they inevitably bring in their wake, we begin to wonder if after all they are accomplishing their purpose. If the roads in question could be kept as purely fire protection trails, utilized only by the Forest Service for the transportation of men and equipment during an emergency, they might be justified, but the instant they begin to vary from their original primary purpose, the ultimate fire hazard more than counterbalances any good that might ensue from their construction.

Our neighbor to the north, the Quetico Provincial Park of Ontario, polices its 6,000,000 acres of lake and forest country entirely by plane, and inasmuch as the Superior is an identical area from a topographical standpoint, there is no reason why this highly efficient means of protection could not be used advantageously here. In a country with as many possible landing places as the many lakes here afford, it is possible in practically all cases to approach closely enough to a fire with a plane carrying men and pumps, to control it very quickly and easily. I have many times seen a Canadian plane spot a fire and within a few minutes drop to within a few hundred yards of it, in a number of cases close enough to reach with a single length of hose. Usually, the plane is on the job before the fire has gotten under way and putting it out then is an entirely different matter from what it might be several hours or days later.

It is true that there are a few isolated areas in which lakes and possible landing places are not numerous enough to permit of this type of control, places in which roads would be the only efficient means of entry for men and equipment, but there are many other areas, particularly those which make up the very choicest of the canoe areas in the Superior, where the only logical means of fire control is by use of planes. Contrast the speed of the two systems. On the American side a fire is spotted by the lookouts and word telephoned in to headquarters. Trucks and a crew of men must be rounded up, tents, canoes, equipment and food supplies, must be gotten ready and trucked to the nearest point to the fire in question. Then comes the unloading and the slow work of paddling and portaging to the scene of the blaze. When it is finally reached after many hours of delay and perhaps several days, the fire has usually spread to a broad front, necessitating weeks of work and the loss of thousands of acres of timber. A plane could have been there in a fraction of the time that it took to even get started. Compare the enormous fire damage of last year in the Superior and its environs with the low fire record of the Quetico for 1933 and it is not hard to be convinced of the superiority of their type of control. With the splendid example of plane efficiency continually before us, it seems little short of ridiculous to still adhere to old time cumbersome methods still in use in our forest.

It is true that at times private planes have been pressed into service on bad fires in the Superior for patrol work and for freighting in of supplies and equipment, but this use has never been resorted to until fires have gotten beyond control. The very fact that they have been made use of in great emergencies is proof that their efficiency is recognized by Forest Service officials. However, if planes were continually on hand to cooperate with the lookouts and to locate definitely small blazes which are continually springing up, half the battle would be won. The other half would be won when we have reached a state of efficiency where a plane could be shot into a fire within the hour of its discovery, before it had a chance to get under way. Anyone knows that the secret of fire control is to spot a smoke early and kill it before it had a chance to spread. A small fire can be easily put out by a couple of men with a hose and pump or even with axes and grubhoes, but let it cover a half mile front in a wind and nothing short of a miracle and hundreds of men can stop it.

There is no question but that the efficiency of air plane control of fire has been well demonstrated on both sides of the border and that the Forest Service is cognizant of it. However, the fact remains that only in great emergencies has the plane been resorted to on the American side. Although there may be something to the explanation of certain Forest Service men that the interpretation of the federal statutes controlling the activities of the Forest Service, prohibits the ownership of planes as a departmental function, nevertheless, there can be no valid objection to the hiring and use of private ships for this purpose.

In addition to the added efficiency of airplane patrol, in the last analysis, the most important factor is whether we want the Superior cut up by countless fire protection trails. Here is the last great wilderness lake region on the continent, an area increasingly important from a recreational standpoint, and one which depends chiefly for its charm on the very fact that as yet much of it is undeveloped wilderness. Every road which is put in robs it of some of its appeal. If roads were the only possible means of fire control, there would be little argument, but the fact that we are overlooking a form of protection infinitely more satisfactory and instituting in its place a method that not only does not prevent or control fires, but also detracts immeasurably from the esthetic value of the country, should make us pause and take stock of our present policy.

If the present rate of road building and improvement goes on, it is safe to predict that in ten years, there will be no part of the Superior which cannot be reached by automobile and though the country will be filled with resorts and private homes, its present charm will be gone, for it will no longer be a wilderness, merely another of many vacation lands. Now it is different and has an individuality all its own. Open it up with a road to every lake and building site and it will be just like all the rest of the country.

During the past ten years, the populations of the middle west have looked increasingly to the Superior for their recreation, for in addition to being unique in its character of primitiveness, it is also more centrally located and accessible than any other vacation area in North America. Without doubt, in a short time, the recreational possibilities of the region will far outbalance any other resource. According to Ernest Oberholtzer, head of the Quetico Superior Council, "No other lakeland of America, however lovely, has such riches, both in associations and natural endowments as the Superior National Forest. When we consider the fact, that the tourist industry of the state runs close to $75,000,000 annually and that no small part of this revenue comes from the forests of the north, we begin to realize that here is a resource that cannot be regarded lightly." In view of that alone, we should think twice before continuing with a policy for the Superior which ultimately will be of detriment, not only to the forest, but to the people of the entire middle west. And the constant building of roads comes under this category. The I. W. L. A. can be of inestimable service if it gets solidly behind this movement to block for all time further proposed road extensions, built under the false guise of fire protection. Unless public opinion is roused to the point where it will demand a change of policy, the steady encroachment of trails will go on, and now under the new appropriations, more and more rapidly, until the old Superior which we have come to know and love, will be gone forever.

A New Policy Needed for the Superior

Minnesota Conservationist
MAY 1934

THIS IS THE *second issue statement article that Sig wrote. In this article, we can see his analytical abilities sharpening as he makes a direct attack on a Forest Service statement.*

Elizabeth reflected on Sig's conservation abilities saying, "Sig could express himself in ways that equally good conservationists could not. He couldn't write the way he did, with integrity, were it not for his scientific knowledge and background."

The Minnesota Conservationist was the predecessor to The Minnesota Volunteer, *the official publication of the Minnesota Department of Natural Resources.*

IN A RECENT ARTICLE, F. W. Tinker, Regional Forester for this district, made the following statement: "The forest soil of the nation has never carried its full share of the permanent population and it can provide almost unlimited work, largely of a liquidating nature. Communities established in the National Forests could be given sufficient woods work to assure a cash income adequate to provide the necessities which could not be produced on the land." After this pronouncement of theory, he goes on to explain its workings in regard to the Superior National Forest property.

"A plan recently completed for an area of about 170,000 acres in the Superior National Forest, indicates 1,703,150 man-days of six hours each, will be required to do all of the work necessary to make this land fully productive. The work needed will keep 200 forest workers busy 150 days of the year for over fifty years. The community of 200 families, including probably 800 people, would be established on an area of about 1,400 acres of soil suitable for gardening near the center of the forest tract. The use of surplus labor to improve and make productive the forest properties, would relieve unemployment and reduce permanently the congestion of population in the industrial centers."

At first reading, the plan would appear to have nothing in it but merit, for assuredly, any project which would ultimately mean permanent employment and an increase in the forest products of the Superior, must be worthwhile. Upon closer examination and analysis of the motive behind this plan, which has been the result of years of careful investigation and research on the part of the Forest Service, it can readily be seen to be fraught with grave danger for the last great wilderness area of the Middle West.

From the standpoint of timber production only, the idea is admirable, but through the eyes of men who would like to see the Superior left in as primitive a condition as possible, it has dire significance. It is indicative of the entire attitude of the Forest Service in regard to the National Forests entrusted to their care and because of the interpretation of

A NEW POLICY NEEDED

the law creating such areas which stipulated that they were primarily timber preserves, the administration of which should be along the lines of increased timber production, we cannot entirely blame them for losing sight of the purely aesthetic values.

Since its creation by President Theodore Roosevelt in 1909, the Superior has been placed in the Forest Service catalog as an area of timber of a certain type, merely another block of potential production. With it have been placed all other National Forests and they have been administrated similarly with this end in view. The Superior was merely another forest tract, an area with no particular individuality or appeal, one which could be operated most efficiently along the lines laid down for all other regions coming under the same category.

For ten years, nothing was done to the Superior. Then came the boom days of building and development after the war and the administration at Washington, urged by the clamor of individual concerns who could see a personal profit in the opening up of the border country, suddenly awoke to the fact that there was work to be done. Since that time, development has gone on apace, in spite of the constantly growing sentiment of a public which is swiftly beginning to realize that something is wrong. Each year sees an increase in the tourist population of the area and with the growing interest in the possibilities of this great wilderness of lakes and streams, the people of the Middle West are beginning to wonder if after all, the Superior has not a greater value to the country at large than as a timber production unit.

Occasionally, conservation organizations, such as the Izaak Walton League, the Quetico-Superior Council and others, have fought the ever increasing program of development and have in a few cases won compromises. This has been particularly true with respect to roads and power development. During these long drawn out controversies, there has been much bitterness on both sides and no doubt, the Forest Service and the administration at Washington has often been in the dark, as to the reasons for opposition to a policy entirely within keeping of the usual procedure for the administration of such an area.

What has never been adequately brought out is the fact that the Superior National Forest cannot be classed with other National Forests and therefore deserves a different and individual treatment. It is as ridiculous to put the Superior in a class with the western forests as it would be to apply the same development plan to a desert region of the Southwest. Yet that is exactly what has been done and the Superior, until recently, has been part of a western forest district. As we all know, until the creation of the Lake States District, Mr. Tinker had his office in Denver and it was prefectly natural that with the western forests under his jurisdiction, the Superior would permit of no different handling than any other timber tract. To administer the lake wilderness of the Superior like any typical western forest is a grievous mistake, for here is an area unique in itself and nowhere on the North American continent can we find its equal.

Here is a wilderness lake country of unequalled beauty and charm, thousands of lakes and streams intimately connected and interlaced, a paradise for the wilderness traveller. The strip of country encompassed by the Superior National Forest and the area immediately north, the Quetico Provincial Park of Ontario, takes in the very finest of the canoe country of the continent. Nowhere else this side of Hudson's Bay can one find such beautiful lakes, rocks and forests and certainly no area compares with it in game and fish population. More and more the congested districts of the Middle West are turning toward it for their recreation, for it is the one place within reaching distance of the great centers of population where this form of vacation can be enjoyed.

Here a man can take a canoe and disappear for a few days or several weeks and live in a real wilderness, a wilderness, however, which under the present policy of development is rapidly undergoing change. Ask any one of the thousands of visitors who have come to the Superior during the last few years, what is it about the country which appeals to him most, and he will invariably answer, that it is not the fish and not the scenery, superb as it may be, but the fact that here is one spot where he can get away from crowds and enjoy primitive wilderness conditions.

These growing numbers of wilderness devotees find it increasingly hard to understand that this area is being groomed for an entirely different purpose, one which disregards a very real need of the dwellers in our cities. While they understand perfectly well that timber is a necessity, they also wonder if after all there might not be a more important function for the Superior. Prof. Aldo Leopold, former forester and present head of the Department of Game Management of the University of Wisconsin, once said: "Wilderness is the one kind of playground which mankind cannot build to order. The really wild places within the reach of the centers of population are gone. As a nation, however, we are so accustomed to a plentiful supply, that we are unconscious of what the disappearance of wild places would mean, just as we are unconscious of what the disappearance of wind or sunsets would mean. In all the category of outdoor vacations and outdoor sports, there is not one, save the tilling of the soil, that bends and molds human character like wilderness travel. Shall this fundamental instrument for building citizens be allowed to disappear from America simply because we lack the vision to see its value?"

He goes on further to say: "Acceptance of the idea of wilderness areas entails, I admit, a growth in the original conception of National Forests. The original purposes were timber production and watershed protection, but the whole subsequent history of these forests has been a history of the appearance and growth of new uses, which when skillfully adjusted for the primary uses and to each other, were one by one provided for and the net public benefit correspondingly increased. Public recreation was one of these. It has been proved that skillful administration can provide for both in the same system of forests without material sacrifice of either."

Here is a declaration of principle by one of the foremost conservationists in the country today, a declaration which if applied by the present administration to the Superior, would leave nothing to worry about.

It is true, that a small wilderness area has been set aside in the northeastern corner of the forest, a tract that ostensibly will not be opened to exploitation, except for a certain amount of selective logging and for that much we are thankful. But it is also true, that during the last ten years, the Superior as a whole has been undergoing radical change and is rapidly assuming the status of a semi-cultivated area.

Since 1920, a power project has controlled the Kawishowa River system, a railroad has been built into the Cook County timber preserves north of Grand Marais, innumerable roads have been built, among them the Gunflint Trail from Grand Marais to Lake Saganaga, the Echo Trail from Ely to Buyck, opening up the entire western half, the Fernberg Trail and many short laterals. Under the present plan, more roads are constantly being built, and trails that formerly were designated as fire protection trails only, are

A NEW POLICY NEEDED

swiftly becoming public highways. There is some talk among Forest Service circles of running a branch road from the Echo Trail to Lac La Croix, opening for the first time this hitherto untouched wilderness area.

If the Superior was a typical western timber producing area, the building of roads for fire prevention purposes, the damming of streams and lakes for power, the creation of woods-working communities in its midst, might be sanctioned as a means of securing the highest possible status from a strictly commercial standpoint. But the fact that this forest is something entirely different, an area whose recreational and social factors are predominantly important, makes us pause and wonder if our present policy of administration is not overlooking its prime values, and in the last analysis, it becomes a question of exactly what is the highest use to which the lakeland of the Superior can be put, timber production or recreation. It should be possible somehow to achieve a happy medium in which both factors can be worked out in harmony.

According to Ernest Oberholtzer, Chairman of the Superior-Quetico Council and foremost in the battle against the exploitation of the border waters by the power interests, in surveying the tourist industry of the region: "it would seem that a monopoly resource of such rare and growing value would be guarded as a sacred trust. Timber, minerals, water power, are all relatively common on a continent bulging with natural wealth. As a forest alone, the appeal of the region would have been negligible, but as a lakeland framed in forest and containing all that was best of the past, both flora and fauna, it makes no less call upon us, than our homes and country. Our vanishing inheritance and its influence upon the race is fast becoming a memory. These border lakes, in view of the rapidly changing conditions, can only be regarded as one of the most precious cultural assets left to the present generation."

If we would safeguard for all time the wilderness of the Superior, then we must act quickly and decisively to mold public opinion and thereby demand a change of policy which will take into consideration and place first and foremost among the uses of this unusual area its aesthetic values. While we admit the necessity of increased timber production, we also know that there are many areas, not so uniquely situated or of as great potential recreational importance as the Superior, where such a program could be carried out without depriving the population of the Middle West of its right to enjoy wilderness living. To cut up the Superior with innumerable roads, within which will ultimately be found highly managed plots of timber, to settle in its midst forest working communities, to make of it in other words a highly specialized timber production plant, will be a tragedy to all lovers of the wilderness, a tragedy, whose full significance will not be appreciated, until the last wild place is gone forever.

Cruising in the Arrowhead

Outdoors
MAY 1934

IN THIS ARTICLE, *Sig takes us back into his guiding business. Elizabeth said that it was Sig's sense of humor as much as his woodsmanship that made him a successful guide. She was left alone for long periods of time.* "Naturally, I got lonesome, but there were things that needed to be done and I felt that what he was doing was important. He said, 'I have to be in the woods and if I'm not allowed to be, I won't be worth living with.' "

Was she worried about him on these long absences? "No, but I think I should have been. No, I never worried, I just simply thought that he knew what he was doing." *(According to Bob Olson, Elizabeth worried about Sig all the time. Perhaps because of that, she didn't worry about Sig more during long absences than she did during short ones.)*

DOC'S NIGHT LETTER wound up with: "Will arrive on the noon train. Have everything all set. Plans up to you." And for three hours after that the old warehouse on the shores of Fall Lake buzzed with activity. Grub to be checked over and packed, knives and axes to be ground, paddles tested, pack straps to be gone over for flaws, a sixteen foot canoe to be put in shape, all of the joyous hullabaloo that goes into getting ready for a canoe trip in the Arrowhead Country of Minnesota.

At noon I was down at the train, all togged out in my guiding best, newly hobbed Jefferson drivers, stag pants, and a new checkered shirt. The train pulled in with a roar and Doc, the last passenger at the end of the run, stepped out, preceded by the usual mound of duffle. A farewell to the train crew and he was pounding me on the back as though he hadn't seen me for twenty years. Greetings were short, however, and we piled into the truck which was to take us to the jumping off place of the Border Lakes Outfitting Company at the edge of the little frontier town of Winton.

It didn't take Doc long to get into his cruising clothes, for he was an old timer at the game and this was our fifth trip together. Even before I had started toting the packs down to the dock, he was on hand checking his personal belongings and restocking the old battered tackle box. "Better lay in an extra supply of trout stuff," I cautioned, as I buckled down the last strap, "I've half a notion you'll need it on this trip." He looked at me meaningly over his glasses and proceeded to lay in about all of the brass spoons and dipsey sinkers there were in the place.

We had decided to take the launch-tow to the border this trip rather than paddle up as, for some reason, Doc was more anxious than ever to be back on his old stamping ground. The launch was purring softly as we stowed the last of the packs and tied the canoe in tow. As we backed out of the landing, he settled himself comfortably on the pile of duffle, lit his pipe and his face was a joy to see. The driver turned due east and with a roar of the exhaust we plowed straight up the lake toward Basswood and the border.

"Where to this time?" asked my partner. "I suppose you've got everything all mapped out."

"Not exactly," I answered, "but as we were packing up, I just happened to think of a 24-pounder, that was taken out of Trout Lake, not a week ago. That's been worrying me just a little and I think we should get together on it before we go much further."

Doc was on his feet before I had finished. "Twenty-four, you said? I don't believe a word of it. There isn't a trout in this country that big," and he settled himself once more back on the packs. I could tell by the tone of his voice, however, that as far as he was concerned, the question of where to go was all settled.

We stopped at Kings Point on the Canadian side for our licenses and then had old Joe Beachard run the launch over to a little island about a mile away, where I always like to camp the first night out. Joe ran us alongside a steep rock on the eastern side, threw out the packs, cut loose the canoe and began to swing out before we had barely time to realize that we were supposed to get out. We scrambled out hastily, waved our farewells and he was gone in a cloud of spray. At last we were alone, and for ten days we would travel under our own power wherever we wanted to go. Doc had climbed to a rocky point and was waving a last time at Joe as he disappeared around a point to the east and I knew that for him this cutting of the last tie with civilization was one of the biggest thrills of each trip. To know once again he was on his own and that from now on it was up to us alone, was, as he had often confessed, worth the whole price of coming up.

"You know," he said as he came down from his rock, "it doesn't seem possible that it is a whole year since we were here last. Seems more like a week or two." We smoked for a while and reminisced and suddenly bethought ourselves of the food and the outfit. Doc, as was always his custom, busied himself with the tent, while I started gathering some wood for supper. Years ago I had taught him the art of putting up a wedge tent alone and from the standpoint of a guide, it was a pleasure to watch him.

While the fire was getting under way, I made a hurried survey of the grub sack, and by the time Doc had the beds blown up and the blankets laid out, supper was almost ready. When he had finished, he came over to watch the final preparations and I could tell by the look on his face that everything wasn't quite as it should be.

"Corned beef?" he said, looking over my layout, it doesn't seem quite right, when for a whole year, my mouth has been watering every time I thought of a walleye." Without another word, I tossed the open can of beef to the whiskey jacks and in no time at all, Doc was casting a bit of pork rind and June Bug off the rocks. His first cast brought nothing, but the second brought a lively swirl. "Now watch my smoke," he said, as he took a longer cast than usual. Sure enough, this time something struck and in a few minutes, a five pound walleye was thrashing around close to shore. It was the work of only a moment to steak him out and by the time the fat was sizzling in the pan, Doc had both strips seasoned and floured, and again our supper was on the way.

To the uninitiated, the above account may sound a little too fishy to be true, but during the many years of my guiding in the Arrowhead country, I have seen it happen so many times that, to me, it is far from unusual. And off this particular island, where we were camping, I have often caught my limit of good sized pike, as fast as I could reel them in. Of course, there have been times when a man couldn't get a strike on anything, but that happens even in the best of lakes.

Golden brown fillet of pike, mashed potatoes, cornbread fresh out of the reflector oven, and coffee! As I think of it now, with a winter blizzard howling outside my window and the thermometer down to 42 below, it almost makes me weep. Yes that was real food, and it is what the average cruiser in the border country has to put up with regularly.

In the morning we found that a brisk wind had blown up out of the south, which meant that we would have some stiff paddling to do to reach the mouth of the Basswood River, three miles to the southwest. After an early breakfast we broke camp, loaded up and were on our way. An hour of choppy waves, slapping white caps, sneaking around the lee sides of islands, and we could hear the roar of the first rapids, the upper falls of the Basswood River. Landing at the white portage sign just above where the water begins to boil for its downward plunge, we dug our hobs into the trail and we were off on the first carry. Doc loved the bite of a pack strap and though his shoulders were still soft, I could tell by the way he singled out the heaviest pack, that the year of inactivity hadn't at least dampened his spirit. We made the quarter mile portage with little trouble and, as we were shooting the next little swirl, we noticed a cow moose feeding in the shallows of a little weedy bay just below us. Changing our course quickly, Doc dug for the movie camera, while I guided the canoe. The cow hadn't seen us and was feeding again with her head completely under water. By the time we were within fifty feet, the camera was buzzing, and this time, when she came out of the water, the sound caught her ear. One startled look, eyes wide with surprise and she whirled, crashing off through the muck in a cloud of spray. "Thirty feet on that one" yelled Doc exultantly as he stowed the camera away and grabbed his paddle. What a break the first day out!

A few more portages found us at last on Crooked Lake, the most beautiful of any of the lakes on the whole western boundary route. It was mid-afternoon and we decided to make camp on the point just below the twin falls of the Basswood River, where it empties into the main body of Crooked. While I was busying myself with getting our evening meal, Doc decided to take a try at the big great-northerns which are always found below any rapids or falls of any size in the border country. He hadn't been gone half an hour, when I heard a yell. I couldn't hear what he said because of the constant roar of the falls, but I knew something must have happened or he wouldn't have called me. I could see that he had something on and the way he danced around on the rocks, first running this way and then that, with his rod all but bent out of shape, convinced me that he had hooked something worth worrying about. Moving the reflector oven away from the heat and putting on another stick of wood, I ran toward the point. "Come on," he yelled, "I've got a whale, twenty pounds if he weighs an ounce."

I stood on the rock above and watched. It was a shame to spoil his fun and by the looks of his line, I knew that here wasn't any ordinary fish. What made it doubly interesting was the strong current below the falls. If the fish was of any size he would have a time landing him, for even a five pounder would give a real battle. I yelled encouragement and the battle went on, the old rod grinding and pumping as though this were a salt water tarpon. Finally the fish began to tire and slid out of the foam into an eddy alongside the rock on which his captor was standing. It was a big one,

CRUISING IN THE ARROWHEAD

a great northern pike of probably fifteen pounds and when it lay there, fins fanning and jaws wide open, it looked fierce enough to suit any fisherman. Far too large to eat, just then, we released him with our compliments. "I need some food," was all Doc said, "he took everything I had!" And I believed him.

The following morning we pushed up the winding, wooded channel of Crooked Lake. The south wind was now in our favor and we travelled with little effort. A short distance beyond the falls, we stopped at the great bluff of the western shore to examine the Indian paintings of moose, caribou, pelicans, and many strange heiroglyphics of which we could neither make head nor tail. These pictographs of the border lakes have no known origin and not any of the present day Indians seem to know anything about them or their interpretation. This we do know, that they are thousands of years of age and resemble in many ways the stone age sketches found in the caves of France and Spain. Later on that day we passed Table Rock, the site of a peace treaty between the Sioux and Chippewa tribes, and then pitched camp on a bare pine shaded rock just opposite one of the finest bass lakes on the border, Bart Lake.

After supper we decided to make the short portage and try the evening fishing for bass. Here was a different type of water . . . clear and cool, lily pads and windfalls, everything as it should be. At the end of the portage was a tiny beaver dam and some freshly cut poplar felled into the lake, and it was here that we got our first action. Doc was using a pork chunk, and I, a lowly green frog. My bait hadn't more than touched the water at the end of the first windfall before there was a boil and I had a two pounder. While I was playing this one Doc grunted, and out of the corner of my eye, I saw him set his hook into another. There was only one thing to do, clamp my rod between my knees, and fish or no fish, take a paddle stroke out into deeper water. This I decided to do, and no sooner had my line slacked than my bass came out of the water, gave a shake of his head and threw the frog clear out of his mouth. That settled that and I reeled in all but the last six feet of line and concentratead on being a good guide. Doc had a nice one on and a short time later landed a three pounder.

By the time the sun was getting low in the west we had caught our limit and were satisfied.

One thing about these northern bass. Although they seldom get over four or four and a half pounds in weight, due to the fact that they live in the cold clear water of these lakes where stagnation is unknown, they develop a strength and ferocity and cleanness of body seldom found in the bass of other sections.

But it was really trout we were after, and a big one, so a couple of days later found us setting up camp on a beautiful island in the very center of famous Trout Lake of the Quetico. Trout Lake, what memories that name holds for the fishermen of the border country! From our camp, we could see most of the lake and there, just a quarter of a mile to the east, was the best hole of them all, a hole that has produced more and larger trout than any other spot in the lake. That night we spent putting camp in order and I showed Doc the blazed tree on which most of the records have been inscribed during the past few years. A. R. Cahn, 26 pounds, 1927; Dr. Chas Bacon, 21 pounds, 1928; James McManus, 19 pounds, 1928; J. R. Smith, 23 pounds, and many others. It was enough to get any fisherman excited just to read these terse accounts of former victories, and we spent the evening working out our plan of attack.

The next morning Doc rigged up his best 30 pound test line, with a shiny brass K & B spoon, of a type long used in the north, a four ounce dipsey sinker and his stoutest rod.

CRUISING IN THE ARROWHEAD

Today we were out for meat, nothing under thirty pounds. All morning long we trolled, criss crossing back and forth over the old hole, but not a thing did we get but snag after snag. Toward noon we caught two small ones, three and four pounds respectively, and just before we decided to go in, a five-pounder, which helped some. We paddled back, decidedly lower in spirit than when we had started out that morning. The afternoon we spent smoking the three trout we had, in a little smoke house which the old camp site afforded. Right here I must say that those who have never tasted freshly smoked trout, have something to look forward to, and I am almost ashamed to admit that before we rolled in that night, the biggest share of those trout was gone.

It was not until the evening of the following day that we got our big strike. The first time over the hole nothing happened. This was our last night on Trout Lake and it began to look very much as though Doc would have to postpone his big one until another year. We had taken plenty of small trout, all under ten pounds, but nothing really worth boasting about. I remember vividly just how it happened. The sun was getting pretty low and the loons were beginning to call. One loon in particular seemed to be more derisive than usual and, just out of spite Doc reeled in his line, spat on the spoon in an "I'll show you" gesture and began to let his line out once more. The charm worked, for no sooner did it reach the bottom than it went taut. At first we thought it was a snag and I backed water swiftly to save the lures and the sinkers, but then it started to move out toward the deeper water and I knew that we were fast in one of the old lunkers which has made the lake famous.

I remember jotting down with a stub of a pencil on the thwart before me, the notation, 6:37 P.M. The fish was a big one and he bored for the bottom in the most approved fashion. Once he made a rush for the shore and I backed water gently to help Doc curb him, then out again toward the open lake. Twenty minutes went by and still no sign of weakening and we both began to wonder what he had actually hooked. "Bet he weighs 35 pounds if he weighs an ounce," spoke Doc as he pumped away at his rod. "I've caught big fish down in Florida and I know how they feel at the end of a line. This isn't any ordinary trout." I, too, had seen many a fish caught, and knew by the looks of the rod and the straining muscles in the back of Doc's neck that he was probably right. By 7 o'clock, the big trout was weakening and Doc began to reel in cautiously, but just as we thought we should be able to see him, there was a great swirl in the clear water and out went every foot of line that had been regained. It was now only a matter of minutes, for after the last spurt all fight had gone and he came in easily. I'll never forget the first glimpse we had of him, his huge silver grey body, broad tail and outspread fins, looming up ghostlike beneath the canoe. As he edged in close, I leaned far over, slipped both hands into his gills and dropped him into the bottom of the canoe. One or two convulsive flops and it was all over. Doc was breathing hard, and I didn't wonder. It had been a real battle and now he could write his name with the immortals on the blazed pine near the campsite. When we got back, we weighed him carefully, and that evening, by the light of the fire inscribed a new legend— Dr. John McKenzie, weight 26 pounds, 6 ounces, 1932, time 37 minutes.

   The next day, we skinned the trout out, smoked every sliver of meat for our return trip, packed up and got ready to go. Doc was as happy as a school boy, but at my suggestion that he try it again said, "No, this is enough for this year. If I get another big one now I won't have anything to come back for."

And he was right, for now I am dead certain that before many more months roll by I'll get another wire reading something like this: "Dr. John McKenzie weight 35 pounds, time, one hour 30 minutes, 1934," and I won't have to guess where he is heading for, or what he's been dreaming about during the long winter months that have passed.

En Roulant Parts I and II
Sports Afield
JUNE AND JULY 1934

THIS IS THE ONLY *two-part piece in the Sig collection. Both "Papette" and "Fortune at Lac La Croix" had brief summaries at their beginnings, which seemed like summaries for a part one, but they were merely lead-ins for the main story. Walter J. Wilwerding and Charles Phil Hexom were the illustrators for "En Roulant."*

Within the pages of the story, the magazine describes the author as follows: "Sig Olson ("En Roulant") is well known to SPORTS AFIELD readers by virtue of his previously published stories, which include "Papette," "Trail's End," "Confessions of a Duck Hunter," and others. Having guided canoe parties in Quetico Provincial Park of Ontario (the area about which "En Roulant" is concerned) for years, he knows intimately the country about which he writes. He has paddled his canoe over the same lakes, has shot the same rapids, and has cruised the same timber.

"When Sig Olson made his first canoe trip in the Quetico-

EN ROULANT

Superior country, nobody knows — but it was a long time ago. He has always wanted to write this story of the last of the voyageurs. Has virtually been a voyaguer, himself, for many years . . . a new kind of voyageur, however. When it became difficult for him to continue guiding, because that occupation took him away too long and too often from his family, he set up his own canoe trip outfitting business. Now he makes voyaguers out of adventurers from the cities. Lives for, and in the North. His home is in Ely, Minnesota, where he teaches biology and zoology in the Junior College.

"For years, Sig Olson has been one of the leaders in the fight to keep the Quetico-Superior country an unspoiled wilderness. By virtue of several college degrees and much practical experience, he is recognized as one of the leading exponents of game management and practical conservation in the country. His wife and two boys are as thrilled by the North Country as he is."

Sig was a student of history as well as an ecologist. He saw the human role in the wilderness and in all of life and understood that we need to have a perspective that includes the human race if it is to save all the other life forms. His classes in biology were field trips that blended science, nature, and history. He was a bridge between the men of the past and the men of the future. He felt for the voyaguer, the Indian, and the explorer. He read Daniel Boone, Lewis and Clark, and the other great explorer stories of America, and he walked in their footsteps as he explored the trails of the North. But it was the canoe routes that eased him into a relationship with history. He always felt that the rhythms of earlier paddlers were still present, and when he was in harmony with his canoe, he would blend with those images and spirits of the past.

Part I

THE REAL STORY of why French LeBeau and I ran the log drive on the Quetico River has never been told, and there are those not knowing him, who condemn him utterly. To me, what he did that day was justified and when I camp in the beautiful timber on McAree, Frenchy's timber, I feel that I understand. Sometimes, on clear cold nights when the stars are out, I try to hear what he so often heard at McAree and I think of him then as paddling with the men from Trois Riviers, heading for the big divide and the Northwest.

I remember well one clear moonlit night, when we were camped on the barren shores north of Saganaga, how he called to me time and again, asking me to listen with him for the weird ghostly singing of the voyageurs.

"You cannot hear dem?" he questioned unbelievingly.

"No, Frenchy," I was forced to answer, "only you can hear them."

How disappointed he was, that I could not share the joy that was his. "De singing, eet ees quite clear tonight," he would say, but no echoes of "En Roulant," the paddling song of "La belle Françoise" did I hear, nothing but the soft lapping of the waves against the rocks. At such times Frenchy was transported. He really believed that he could hear the singing of the voyageurs and by the look in his eyes, I knew that he heard something. Sometimes, even in the dead of winter, on nights when the mercury dropped from sight and tree trunks cracked with the frost, he would listen for the tinkling bells of their dog teams.

For many years, Frenchy and I had cruised the wilderness lake country of the Quetico in his Majesty's Service, years as happy and carefree as only men who have lived in the wilderness know. During that time, I came to understand him, the real Frenchy, and to love him for what he was and what he symbolized. I can see him now, black little French Canuck, that he was, sitting perched on some rock overlooking the lake, singing some half forgotten song of the

old days, and dreaming always of the days when his forefathers had traveled these same waterlanes in the service of the Hudson's Bay Company.

He often told me of those early days and his eyes would light up with eagerness as he pictured the fleets of great canoes from Quebec and Montreal, and told me tales of Grand Portage on Lake Superior and the country far beyond. He knew the camp sites they had used, and one of these at McAree above its outlet into Lac La Croix meant more to him than all the rest. Here was some of the most beautiful timber on the Quetico. He would walk through it, feeling of the big rough trunks of the Norways, running his hands up and down their straight reddish holes as though they belonged to him, which in truth they did. I believe, he actually talked to those trees and felt that they knew him. To those who have lived much in the cities, this is hard to understand, but in woodsmen, I have often seen it, a kinship with inanimate things that almost approaches worship, a feeling of oneness with the earth and completeness that comes with much living under primitive conditions.

Back at headquarters, the boys thought Frenchy a little queer and perhaps slipping just a trifle, but I knew better. To him the country had become a religion and though he worked in the present, it was as a voyageur that he lived, a voyageur of the old company. In his veins ran the pride of the old stock, a strain of men to whom the very name Voyageur meant everything worth living and fighting for. To them the country had always belonged, its trees, and lakes and rivers, and the Quetico was part of it, a last bit of the old lake wilderness as it used to be when they traveled it two hundred years ago. To Frenchy, every portage, worn deep by their moccasined feet, every camp site with its blackened fireplace, every landmark was sacred, relics of a past of which he was still a part. His was the work of preserving this last remnant of the old days, keeping without change the waterlanes and shorelines they had known so well.

The longer we cruised, the more this sense of ownership and responsibility grew upon him, until toward the last, it became almost a mania. Always restless, always on the move, we covered twice the ground of any other pair of rangers on the force and the green unburned timber of our beat, showed well the results of our vigilance. And the virgin forests on the shores of McAree had become to Frenchy the embodiment of all that he felt for the Quetico. We made the old camp site that meant so much to him, more regularly than any other point and unconsciously as the years rolled on, all events in our woodsman's calendar were dated from "when we were on McAree."

When tourists began coming into the Quetico, shortly after the war, our fire problem became more acute. Small fires broke out frequently in spite of our care and we had constantly to be on the lookout. And McAree was more than ever on our minds. We might be miles away, far toward the country of the Saganaga, but every morning, no matter where we were, Frenchy's first duty was to climb the highest hill he could find for a look to the west and the timber that was his. At the slightest sign of smoke that way, our plans would be changed and sometimes we travelled many miles to find that all we had seen was the smoke from an oversized camp fire. The last spring we were together, fires were everywhere, and no sooner had we put out one smudge, than another sprang up in its place. Then one day the inevitable happened.

We had come west from Saganaga, along the international boundary through the Knife-Ottertrack chain of lakes to Basswood, then turned north toward the country of Ansellette. It was late in May and for days the air had been heavy with smoke. In the mornings the sun rose a blazing ball of red through the haze and at night it was the same. We were both worried and had reason to be, for not a drop of rain had fallen since the breakup of the ice almost a month before, and the woods were dry as dust. One night found us at the Cone Lake ranger station, planning on working west to McAree the following day. The wind was from the east, hot and acrid, and after days of fire fighting, we were both on edge and restless.

The next morning while I was cooking breakfast and packing up, Frenchy as was his custom, climbed the hill in back of the cabin for a look toward McAree. He hadn't been gone ten minutes when I heard a yell and a few moments later, he crashed through the brush and stood before me, wild-eyed and breathless. One look at his face and I knew what had happened.

"She's on fire," he exploded, "She's burn, my timber on McAree."

We hastily grabbed a mouthful of food, threw the packs into the canoe and paddled desperately for the west end of the lake. A three-quarter mile portage, we made without stopping for breath, crossed a little beaver pond and made another rocky trail to the broad island dotted expanse of Trout Lake. With the wind at our backs we made good time but it seemed hours before we covered the four miles to the Crooked Lake Portage. When we hit the waters of Crooked Lake, we could see plainly a white column of smoke rising steadily to the west, but could not tell exactly where it was. "Perhaps she's west toward Namakon," and the thought gave us both new strength and hope.

At the end of Crooked Lake, we portaged around the roaring falls of its outlet into Iron Lake and then at last were on the rocks above Rebecca Falls on McAree. It was true and we could see a column of smoke billowing wildly from around the second point, just across from the old camp site.

When we got there, half an hour later, we found that the fire already had a broad front and was burning fiercely in a thicket of green balsam and spruce. We saw at once that there was little two men could do without pumps and equipment.

For several hours we fought trying to cut a fire lane in the path of the advancing blaze. Frenchy swung his axe like a wild man and was everywhere at once, but when the flames leapt across and started burning the brush behind us, we knew we had come too late. There was only one thing left to do, head north to the logging camp on the Beaverhouse and there call Fort Francis for planes, pumps, and men. Frenchy did not want to leave, wanted to stay and fight that thing alone, but I finally persuaded him and we left. It was early afternoon and with good luck, we should make the trip before dark. We might get help that night, if we hurried.

The swollen rapids of the McAree River, we shot without a scratch and then were paddling swiftly on the wide open waters of Lac La Croix for the Indian Village at the mouth of the Snake River, seven miles away. That was the longest pull of all and we went by points and islands at a pace that seemed interminably slow and not once did we look behind us or speak a single word. Paddling, the way we were going, left little room for else.

Coming across that last long open stretch, I had wondered if there might not be a chance of rounding up a crew at the Indian Camp, but Joe Moose, who met us at the landing quickly dispelled that hope, for he informed us that everyone except three old squaws and himself had gone down to Lake Vermillion for the Pow Wow. So it was out.

It was here too, that we heard the first news of the log

drive on the Quetico River. Joe, it seems, had just returned the day before.

"No can do," he explained, "de riviere, she's full of logs. No canoe go up de Beaverhouse today, two tree day, mebbe more."

Our further questioning brought no hope. He merely shook his head and kept repeating, "No can do."

Two or three days, that was impossible. All the timber in the Quetico could burn in that length of time. We could circle back by way of the Wild Goose, but that would take too long. Frenchy must have guessed what I was thinking.

"We cannot go no odder way, dees tam we tak a chance."

We had seen many log drives north of the Quetico, Frenchy and I knew what a chance it was. We also knew that sometimes even in the best regulated of drives, a lull might occur due to a dying of the wind in the later afternoon, a lull that might last an hour or half a day. There was just a bare chance that we might be lucky. If we did not reach the Beaverhouse before the drive came down again, well, we did not reach it, that was all. Years ago, we had found a broken canoe below a drive on the river Siene to the northward, a broken canoe with a sodden pack sack tied to one thwart, nothing more. "Damned fools," we had said then, and now we were going to try it.

Frenchy stood impatiently by the canoe, his dark face tense and hard. He did not have to make up his mind. To him there was no question to decide, it was up to me. Joe Moose again shook his head, "De timber, let eet burn," he said, "You cannot mak dat treep today." I turned and looked toward the east end of La Croix toward the shore from which we had come. A white pillar of smoke stood out against the blue of the sky, Frenchy's timber. There was only one thing I could do.

That afternoon, we shot rapids on the Snake that ordinarily we would have never dreamed of trying and about five o'clock were packing across the last portage between the Snake and the Quetico. As we drew near to the river, we became more and more conscious of a dull drumming note in the air, a sound like the roar of a distant falls when approaching it through the timber. We knew only too well what it meant, the drive was still on and Joe Moose was right. The roar increased in volume as we neared, grew louder and more menacing, until the air was vibrant with the boom of a great barrage.

Before us lay a steep climb to a rocky ledge and we dug our toes into the trail. The noise now was deafening and the air damp with mist. We climbed breathlessly, topped the summit and there below lay the river at last, a river of churning logs, thousands and thousands of them, on their way to Fort Francis and the mills a hundred miles below. Not a ghost of a chance to make the Beaverhouse and the timber on McAree burning up behind us. For the first time in years, I heard Frenchy swear. He stood alone at the edge of the swirling water talking softly to himself and staring fixedly up the river. There was nothing we could do. Our only hope was to wait for a lull in the drive and trust to luck.

Most of the rivers in this section of Canada are really long chains of lakes, the only swift water being where one lake flows into another over a falls or rapids. The Quetico was no exception. Originating in the rambling body of water bearing its name, it plunged in a foaming rapids to the great Beaverhouse, through which it flowed with no perceptible current, and then down through a series of smaller lakes, each with its own wild discharge to the Namakon River below.

We had come out at the third rapids from the outlet of the Beaverhouse and below us was a churning millrace of white water, plunging timbers and spray. Upstream, where the river widened out into one of its lakes, quieter water and a solid raft of logs, moving slowly toward our gorge. If the wind would die just a least bit, the logs on the Beaverhouse, above the great sluice that was there, would stop and then a lead would open up and we could take our chance.

I joined Frenchy at the edge of the water and together we watched the logs go through. Not until they were within a hundred feet of the first down slope, did they begin to feel the pull of the current and increase their speed. At the very brink, they seemed to pause as though in conscious hesitation before taking the plunge. Then they would start, slowly at first, gradually gaining momentum, until by the time they were in the center of the melee, they were travelling with the speed and force of huge projectiles. From rock to rock, they bounced and boomed, splintering massive butts in their eagerness to reach the quieter water below.

Occasionally, a timber larger than the rest, would stick in mid-stream, balanced precariously on some hidden pinnacle of rock. Usually, it was jarred loose by another plunging log or else ended up with the force of water behind it, to drop with a crash upon the logs beneath. A canoe would act just that way, if it went over. Once a dozen logs wedged crosswise in the stream, and the river, suddenly dammed, shot high behind them in a green white funnel of spray. Then came a log larger than the rest, up ended against the tangled jam, hung there a moment and fell. With a sound like that of exploding dynamite, the logs separated, fought for a confused instant with the current, straightened out and sped on down stream.

For an hour, we watched those logs go through, then suddenly realized that they were slowly becoming less. It was the beginning of the lull we had been waiting for. Climbing the rise behind us to make sure, we found that the raft had actually broken and that a short distance up the stream from the gorge was a long open lead running straight up the center of the river, a gap that was widening every instant. The banks were still crowded for half a mile above, but the stronger current in the middle was rapidly clearing out its channel.

"We weel go," exclaimed Frenchy, excitedly, "we cannot wait no more." I too, felt the strain and we carried the canoe and the packs to the foot of the lead ready for the start. In another hour it would be dark and then we would never make it.

Part II

Pushing a small raft of blocking logs out of the way, we slid the canoe into the water and were off paddling desperately against the powerful undertow of the rapids below us. Once free of its deadening pull, we made good progress, zigzagging warily up stream, dodging single logs set on ramming us and running away from the loosely flung groups of four and five, determined on hemming us in.

A half hour later, we rounded a bend and were greeted by the roar of the second rapids, the wildest piece of water on the Quetico. An occasional log boomed its way through, but there was not the sustained cannonade there had been earlier in the afternoon at the lower gorge. The wind on the Beaverhouse no doubt had shifted and for the moment the drive would wait. Fast water loomed up white and threatening before us. A few logs were still coming down through the sluice and we pulled to one side to await our chance. The near ones slithered swiftly toward us, would loom for an instant black and threatening and then with a push from Frenchy's watchful paddle would slip into the main stream pulling their white seething wakes after the main stream pulling their white seething wakes after them. The intervals between logs became longer and longer and our chance had come. We stole out quietly as though to take the river by stealth, then stroked deeply quartering the cross currents of mid stream. A timber to the right announced its coming. Raising my paddle, I speared the advancing hulk with all the strength I could muster and got a push in return that sent us shooting into the safety of the portage.

Frenchy was jubilant. "Good wan," he shouted as he hopped out of the bow, "de nex' wan we mak' too and den we mak' de Beevairhouse."

"Listen," I answered, as I lifted the packs out of the canoe. From up stream came a dull boom, followed quickly by another and then still others in quick succession. Frenchy's face blanched. The lull was over and a new drive was starting down. We had a bare chance if we hurried and could catch the open lead above before the oncoming logs had filled it up again. The shadows were lengthening as we sweated across that last portage and had it not been for the ominous reminding undertone of the river, it would have seemed as quiet and peaceful as any other afternoon in the Canadian lake country. The call of the loon came faintly over the hill, the long drawn call of evening in the north, and for the moment what we had planned to do seemed madness.

At the end of the portage, it was as we had feared. The logs were coming down again and as far as the next bend a mile above, the river appeared to be choked with them. Still, from the shore we could not tell, and Frenchy cut swiftly into the brush to climb a knoll for a better view.

I was looking at my map to get our exact location, when I heard him sing out, "Open water up de shore a quarter mile from here," and then he was back. We lost no time in loading on our duffel and stumbled in the growing darkness along the shore. It was foolhardy to even think of trying to work up through that lead with the logs still coming down, but I had not the heart to fail him now. The foot of the open lead however, proved to be much further than he had estimated it, due to the fact that we were forced to work around a muskeg swamp bordering that section of the river and by the time we had shoved the canoe into the water once more, it was almost dark.

The first few hundred yards, we made with little effort. Then to our dismay, the lead ahead began slowly to close. The logs above were forcing those of the main raft together. We pushed forward, pried and heaved with our paddles, but not an inch could we make, the lead was closed.

"No use," I finally yelled, "we've got to go back."

I stood up then to take a look around and found that the worst had happened. The lead behind had also closed and we were bottled up tightly, a solid part of the great raft. In half an hour, unless we could somehow work our way back, we would go through the rapids. Already, we could hear the advance going over.

Up the river, a dark mass of logs was swimming slowly around the bend and not a sign or the slightest indication of an opening anywhere. With every minute that elapsed, we became more completely wedged in. The logs were pressing us close and the sides of our light canoe gave dangerously. If we only had something to work with besides our paddles.

With calked driving boots, we could probably have run to shore, but with the smooth soled cruisers, we wore, it was next to impossible. One slip and you would be forced underneath to drown. I remember distinctly of spotting at the time two big Norways on the south shore, one just below us and the other at a bend, just above the rapids, a quarter of a mile downstream. The gloom was settling and the flies and mosquitoes had found us with a vengeance.

There was only one thing left to do, get out on either side of the canoe, lift it bodily onto the logs of the raft and then by sheer force, using it to support us, slide it along on top toward the shore. We stepped out carefully onto the shifting timbers and with much difficulty succeeded in pulling the canoe out from the vice in which it was held. The first fifty yards, we made with little trouble, then a small lead opened suddenly before us. It was a temptation and we hesitated getting back into the water after the battle we had had in getting out, still here was a chance for speed and we took it. No sooner had the canoe slipped in, than we saw our mistake. A huge pine log broke away from the main raft and slowly slithered toward us, a solid ton of moving weight against our sixty pounds of shell. Just before it struck, we leaped out onto the nearby logs, lifted the bow, and allowed the three foot butt to slide underneath, tilting the canoe at a dangerous angle. We tried desperately to right it, but it pulled from our hands and slipped into a natural trough between two logs, where it was wedged securely. We tried to lift it out once more, but it was as immovable as though anchored to the river bottom itself. There was little hope for the canoe now, for with every log that came down, the pressure increased. A rib cracked with a sharp snap.

If our situation was dangerous before, it was doubly so now. Our one remaining hope was to somehow make our way over the treacherous shifting logs to shore and that without the canoe. We had been moving steadily and had already passed the first of the Norways, I had marked. Half of our time was gone. A pair of ducks whistled by swiftly overhead.

"Fish ducks," remarked Frenchy.

And I remember hearing a white throated sparrow calling long and wistfully from up the shore. Queer how one notices little things at a time like that. Everything seemed natural and as it should be and there was Frenchy humped over in the bow filling his pipe as unconcernedly as though he was drifting into camp. An inertia seemed to have taken hold of us, the inertia and partial paralysis that sometimes seizes one in a dream, when confronted with the need of quick and sudden action. Why didn't we do something? Why didn't something happen? It did not seem real and all the time the steady booming of the logs down below. The flies were getting terrible.

Frenchy wiped his face, "My han'," he said, "She's cover wid blood."

"They're getting bad," I admitted, "pretty bad." As though it mattered.

Suddenly Frenchy was on his feet. "Les go," he snapped, "eet ees our only chance."

I looked again at the softly slopping logs, milling and grinding against each other in the dusk and hesitated. Still, here was action, anything better than waiting and we tore into the packs for our notes and maps. Stowing them safely in the backs of our shirts, we were ready to go. Three hundred yards of shifting logs, moving and turning in the current, a carpet of brown in the gloom. We went over the edge cautiously, Frenchy on one side and I on the other.

Running to the tip of the log wedging in my side of the canoe, I jumped for the next a lopsided white pine butt. The instant it felt my weight, over it went and I was in the water fighting for my life. A frantic heave and I pulled myself half way out but no further. I was held tightly between two logs. My struggles caused them to roll over toward me. I tried to yell, but could not, my breath was gone. Then they separated and for the moment, I was free, lying crosswise on a raft of small logs, that submerged every time I shifted my weight.

Then, I thought I heard a scream and turned my head to look. There was Frenchy a few rods away in the same predicament. The second tree slid by. We were getting near to the rapids. Damn these small logs, where were the big ones now? I tried crawling toward the dark outline of the shore, snaking myself along inch by inch, but found that the increasing current robbed me of every foot I made. When next I looked aorund, I discovered to my horror that I was really closer to the canoe than when I had started to crawl. The minutes were slipping by and at the rate we were going, the rapids would find us in a far worse position than if we had stayed with the canoe. I started back the way I had come. Frenchy was already there and a moment later, I too pulled myself into the canoe.

We were now rounding the bend above the chute and already could see the quickened movement of the logs around us. I stood up once more to take a look down stream. The west was still a lurid mass of color. It would be a fine day tomorrow. Frenchy asked me what I had said. I did not realize that I had spoken out loud. As we rounded the bend, the roar of cannonading logs hit our ears. It was as though we had never heard them before.

"Mon Dieu" gasped Frenchy, "eet ees de end." He jumped to his feet, but collapsed, one leg doubled queerly under him.

"What is the matter?" I called, as I climbed hastily over the packs toward him.

"My leg," he answered, his face contorted with pain, "she ees broke above de knee."

For the first time then, the full significance of our predicament crashed into my consciousness. We had been through so many tight places together, Frenchy and I, and somehow I felt that everything would work out, but now it was different. For once I was alone.

"We must try it again," I yelled into his ear. "I can drag you over the logs," but he shook his head. "Non," he answered, "de two of us, we cannot go, dees tam you go wid out me."

I pleaded with him, begged and threatened, but he would not move. The roar was getting louder and we were moving faster than before. Part of the raft was slipping over the brink. It was time to go. I grasped Frenchy by the shoulders and tried to lift him to his feet, but his powerful hands were gripped firmly onto the gunwales. Finally, he said, "you mus' go, partnere, de timber on McAree. We cannot bot go down, and you might mak' de shore. I stay wid de canoe."

That I knew was final and gave his arm a farewell squeeze, Frenchy of McAree. Perhaps his chance would prove better than mine. One wild leap for the logs and I was down between them scrambling madly for a foothold. Regaining my feet, I ran the full length of a long boomstick, leaped a ten foot gap and crawled gasping for breath onto a jammed mass of tangled, upended timbers. How I got over that mess of logs, I do not know, but suddenly realized that the logs under me were not moving with the rest of the raft, but were jammed and solid on something underneath and that for the moment, I was safe. I rose carefully to my feet and looked out toward the center of the stream, the way I had come.

Far out in the gloom was a darker mass, the canoe, and huddled in the bow was Frenchy. I yelled wildly, perhaps he would turn just once. For answer, above the din of water and crashing logs below, came strong and clear the strains of "En Roulant," the paddling song of the voyaguers. The

next instant, a great section of the raft slipped smoothly over the brink and he was gone.

For a long time, I lay on my little island of logs, too sick at heart to move and not caring much whether the logs gave way or not. Gradually, however, the drive abated and when the river around me became clear of timber, I swam to shore. It was after midnight when I stumbled wearily into the camp on the Beaverhouse. "Damned fools," they said, when I told them my story, "fools to take a chance like that." Of a sudden the bunkhouse was stifling and I stepped outside.

The barrage was beginning again far down stream, a hollow reverberating rumble, a symphony of death to the old wilderness and to Frenchy, the last of the voyageurs.

Perspective — The Continuation

THERE WERE MANY parts to Sig's life: his family, his teaching, his adventures, his philosophy. In other volumes of this collection, we will examine his maturation as a writer-philosopher.

After 1934, Sig became a college dean and made some important decisions about his writing career. With teaching, guiding, writing, and a growing political awareness, Sig had to make some hard personal decisions.

Following the war, Sig was an ecologist and writer. At this time he became a full-time warrior in the political battles of canoe country — battles over acquisition, development, air flights, and protection. During those years, Sig divided his time among Ely, Washington, D.C., and Canada.

From 1955 to 1964, Sig was in the process of defining

PERSPECTIVE — THE CONTINUATION

wilderness in both philosophy and experience. There were an extremely large number of visitors in canoe country compared to Sig's first visit in the 1920s. The crowds and the increased use of motors changed the canoe experience in a negative way, while recovery from the effects of early logging practices actually made it a more beautiful place.

Sig began his career as a book author during this time. He also joined a loosely knit group of canoeists who called themselves "the voyaguers" for an annual far north canoe trip. This period culminated in the Wilderness Act of 1964.

The passage of the Wilderness Act left a loophole that kept the Boundary Waters in a sea of controversy and conflict over mining claims, logging, development, power boats, and snowmobiles. The very essence of canoe country needed to be defined and put into law. This was accomplished in 1978.

The last period of Sig's life, from 1978 to 1982, was one of honors, recognition, and the development of a legacy. There was the Sigurd Olson Institute, and there were challenges that Sig voiced for future generations.

The other books in this series will focus on these aspects of Sig and canoe country. We will look at Sigurd F. Olson as the bridge between our historic use and our present-day values of wilderness.

About Mike Link

On the first canoe trip that Mike Link guided, he met Sigurd Olson and his life was altered. When Sig said that he could tell a person's skill by watching just a few strokes, it made the paddle across Fall Lake Mike's most difficult passage. He wanted to look good to the "old guide."

As the years passed, Mike and Sig would sit together in the writing shack, share Elizabeth's lemonade, and discuss their hopes and dreams.

Mike has written numerous books with his wife, Kate Crowley, including *Love of Loons*, *Boundary Waters Canoe Area Wilderness*, *Apostle Islands National Lakeshore*, *Lake Superior's North Shore* and *The Sky Islands of Southeast Arizona*. He is director of Northwoods Audubon Center and teaches ecology at Northland College and the University of Minnesota at Duluth. Mike has been a naturalist since 1971 and a writer since 1965, but no assignment has been as challenging or rewarding as this opportunity to share his love of Sigurd Olson.

About Dan Metz

Illustrator Dan Metz was born in 1951 and developed his keen artistic sense at an early age. A specialist in paintings of North American big game, Dan is also noted for sharply detailed scratchboard drawings. Dan's work reflects his travels throughout the mountainous West, the Pacific Northwest, Canada, and Alaska, where he has followed his animal subjects and studied their habits and habitats.

Dan's paintings and drawings can be found in hundreds of books and magazines. He has displayed his work at the Smithsonian in Washington, D.C., the Leigh Yawkey Woodson Art Museum in Wausau, Wisconsin, and the Southern Alleghenies Museum of Art in Loretto, Pennsylvania. He was awarded Best of Show for paintings in the 1981 Minnesota Wildlife Heritage Show and the 1985 Wildlife and Western Exhibition.